THE
COMING STRUGGLE
FOR LATIN AMERICA

BY CARLETON BEALS

CONTEMPORARY CHRONICLES

The Coming Struggle for Latin America

America South

The Crime of Cuba

Rome or Death: The Story of Fascism

Mexico: An Interpretation

TRAVEL AND DESCRIPTION

Fire on the Andes

Banana Gold

Mexican Maze

PERSONAL EXPERIENCE

Glass Houses: Ten Years of Free-Lancing

Brimstone and Chili

BIOGRAPHY

The Story of Huey P. Long

Porfirio Diaz: Dictator of Mexico

NOVELS

The Stones Awake

Black River

Destroying Victor

THE
COMING STRUGGLE
FOR LATIN AMERICA

BY

CARLETON BEALS

Philadelphia   New York

J. B. LIPPINCOTT COMPANY

London   Toronto

38- 27709

CONTENTS

I   THE MIKADO LOOKS SOUTH   13

II   SWASTIKA OVER THE ANDES   45

III   THE BLACK SHIRTS MARCH   86

IV   THE BRITISH LION RETREATS   105

V   RED STAR SOUTH   133

VI   FRANCO INVADES LATIN AMERICA   159

VII   THE GOOD-WILL RACKET   175

VIII   OUR NEW ROLE: SALESMAN OR REVIVALIST?   217

IX   DON QUIXOTE RIDES THE PAMPAS   247

X   WE FIGHT FASCISM   275

XI   ARGENTINA'S IMPERIALISM   316

XII   WHAT DOES LATIN AMERICA WANT?   353

INDEX   381

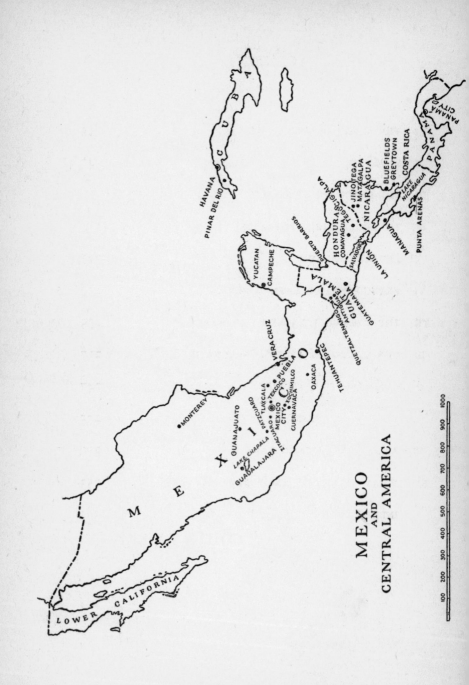

MEXICO
AND
CENTRAL AMERICA

SOUTH AMERICA

THE
COMING STRUGGLE
FOR LATIN AMERICA

CHAPTER

I

The Mikado Looks South

THE Japanese are great fishermen. In Latin America the Japanese are also great barbers. They are great spies. They fish and fish and spy and spy. They cut hair and spy. They shave people and spy. Scratch a Jap fisherman, and you'll find an imperial naval lieutenant. Scratch a Jap barber, and you'll find an imperial army officer. At night, by the light of accordion-pleated paper lanterns, they do nothing but paint long step-ladders of news very important for the Mikado and his klan.

All this may be true. I don't know. In some few cases, I have a hunch that it is true. All nations, including our own, hire spies to nose around foreign arsenals and bridges. Mostly, I suppose, Japanese fishermen and barbers in Latin America are just poor immigrants trying to get along. However, given the greater fanatical patriotism of the Japanese, every citizen can be more easily used to promote the greater purposes of the fatherland.

Certainly our army and navy intelligence departments believe that nearly every Jap in Latin America is a slick spy. Some years ago I walked along the rattly board veranda of the army administration building in Ancón, the Canal Zone, to talk to the major in charge of the Intelligence Service. His special task, although his office is a clearing house for all Latin America on south, was to keep track of undercover work on the Zone and in adjacent Panamá.

Quite aside from the importance of his duties, he shivered with pleasurable excitement at his world of half-shadows and mysterious plotting. In Panamá, he told me, nearly every nation on earth has men sleuthing about—England, Soviet Russia, Germany, Italy, Poland—these were nations he mentioned. But the Japs were his worry. He saw a Jap spy under every chinaberry bush. Of every hundred Japanese in Panama City and Colón, his files reported, ninety-odd were spies, ready at the drop of a pin to die for the Mikado. The good Major's office distinctly had an aroma of dead fish-scales and bay-rum.

I have known spies, in Panamá and elsewhere. Some pose as wealthy men, with fake titles, and maintain swank bachelor apartments where the wives of officials and army and navy officers can divest themselves of their fashions and their ennui. International spies lounge around fashionable bars, often in the company of munitions salesmen, who frequently combine both professions. The association is mutually helpful as well as congenial.

The whole racket is full of humbug. Spies draw good salaries, turn in big expense accounts, are very favored by Aphrodite, and send home, in the case of the Canal Zone, maps anyone can buy in any good stationery store. They copy off official reports anyone can obtain.

Any responsible American can get permission to go through the secret canal fortifications as I did. Some visitors are later indiscreet. Their information is rarely technical, but it is enough, coupled with a close perusal of newspapers, for officer transfers, troop movements, Congressional appropriations and what not, for a spy, without at all risking his hide, to be able to send in reasonably accurate information regarding the number of soldiers quartered, vessels, airplanes, the location, size, age and range of batteries, and other sundry data. Most of it costs the various governments far more than it is worth, though in case of war it might be invaluable to have a key man around the sand lot.

According to the Major, the Japanese are the most active. This may well be so. For Japan, though not seeking trouble with the United States, though constantly denying there is any reason for trouble, is going on the theory that, reason or no reason, we—never themselves—intend to create friction, that conflict is inevitable. Army and navy officers and patriotic politicians are born with such ideas and believe them so implicitly they usually turn out to be true.

As Tokio's trade with Latin America increases, as it has been doing, the Japanese may even come to believe—if we try to set up a too closed-door policy such as they are enforcing in the Orient—that it is worth fighting for. Already they are quite convinced that we have shown more unfriendly aggression than they have. They argue that they have planted no garrisons in Latin America as we have under their noses in China. They have no gun-boats on the Amazon, La Plata or Magdalena Rivers as we have on the Yangtze. They have no fortified over-Pacific colonies near our shores as we have near theirs. They fear that eventually we intend to force the issue to the point of war.

They do not intend to be caught napping. If the evil day is to come, they are aware that our vital line would be, not the coast of California, Oregon or Washington, where they would stand short shrift, but in Latin America, and they have not been idle. They have been looking over the ground there methodically, pushing their interests, getting in on the ground floor.

Even so, to see a Japanese spy under every bush is a bit

absurd. A married roué never trusts his wife because he can't conceive of a virtuous woman. A spy sees in every other foreigner another gum-shoe sleuth. I am not in the least desirous of deriding those Congressmen, afflicted with gastritis and publicityitis, who every so often see an evil Jap grinning under the bed. Nor am I in the least desirous of poking fun at our intelligence services, but the truth is that out of every hundred Japs in Panama City and Colón, probably 98.264 percent are merely honest, hard-working individuals, anxiously taking home the herrings and crabs to the little woman and the tiny slant-eyes.

But even reversing alarmist statistics, it is certain that the Japanese have on occasion used the fishing industry to gain valuable information of nearly all the islands, coasts and harbors of Latin America, including Caribbean shores.

Much of this spy work is also bunk, for excellent charts exist of much of the area. Even so, it is of value to have exact knowledge, not merely of depths, but of climate, currents, tides and prevailing winds, and planted mines. The Japanese have thus created a large corps of young officers personally familiar with all the ins and outs of the southern shore-lines.

Some years ago, a large American corporation with far-flung interests all around the world set its best negotiator of concessions, a wealthy Cuban occupying a high government post, to tackle the job of getting a foothold in Japan. Diplomacy was promptly invoked. K. Uchyama hurried over from Japan to Cuba to sign a special favored-nation trade treaty. Japanese fishermen were allowed to swarm about the landlocked harbors that abound on both sides of the island. Presently the Cuban official became Plenipotentiary Extraordinary to Japan. The American corporation didn't get its concession, but the Japanese got their soundings.

The Japanese have practically a monopoly of fishing off most of the long Mexican coast-line, and have been granted two shore bases in Lower California. J. Yamashito and Y. Matsui came over to sit with the Mexican Fisheries Commission, and Japanese explore the coast. The Kyodo Fishing Company has a fifteen-year shrimp and lobster concession. The Nippon Suisan Kaisha Fishing Company, its stock largely government-owned, operates with a fine fleet out of Guaymas. In the Gulf of California is the Japanese trawler, *Minata Maru*, equipped with fathomer, radio, etc., three other trawlers and eight tenders. According to Mr. L. Kane of the marine department of the Los Angeles assessor's office, these vessels have carefully charted the whole Gulf and have inspected and mapped many land sites, suitable for aviation and other war-like purposes.

Japanese fishing fleets are busy off Panamá and Central America. A large concern is the New Amano Fisheries Ltd., owned by Yoshitaro Amano, with extensive business interests strung along the Pacific Coast countries. The chief vessel, the *Amano Maru*, a 100-foot steel tuna clipper, is equipped with a powerful Diesel engine and a strong radio sending and receiving set.

Recently confronted with new restrictive legislation in Panamá, the fishing interests, with the aid of the Japanese government, negotiated with Costa Rica for a new base, and the price of fish went up in Panamá. Incidentally this also did away with the American tuna-fishing industry there —a much larger activity. A Japanese-Argentine fishing company operates in the South Atlantic. In Colombia, Ecuador, Perú and Chile there are large Nipponese fishing fleets. Recently Japan sought from Ecuador a permanent concession of the Galapagos Islands, southeast of the Panama

Canal, but Ecuador settled it by allowing no foreigners whatever to land there.

2

Overpopulated Japan has sent many of her hardy sons to Latin America as permanent immigrants. Probably only in México and Cuba are there more Americans than Japanese, and even in those two countries the numerical superiority is not large. Probably in all Latin America there are nearly 350,000 Japanese.

México has a strict exclusion act against Orientals, but through bribery of officials, Japs continue to trickle in. There are numerous Japs in Central America, still more in Panamá. Throughout the Caribbean area you find them fishing, cutting hair, running restaurants, stores and estates. Not many in Venezuela, quite a few in Colombia and Ecuador, but in Perú they are of great importance, comprise the largest foreign colony. If only the official count of 22,600 is accepted, they are nearly half of the total of aliens there. However, they number many more. Exact figures for the number of other foreigners exist, but the Japanese have not been required to register with the authorities as are Americans, Englishmen, Germans and other lesser breeds. Competent observers say the Japanese in Perú total at least 60,000 (as compared to 1,229 Americans), or 25 percent more than all other aliens together. Huaral, on the coast, is completely a Japanese city.

The Brazilian 1934 constitution excluded Orientals, but the provision was never effectively enforced against the Japanese. They now number nearly 250,000. Having introduced many of their own plants and trees, such as the feathery bamboo and water lilies, these, with rustic tea-gardens, give parts of the Brazilian landscape an almost

Japanese appearance. They constitute 18 percent of the population of the great city of São Paulo. Proof of their energy is that, outside of coffee-growing, the Japanese are responsible for 29 percent of Brazil's agricultural exports. This is indeed remaking the country.

Recently our State Department rejoiced over the cancellation of one of several Japanese agricultural settlement concessions. But in May, 1938, the ban on Japanese immigration was largely lifted. The state of São Paulo has an agricultural labor shortage of 300,000 hands this year, and the Japanese have been found to be by far the most efficient workers.

Good-sized colonies of the sons of the Rising Sun are also found in Argentina, Uruguay, Chile, and particularly Paraguay.

Whether by intention, accident or perhaps merely with an eye to future profit, many Japanese have settled in highly strategic zones. In México they cultivate large areas in Lower California, Sonora, Michoacán and the Isthmus of Tehuantepec. A Japanese friend of mine, a dentist, has made a good living in Tehuantepec.

In Colombia they have a settlement of several hundred near Cali in the Cauca Valley, adjacent to Panamá, and are trying to purchase 400,000 acres more for colonization.

In Costa Rica, a Japanese official recently rented a large flat acreage near Puntarenas for cotton experimentation, and Jap laborers were imported from Chimbote, Perú.

Alarmists have claimed that the sites in Cauca and Costa Rica are level, so chosen as to serve, in case of an emergency, as airplane landing fields. Both are two hours' flying time from the Canal Zone.

In Perú, Japs own 18,000 acres of the 30,000 cultivable acres in Chancay province; are thickly scattered through the rich rubber regions of Acre Province on the borders of Brazil, Perú and Bolivia. They own all the water front and land adjacent to Chimbote. Though undeveloped, Chimbote is the first good salt-water harbor on the Pacific south of the Canal Zone. Japanese goods and Japanese immigrants are easily smuggled in there.

Most Japanese immigrants have come over poor, often contracted for by large plantation owners as field hands. Juan Leguía, son of the former dictator, made large sums importing Jap laborers for the Chicama Valley estates— in flagrant violation of the laws.

But Japanese newcomers do not long remain underprivileged. Competent, industrious, frugal, loyal to each other, as a rule they rise rapidly. In any case, they soon get into some independent activity, be it peddling peanuts or novelties or cutting hair. Japanese barbers infest Panama City. There is hardly a town in all Perú, however remote in the Andes or the jungles, in which the barber is not a Jap. They are great tailors, and their establishments are sprinkled from Mexico City to Buenos Aires. In Lima they own over two-thirds of the saloons and bread stores.

They go in for restaurants—usually better appointed than Chinese establishments—and for retail business, selling chiefly Japanese goods. In Lima, Perú, they dominate much of the retail trade picture, and few outlying towns are without a Japanese store. In some coast towns only Japanese is spoken.

Particularly adept at agriculture, they acquire large estates. In México and Central America they are the proprietors of big rice, sugar and coffee plantations. In Ica, Piura and other coast provinces of Perú they own fine rice, cotton, sugar and cattle estates. One will also find them farming and trading clear up in the Andes, along the rivers, and in the furthest jungle reaches of the trans-Andean region of the Amazon headwaters. All told they are a highly civilizing influence. In Paraguay they have recently acquired large tanin and cotton properties.

In Brazil they own large rubber plantations, many of them gained through liberal State concessions, also rice, sugar, banana and coffee estates. The *Compañía Nipona de Navigación* owns a million rubber acres in Pará. Largely through Japanese initiative, the new cotton-growing experiment in Brazil has progressed by leaps and bounds. In 1932 Brazil grew only a few hundred thousand bales of cotton. This year Brazilian production will probably total more than 2,000,000 bales. 6,000,000 acres are now under cultivation, and in a very short time the production is expected to surpass that of the United States—thanks largely to the Japanese.

The Japanese have also been instrumental in introducing silk, tea and rice crops into Brazil. The output is rising rapidly in all three lines, promising further to revolutionize Brazilian economy by providing new important exports and bringing contacts with new markets and new countries.

More recently Japanese have gone in for engineering projects, bidding on public works, dams, city water supplies, harbor improvements, etc. In most cases their bids have been the lowest, though often political pull, bribery by others, or U. S. diplomatic pressure, have caused such bids to be thrown out.

Japanese capital is drifting into cattle and sheep ranches, textile mills and mining properties. They have made persistent efforts to get control of manganese and oil properties, some of which are intricately held through native dummies. They have meat packing establishments in Argentina. The Taisei Fur Company of Nagasawa has an important branch in Buenos Aires and agents in Uruguay, Brazil and Chile. Various officials in Panamá, Argentina and elsewhere have held out to Japan the glowing possibilities for further investment.

Japanese capital, though, is still weak on banking service. The Yokohama Specie Bank maintains branches in Brazil; and the Bank of Taiwan has representatives in Argentina, Brazil and Uruguay. Though the Japanese elsewhere lack facilities, they maintain excellent relations with correspondent banks and have made up for any lack by means of credit arrangements carried on by Japanese Chambers of Commerce, which have now sprung up in all large centers.

The Japanese have a fine fleet of passenger and freight steamers plying both coasts, the leading lines being the Nippon Yusen Kaisha and the Osaka Shoshen Kaisha.

Some years ago at Callao, Perú, in the company of a Japanese friend, I boarded one of the largest passenger liners. The crews work for a few yen a month, sleep on mats, and are content with a little rice and fish. Each vessel carries a far larger officer personnel, with many more titles and more assistants than our boats do.

The captain of the vessel explained to me that as the Japanese merchant marine is constantly expanding, young fellows, eager to learn, will gladly work for a few dollars a month so long as they can have a badge, for officer experience counts for advancement in the imperial navy.

He praised their frugality, industriousness, loyalty and particularly their shore conduct.

"Go ashore in any port, and you will see the sailors of all nations making a bestial nuisance of themselves. They bother decent women; they get drunk; they parade the whore houses; they provoke senseless fights. The various consuls are constantly having to get them out of jail.

"Rarely if ever do you see a Japanese sailor making such a spectacle of himself. He is deferential to the people he visits. When a respectable woman comes along, he quietly moves clear off the sidewalk. I'm not saying they're all saints, but they do not throw their money around. They don't make any ostentation of improper doings. They don't get drunk in public. They don't, as you say it, paint up the town. We are a disciplined people, and we can't afford to splurge foolishly.

"Our men go ashore with a guide book. They look up the points of interest. They try to learn all they can about the country. They study the language. They usually take their lunches along from the boat so as not to spend needlessly. They find a nice hill with a few trees and a view on which to eat it and take time to enjoy the beauty of their surroundings.

"When we do things, it is always with an intelligent purpose."

As a result of cheap labor set-up, Japanese boats cut heavily into the freight trade, even as carriers to American ports. A few years ago the Grace Line made considerable effort to develop the vegetable ivory traffic. When it had grown to good proportions, the Japanese promptly handled it for a third less.

Such are the Japanese greyhounds of trade in Latin America.

3

Phenomenal have been the general Japanese trade efforts, the results on the whole highly gratifying. Cheap textiles, cottons, silks, rayons, cameras, dolls, toys, drugs, munitions, boats, sporting-goods, paper products, dress goods, electric materials, notions, thread, buttons, light bulbs, pencils, tooth-brushes, flags, jewelry, stockings, knit goods, parasols, perfumes, crockery and fine china, glassware, kitchen utensils, slippers, needles, wool, combs, brushes, cutlery, dried fish, shrimps and mushrooms, lip-stick, cold cream, powder, artificial leather, celluloid, handbags, trunks, mats, baskets, carved boxes, straw fans for charcoal braziers, straw mats, lacquer ware, art objects, even delicately traced pornography —such are some of the numerous products which have rained on Latin America at low prices.

The Nipponese have also perfected the small Datshun car for sale in Latin America, particularly in Chile, at a cost two-thirds that of the cheapest Yankee type. Perú has bought cement and steel products, sheet-iron, nails, wire from Japanese factories. Tokio nails hold together crates of Cuban oranges. Mikado-style radio sets provide audiences for Mr. Roosevelt's periodic Pan-American good-will messages to the great democratic southern governments run by cut-throat dictators. Japanese phonographs and records in Perú, Chile and Argentina grind out American jazz, crooning and swing for peoples with a far deeper musical understanding than Americans. Don't look now, Akron, Ohio, but Ecuador and Colombia are buying Tokio auto tires.

Ruben Dario, Latin America's greatest poet, was born by candlelight in the little thatched village of Metapa, Nicaragua. Now you can copy out the record of his birth by the light of Japanese electric light bulbs.

When I was in Panamá, it was possible to buy a passable Japanese tennis racket in the U. S. commissariats for fifty cents. Silk shirts sell four for a dollar.

Many a snobbish Lima or Buenos Aires girl shows off her silk stockings and undies, which she brags of having bought at the swank French shops when in reality she sneaked into a Japanese store.

The Japanese are clever at imitating preferred native goods, textile patterns and weaves, as well as French, German, English and American goods. Mickey Mouse went south to Rio and Santiago on glassware, crockery and toys. Snow White and the Seven Dwarfs have already traveled to Osaka and back south in new designs on Japanese goods. A Japanese town, re-baptized USA, permits the Japanese to print on their wares, "Made in USA," without violating certain trade laws.

The low cost of products has permitted Oriental merchants to tap markets never before reached by European or American goods. Since the general standard of living, as in Japan itself, is low, the eastern merchants have made it possible, for the first time, for the large masses of the Indo-American population to buy imported goods. The Japs have found it highly profitable to carry on sales propaganda among large blocs of the low-paid indigenous population to which United States business cannot afford to sell. It is claimed that the Nipponese goods are inferior. But a man who earns only fifty cents a day is obliged to buy the cheapest quality.

But besides opening up this low-grade market, more extensive than any other, the Japanese have gradually forged ahead in the preferential market.

The low cost of Japanese products is made possible by devaluated currency, State subsidies, low overhead, low shipping costs and cheap labor. The Japanese government gives direct aid of many sorts to over-seas commerce. Practically all exports are handled by a centralized agency, the Japanese Central and South American Export Association, headed by Ruyuzo Asama, which enjoys financial, technical and diplomatic assistance from the government. Distribution costs are correspondingly reduced. Sales propaganda is unified; fewer agents are required. Merchants need to spend less on sales promotion because the network of Japanese retail stores throughout the remote corners of the countries at once provide a wholesale outlet. Shipping costs are minimum.

Nor do the Japanese, like the Americans, go in for expensive showy offices. The American concern sends down a high-priced representative, rents fine offices, outfits them with luxurious furniture. Perhaps a local company is organized with plenty of watered stock. All this fancy overhead must be met by marking up the sales tags. The Japanese sell cheaply, with a minimum of promotion costs and of showy extravagance.

4

Labor costs all around are much lower for the Japanese. When a member of the League of Nations, Japan steadfastly refused to accept the Geneva Labor codes.

Take the textile industry. In our own country it is one of our worst-paid industries, the average weekly earnings, including high-priced employees, managers, etc., in 1936 was only $13.60. But in Japan, girl textile operators receive $1.32 a week, the 32 cents being deducted for food, and are given their lodgings and medical care.

The American textile industry is chaotic, cluttered up with antiquated mills, factories in anti-economical sites. Japan, with no sacred idols of laissez faire, has been able in a few short years to put her industry in an insuperable position. In 1930 the government established a Rationalization Bureau. It promptly eliminated wasteful competition and costs in purchases of machinery and raw materials and in sales. Export associations, with private and governmental personnel, were given control over export prices and volumes, not only as a whole, but with respect to particular markets and countries, so as to be able to under-sell any competitor anywhere. Production associations have thus rationalized the cotton, silk, wool and rayon industries. Rationalization has reduced production costs, purchasing and marketing expenses, and has concentrated control of production and marketing in such wise as to provide aggressive entry into the world markets.

The Cotton Spinners Association thus controls 97 percent of all Japanese spindles and nearly half of all wide looms. It regulates production, prices, contracts and working conditions, which border on serfdom. The worker who quits without permission can find no employment elsewhere. However, hours have been greatly reduced (along with wages), but from 1924-34 output per worker increased 100 percent, while declining in the United States.

Today Japan ranks third in the world in the number of spindles, second in amount of cotton used, first in the quantity of cloth exported. American mills often operate less than 50 percent of capacity, and even so there is no intelligent relationship between the volume of production and the prospective market. Japanese mills regulate production to probable consumption to a nicety, but except for two depression years, mostly they have not been able to keep up with demand, and more and better machinery is being built. Most spindles are of the modern high-draft ring type, and the large Toyoda Model Loom Works in Nagoya, and the Toyoda Automatic Loom Works in Kariya, as well as most other mills, have high speed looms. This machinery is equipped to handle a larger proportion of cheap

Indian and Chinese cotton than that of any other country in the world, which in itself is a guarantee of lower costs. The Japanese cotton goods industry is probably the most efficient in the world.

Though Japan is our third largest market in the world —she buys far more from us than we from her, so that without her assistance our world trade would tend toward the red—nevertheless what she does sell us hits certain industries very hard. Japan, even with a gentleman's quota, sells us more textiles than all the rest of the world combined, about $147,000,000 worth in 1937. This importation displaced about 10,000 American workers, and due to Japanese competition in foreign markets about 20,000 more were thrown out of work. This lost buying power threw still others out of jobs and keeps them out of jobs.

If the index number of American spindles in 1913 is taken as 100, then in 1934, the index is 96.4. Over a period of twenty-five years our industry has declined. In 1926, a peak year, the index number was 117.7, so that decline from prosperity days is sharply marked.

During the same years the number of Japanese spindles steadily increased—which meant new and far more efficient equipment being constantly installed, a far larger percent than in the United States. Thus if Japan's spindle index number for 1913 is taken as 100, then in 1926 it stood at 244, and in 1934 at 400.[1]

Thus, in 1922 we exported 587,492,532 square yards of

---

[1] COMPARATIVE INDEX TABLE OF NUMBER OF SPINDLES IN THE UNITED STATES AND JAPAN

	United States	Japan
1913	100	100
1926	118	244
1934	96	400

cotton cloth; in 1934 we exported only 223,481,481, or about 60 percent less. Japan's cotton cloth exports slumped slightly during two depression years, but from 1931 to 1933 jumped up higher than ever from 1,414,000,000 square yards to 2,089,000,000 while the United States and European exports were declining heavily. In other words, our foreign trade in cotton goods has slumped far more even than our slump in productive capacity and slump in output.

Earlier Japan bought her raw cotton mostly from us; now, since our crop controls have rigged up the price, she buys the bulk of her needs from India, Perú and Brazil. We are dealt a double blow.

Thus to the Philippines in 1929 we sold 93,000,000 square yards of cotton goods; Japan sold only 23,000,000. But in 1936 our sales had dropped to only 39,000,000; Japan sold 56,000,000. We lost 75 percent; Japan gained over 100 percent.

The picture in Latin America is even worse. In 1931— that was a bad year for us—the United States sent south 123,000,000 square yards; Japan sent only 13,200,000. By 1935—a relatively good trade year for us—the United States sales in those quarters were only 81,300,000 square yards; Japan's 177,400,000. In five years Japan's cotton-goods sales to Latin America showed a gain of over 900 percent; those of the United States a decline of 40 percent. Last year in Latin America we improved our showing considerably; this year we are slipping again.

The Japanese, suffering from drains in foreign credit due to war, were obliged, during the first two months of 1938, to restrict their raw cotton purchases abroad with considerable injury to the country's export position. By the end of February raw cotton supplies on hand had dropped to less than a fifth of what they had been at that time the previous year, due to a curtailment of 88 percent in raw cotton purchases from June, 1937, to February, 1938. Factories even closed down. Her wool purchases also declined, thus making it more difficult for her to hold her market abroad in all textiles. In March the bars on purchases were lifted, but the lost ground could not immediately be made up; exports continued to decline, though at present they seem to be climbing again, in part perhaps because of the economic straits of England and unsteady prices there. These temporary ups and downs are part of the picture of all international trade in its present chaotic state.

5

In spite of war and difficulties, the Japanese continue to push their commercial campaign in Latin America strongly. Their myriad commercial activities are part of a ten-year plan undertaken toward the end of 1931 by the Japanese government for a large-scale determined conquest of Spanish-American markets. The whole weight of the imperial government has been put behind the effort.

Japanese trade treaties, largely on a barter basis, have been made with all Latin-American countries.

In 1933 Colombia and Japan for the first time in history established diplomatic relations, arranged for a trade treaty, barter and more Japanese settlers.

By coffee purchases Japan bought Salvador's retirement from the League of Nations and her recognition of the Manchukuo government. Washington, which for two years had refused to recognize the Martínez government, seated by an unsavory and bloody coup, veered quickly about, brought pressure and secured tariff legislation similar to that in Cuba. But Japan by buying a large part of Salvador's coffee crop—2,500,000 pounds—succeeded in getting most key Japanese exports taken off the discriminatory schedule. (In Latin America, Japan, like Germany, has been buying far more coffee than she needs—only 40,000 sacks annually —then reselling it in the world market.)

To gain permanent favorable trade conditions, the Japanese government prepared to send over to Salvador no less a person than Kuro Ito, head of the Export Association itself, Tsunetaro Kubota, a large business head, and Tsuyoshi Kasuga, director of the Japanese-Salvador Coffee Propaganda Society, the last named to do the immediate purchasing. Japan offered to buy at least 250,000 yen of Salvadorian products, to take a sales option on Salvador's entire coffee export, if allowed to sell 1,000,000 yen of goods there. Not all of this went through, but Japan has no reason to fear for her position in Salvador.

The United States forged ahead considerably there in 1937 and for the first few months of 1938, but Japan has been busy, and now, along with Germany, has ousted this country in the sale of electric light bulbs. Up to two years ago we had most of the market in this product, now only 10 percent of it.

Nicaragua—though that country still buys more from the United States than from all other countries combined, and the regime which we put in by force through marine intervention still survives in power—has announced that henceforth she will buy her munitions elsewhere. Germany, from 1933 to 1936, doubled her sales there; and Japan's sales, through barter of textiles and manufactures for cotton and wools, increased 500 percent during the same period. In 1937, due to decreased purchases, Japan's trade did not expand so fast, but sufficiently to push France down definitely into fifth place.

In Guatemala, in fact in all Central America, the Japs have registered large trade gains, also in México. A special traveling representative of the official Japanese trade association for Latin America, T. Tahara, maintained offices in Panamá and elsewhere for some time, then was substituted by Takahiro Wabayashi. In Panamá, Japanese exports are second to those of the United States, though the Germans are now pushing ahead once more. The Panamanian consul in Tokio, Julio E. Briceño, recently stated: "Commerce between Panamá and Japan has reached a high level but not yet its highest point."

In all Central-American countries the gain last year in yen was 40 percent.

In México the Japanese have made advances particularly in the sale of electrical goods, notions, drugs, toys, chinaware, etc. They have underbid American engineers on public works. They have offered to take Mexican oil, indicating that they would not permit the expropriated American and British companies to contest its sale. Apparently—though this was officially denied—they made offers to develop the iron deposits of Michoacán and the harbor of Mazatlán.

In 1937 Japan provided 13 percent of the imports of the Dominican Republic. The Dominican consul in Tokio several months ago estimated that this year imports from Japan would reach 20 percent of the total.

In all products in 1933 Japanese sales gains to Latin America were 300 percent more than those of 1931. In 1934, they were close to 400 percent. Exports continued to expand, except for minor set-backs, up until the middle of 1937. Japan's war-economy has since caused considerable recession in her trade with many countries. This decline

however, as 1938 figures begin to show, is a phenomenon
affecting all countries, including the United States. In general, Japan has established a place in the market somewhat
above Italy and France.

Here and there the Nipponese have had set-backs. Here
and there newspapers have occasionally criticized their activities. A few years ago, *La Nación* of Trujillo, Perú, let
out a loud blast against "the Oriental menace." That same
year, *El Telégrafo* of Guayaquil, became alarmed at large
Japanese sales and demanded a commercial treaty that
would guarantee Ecuadorian products in the market. In
Brazil, the now-suppressed group, *Sociedad de Amigos de
Alberto Torres*, had as one of its main slogans "the yellow
peril," but it never found extensive support, for in a country so racially jumbled as Brazil it is pretty hard to arouse
any interest in doctrines of racial purity, and the Japanese
are pressingly needed for agriculture.

In Cuba, which by 1934 had become the greatest cotton
goods market of the United States, but which was menaced
by Nipponese competition, by under-cover pressure, our
commercial attaché pushed through legislation for a differential tariff, particularly on textiles, which decreased in-
versely with the amount of goods any given nation bought.
As we are Cuba's best customer, this gave us a tremendous
advantage (although Cubans had to pay more for textiles),
for Japanese products for a time were charged four times
the tariff on American wares. But this is a dangerous
weapon, for in some other southern countries our purchases
put us only in second or third place.

In Costa Rica, too, the Japanese, though enjoying an unusually favorable trade treaty, have confronted obstacles.

Recently the government refused Japan information regarding facilities on the San José-Puntarenas railway line,

on the grounds that it seemed more pertinent to possible troop-transportation than to tourist promotion. The conservative *Diario de Costa Rica* is quite anti-Japanese, the liberal *Tribuna* rather pro-Japanese.

Costa Rica, one of the few Latin-American countries allowing free-speech, has an ardent anti-Fascist movement; and this, in conjunction with the large Chinese colony there, conducts a severe boycott of Japanese goods. An ironical sidelight in the beginning was that many merchants, heavily stocked with Japanese wares, rushed off orders to American firms in Panamá, the nearest point, and received—Japanese goods.

But even with an active popular boycott, Japanese sales last year in Costa Rica had risen to third place, next to the United States and Germany.

Some years ago England, making a new trade treaty with Perú, asked for only one concession—a restriction quota on the importation of Japanese textiles. But after the agreement had been signed, Perú, very friendly to Japan, promptly ruled that the restrictions did not apply to manufactured textiles.

In Ecuador, Japanese sales also slipped badly last year because of smaller purchases. The Ecudorian law requires that goods from countries who sell 30 percent more than they purchase, shall have to pay a 50 percent surtax duty. Japan fell into this category in 1937 so that her exports declined abruptly from $10,200,000 to $4,200,000. But toward the end of the year, she made heavy purchases to remove the penalty tax, and her sales again expanded.

Throughout Latin America, Japan's brutal aggression against China has raised a great hostility toward her in liberal and working-class circles. The powerful Mexican Confederation of Labor, led by Lombardo Toledano, repeatedly denounces Japanese imperialism, has declared a boycott against Japanese goods, has ordered longshoremen not to load munitions to Japan. Even so, Japanese trade with México has increased, is likely to increase more if the Mexican government sells her oil.

Other workers' organizations throughout the continent have made similar protestations. Unfortunately most of the countries from Argentina to Guatemala, with the exception of Costa Rica, Panamá and, to a degree, Colombia, are ruled by dictatorships, many of them quite savage, that do not permit such elements in the population to voice their opinions.

On the whole Japan's trade, due to the war in China, last year did not show the gains of previous years. If in some places it went ahead slightly, in others it declined somewhat, though not enough to shake the general position gained during the previous half dozen years. In the first two months of 1938, drastic control of imports was inaugurated by the Japanese authorities, and the country's exports fell off one-fifth as compared to the unusually high level of the same two months of 1937. Restrictions were soon lifted, but though export trade improvement did not immediately result, efforts continue unremittingly to better the Japanese position in Latin America.

6

Japan doesn't miss any bets in sales propaganda. Every consul, minister and ambassador is an active trade promoter. Special trade exhibits are constantly on the road. In February, 1938, coinciding with the Central American Olympics, the Japanese staged a big commercial exhibit in Panamá. In numbers of countries permanent museums of Japanese products have been established. Easy facilities are provided for the purchase of goods similar to those on display. Commercial missions are constantly on tour. Toward the end of 1937, two large missions, headed by Yasuhei Konishi, Minister of Commerce and Labor and head of the Konishi Trading Company, toured nearly all South America.

The Nipponese have also learned the American stunt of getting free news space along with advertising. The newspapers to the south constantly are larded with articles on Japan. Various propaganda bureaus also send out free material already translated into Spanish and Portuguese.

American business firms also support several news agencies which send out free releases, but their propaganda as a rule is more directly utilitarian and full of salesmanship. For instance, an article on communications will usually have tucked away in it definite propaganda in favor of telephones, roads, automobiles or whatever it is intended to promote, sometimes even the name of the interested corporation. The Japanese seem quite content to have printed purely cultural articles, stories of Japanese life and travel, without the slightest hint of open propaganda, which the Latins, unlike the Americans, are so quick to discover, resent and deride.

In dealing with Latin-American businessmen the Japanese trader has an eminent advantage. His own civilization, semi-feudal and formalistic, gives him a better clue to the psychology, practices and tastes of the southerners than is possessed by most Europeans and Americans. The gravely formal, courteous, leisurely and punctilious manners of the Japanese are exactly the prized traits of the Latin American in relations with outsiders.

The Japanese envoy or salesman almost invariably has a wider cultural knowledge and background than does the

American or even the European—a great advantage, for Latin-American businessmen are usually highly cultured, set a great store by art, literature and languages. Relatively few American businessmen can talk intelligently or brilliantly about the poetry, painting and music of their own country, let alone that of Latin America, France, Spain and Italy.

Besides numerous Japanese organizations in the various countries, Tokio has numbers of societies for promotion of good-will with Latin America: La Societe Japanaiseen Amerique Latine, the Japan-Argentina Society, the México-Japanese Society, the Asociaça Central-Nippon Brasileina, etc.

These societies and the Japanese government send out lecturers, who speak perfect Spanish, to talk at universities, clubs and elsewhere on Japanese culture, on science, philosophy, history, mathematics and kindred subjects. Japanese poets, writers and painters have been subsidized. Many have gone there voluntarily. Kitagawa, an excellent friend of mine, whose wife was a former Japanese Embassy secretary, is one of the best-known painters in México and is the well-merited head of one of her leading art schools. Japanese theater troupes, musicians, singers are also sent out, even leaders of Oriental religious cults, who find converts in lands growing skeptical from the long abuses of the Catholic hierarchies. Radio programs are broadcast in Spanish and Portuguese.

Not long ago the Japanese government invited forty Brazilian engineering students for a three months' visit. Peruvians, Argentineans and others have also been invited. Such efforts translate into commercial gains. From country after country the Japanese government is now inviting, all expenses paid, special missions composed of the heads of local

Chambers of Commerce and cabinet officials. Such missions have already been invited from Venezuela, Costa Rica, Chile and Honduras.

Nearly all the Latin-American countries have been persuaded to participate in Japanese trade expositions such as that at Nagoya, Kobe, and the Pan-Pacific Exposition in the Aichi Prefecture.

In most of the southern capitals Japanese cultural societies have been set up. Instead of holding rigidly aloof from the local population—as do most American groups afflicted with sentiments of race superiority—the Japanese seek contacts and earnestly try to make friends socially and to spread a knowledge of their native culture. Even in remote Asunción, Paraguay, far up in the interior of South America, may be found the Japanese Cultural Association.

In Rio de Janeiro the Japanese Embassy maintains a Press attaché to promote proper interpretation of the news and to promote publicity for his country and people. About a dozen Japanese professors, their salaries paid by the imperial government, are to be found in the University of São Paulo and the other leading educational institutions.

The canny Orientals also have utilized a sort of Pan-Japanism for the promotion of friendship and trade. Of the 120,000,000 inhabitants of Latin America, not over 25,000,-000 are pure white, though in most countries these are dominant politically and economically; but for more than a century, the trend has been for the Indians and mestizos, i.e., men of mixed blood, to increase in numbers, wealth, influence, and political importance. In countries with large indigenous race blocs the Japanese utilize the argument that they are racial brothers, that the ancestors of the Indo-Latins came from northern Japan centuries ago across the Bering Straits. No North American would thus admit racial equality—the native folk are repeatedly incensed by our attitude of superiority—but the wiser Jap at once admits his close kinship and wins gratitude and confidence.

If this Pan-Japanism, postulated on racial grounds, a "buy in the family" slogan, is now used to gain trade, may it not some day become also a political doctrine? Nations have convinced themselves of far more difficult things.

Hispano-American literati have considerable veneration for Oriental law, religion and knowledge, a mystic admiration for the ancient cultures and wisdom of the East, which they feel is far superior to anything the Occident has to offer. The Mexicans, who for obvious reasons have never liked or trusted us, have always found compensation in admiring Japan. Recently in the official military journal a long article regarding the proper course México should pursue in case of another World War in which the United States and Japan would be pitted against each other, declared that while the sentiments of the Mexican people would all be with Japan because of her far superior culture and her love of the fine arts, imperative practical considerations would require México to remain neutral or ally herself with the United States. Prominent Mexican writers have written books on Japan. The outstanding poet, José Juan Tablada, long experimented with Japanese verse forms.

Many Latin-American leaders see in Japan a happy model to be imitated. That semi-feudal and once politically powerless, though highly cultured, nation has shown that in a few short years the techniques and cunning of European powers can be mastered and full independence from the aggressive West be achieved. Many Latin Americans feel that eventually they can do the same.

Nowhere is there any prejudice against the Japanese as individuals or as a race. The easy polyglot cosmopolitanism of Latin America takes all peoples easily to its heart, and especially the Japanese who come on no plane of superiority. Dr. Samuel Guy Inman quotes a Brazilian diplomat: "In California they seem afraid that Japanese will intermarry with the nationals; in Brazil we are afraid they will not."

Despite Japanese aggression in China, the southern peoples do not fear similar aggression against them. In fact they are happy to promote Japanese trade, would prefer more of their resources to be owned by Japanese capital rather than by that of England and the United States, however much, to please Washington, the politicians may disclaim this. The southern folk would prefer not to have all their eggs in one basket. They recall that despite the welcome Roosevelt good-neighbor policy, since the early days when the Republics became independent, the only country that has seized Latin-American territory by force has been precisely the United States, not Japan.

In September, 1933, *La Prensa* of Salvador, commenting on the coming Japanese trade-war, declared: "The Japanese have decided to intensify their commercial relations with Central and South America, Osaka merchants are putting in orders for coffee, cotton, wool and beef from Brazil and Argentina. May it not be that the new-rising commercial rivalry between Japan and the United States will wage its first battle in Spanish America? It does no harm to let it be known that this would be economically advantageous for our countries."

In July, 1937, the Venezuelan consul general in Tokio, who maintains the ornate trade journal *Asia-America*, published on glossy paper in four languages, declared that Japan is "destined to play a preponderant role in the friendly and commercial relations of the Latin-American countries in the immediate future."

Undoubtedly, according to our own laissez faire doctrines, our faith in rugged individualism, the Japanese or anyone else are fully entitled to get as much Hispano-American trade as they can. The fact remains, however, that increasing trade means increasing emigration, financial penetration and political influence. In these days trade cannot be disassociated from political pressure and dogmas. Few governments today let their merchants paddle their own canoes without State aid—as all American merchants so insist on doing. Instead, governments actively promote trade at all cost. Not only do they promote trade, but they try to create friendly foreign governments imbued with similar economic and political doctrines. This, in fact, is part and parcel of present day international trade war.

For all our pretensions of non-intervention, we have tried to do the same in the past and are trying to do it now.

When we intervened in Latin America, our marines always set up "democratic" governments. Now we merely pretend that the governments down there are democratic. They may be tyrannies, despotism, totalitarian states, as most of them are, but we shout from the housetops that they represent all the noble attributes of democracy. Somewhat frustrated in Latin America, now, instead of establishing "democracies" at the point of the bayonet, we set them up in our own minds. This is a common psychological trait of evasion which has its proper technical name.

Japan, especially since her alliance with Germany and Italy, favors authoritarian governments—the traditional form of the State in Latin America. The Japanese ideas are much more welcome news to southern dictators than any unpleasant prattle about democracy.

7

The sale of munitions invariably brings undue political influence. Usually such sales require the sending of experts, hence direct participation in the various military establishments. Japan has not gone in greatly for armament sales, though she supplied much of Paraguay's equipment during the Chaco War. Some years ago she sold 60,000,000 *soles* of rifles and ammunition to Perú, which was straining to arm for the Leticia trouble. Much of this was outdated French equipment. Early in 1934, the *Latin American Digest* published:

"Perú has been exchanging guano for Japanese arms, and is said to have quite a staff of Japanese officers in her service. . . . *El Tiempo* (Bogotá) has declared . . . that 'Perú has purchased large quantities of artillery from Japan' and that 'these elements of war were transferred from Japanese to Peruvian ships in Panamanian waters,' which merely confirms a story published in the *Latin American Digest* on January 8, 1934—months ahead of any other publication in the world—which, in part, said: 'Japanese arms brought on Japanese steamers were transferred to Peruvian men-of-war on the high seas off the coast of Panamá.' "

This transfer occurred, according to witnesses, off Fort Amador in the Canal Zone, during the Christmas holidays. Much of the Japanese munitions sold to Latin America have been thus pushed in secretly without being recorded in the trade-statistics.

In various quarters Japan gets considerable orders for uniforms, flags, cartridges, shells. Recently she made generous offers to a number of countries to supply them with munitions and battleships in exchange for coffee, vegetable oils, rubber, etc. Agents of Mitsubishi, the Japanese naval constructors, have been very active in Brazil. An unusually magnificent offer was made to that country to build up her navy and merchant marine on a vast scale in return for cotton, rubber and ores. The hurried offer by Secretary Hull to lend Brazil battleships from the American navy—an unheard-of gesture, above all to a dictatorial semi-Fascist nation—may well have been an effort to spike this and German and Italian proposals and promote American sales instead.

At present Japan needs most of her munitions herself, but when the war with China ends she will certainly be looking for a place to dump guns, cartridges, bombs, artillery and other supplies at bargain-counter rates in order to keep her bloated armament industry from collapsing over night.

Politically, Japan's strongest hold is on Perú. This has historical antecedents. Perú has had a long tradition of close relationships with the Orient. Through much of the Spanish colonial period Perú was at the American end of the China trade. All during the independence period Perú continued to trade heavily with Japan. The long dangerous trip through the Straits of Magellan made Perú's access to Europe difficult. Not until the Panama Canal was opened in 1914 did she really come close to European markets and influences.

But the old friendly relations with the Orient, particularly with Japan, have continued. Japanese, alone of all other foreigners, have not been required to comply with many regulations restricting other foreigners.

President Sánchez Cerro showed hearty pro-Japanism on every side. The present dictator, Oscar Benavides, for a time courted the United States, especially during the Leticia trouble, but angered by our apparent partiality toward Colombia, he later let out several loud blasts against American tariffs and loan retirement terms. Now he has become more diplomatic, but his government, despite an American naval mission, remains very much under the thumb of the Italians and the Japanese. When the gold-braided dictator steps out on official business, he is usually accompanied on one hand by the Italian minister; on the other by the Japanese minister. Perú and Poland were the only two League of Nations members who voted against censuring Japan for her invasion of China. The Japanese residents in Perú have offered to put at the disposal of the government, any time they shall be needed, twenty thousand armed and trained men.

Japan is a factor to be reckoned with in Latin America. Quite apart from trade, Japan will have great economic, political and cultural importance there in the future. Her commerce and cultural influence to the south of us— though it may be weakened by defeat in China—in the long run is apt to increase rather than decrease.

CHAPTER

II

Swastika Over the Andes

On a horseback trip through the Peruvian Andes, beyond Ayacucho I came upon a German salesman, Herr
Teufelsdroeck, who had a five year contract to sell drugs
in South American settlements not mentioned on the map.
There are ten thousand such places.

With Indians to carry his wares, he had traveled the
length and breadth of the continent: through the Chaco,
across wind-swept Patagonia, along the granite Marañon
River. He had struggled up Amazon tributaries where scien-
tifically equipped American exploring expeditions get lost.
Under his determined Teutonic tread, the meadow grass of
the Ecuadorian Andes had bent down; he had left tracks
across the hot Chilean deserts; he knew the Paraguayan
quebracho jungles and the mighty Magdalena highlands.
He had gazed upon the noble Iguasú falls. Head-hunters,
bandits, shooters of poisoned arrows—none held terrors for
him.

He was tapping a vast market of primitive folk. Probably
seventy percent of the Latin Americans, living in rural
self-sufficiency, are not users of so-called civilized goods.
Many even weave their own clothes, as formerly in colonial
America.

Herr Teufelsdroeck helped wean these folk from their
native witch-doctors to faith in white pills. In each locality,

sales were perhaps infinitesimal, but with a market of fifty or so million people over a mighty continent, the aggregate would come to a staggering total.

The American salesman—for a wage a scavenger would scorn—would scarcely suffer such dangerous hardships. Our methods are different. Our sumptuous offices in Lima, Rio, Buenos Aires or other large cities depend upon native distributors, who themselves have never tapped the backward rural market. In any case, higher American prices largely restrict our distribution to urban centers—the well-to-do market. But the Germans, like the Japanese, industriously go forth into the wilds to develop markets never before reached.

Courageous, determined, jovial, ever ready for beer and camaraderie—a walking embodiment of Teutonic Kultur —Herr Teufelsdroeck everywhere mingled with the people of the land. The click-heels correctness of the German appeals to Latin Americans, also full of gravity when dealing with outsiders. Of all Europeans, the German—though considered half mad—is the most liked. Precisely because rigid Teutonic discipline so contrasts with the easy-going, beauty-loving native ways, the Germans get on better than the Italians, too close-cousins of the native peoples always to command respect.

The Germans, more than other European folk, have spread into the interior corners of the various republics, have intermingled with the people and taken native wives —a practice Hitler wishes to stop.

Every German pursues a hobby which brings him profitable contacts. He collects reptiles, butterflies, rocks, builds up a herbarium or becomes an expert photographer. He studies archaeology or anthropology or history. He records native folklore or music.

He is a great mountain-climber. When I was in Quet-
zaltenango, two hikers, near the crest of erupting Mount
Santa Maria, stumbled upon a hidden Quiché-Indian pagan
shrine. To keep their secret, the Indians hacked the two
men to pieces with machetes. The hikers, of course, were
Germans.

In Oaxaca, a German hardware clerk was my best source
for material on Porfirio Díaz. He knew every spot the dictator had ever been, where all documents were to be found.
A German coffee-grower in south Oaxaca, a botanical wizard, discovered two trees hitherto unknown to science. In
Guayaquil, Ecuador, a German machinery agent could tell
me the detailed history of the port. In Perú, several Germans have the finest collections—outside museums—of
huacos and other pre-Conquest objects.

Few American residents in Latin America have such
scientific proclivities; on the whole they display little interest in the local history, literature or art. Having little
sympathy for the native people or customs, they foregather
in exclusive American or country clubs, play golf and
bridge, stick to their own national circle and rarely feel
impelled to delve into sociological or other knowledge in
the exhaustive fashion of the Germans.

In most Latin-American countries, except perhaps Cuba,
México and Panamá, there are more Germans than Americans. In México the Germans outnumber all except Americans, Spaniards, Chinese, and, possibly of late, Japanese.
Between 1820 and 1931, according to official figures, 209,-
923 Germans entered Brazil. Since then many others have
come in. In the space of over a hundred years many of these
and their offspring have been entirely assimilated, but if
first, second and third generation Germans are included,
there are, according to some estimates, close to a million

pure-blooded Germans in the country. Like the early Germans in Pennsylvania, they helped push out the frontier, and have built themselves into powerful and wealthy positions.

About 100,000 Germans live in Argentina. The frequent beer-halls, with their neat denim curtains and checkered table cloths, attest to their presence and love of *Gemütlichkeit*. At various times Argentine governments have encouraged German immigration by liberal land grants. But few Germans have tilled the soil long; they soon become owners of large estates. Socially they comprise a class much superior to the Italian, Polish, Spanish or Russian immigrants. They are dedicated to business and banking and the professions of engineering, medicine, dentistry and teaching.

The first German settlement in Chile, planted in Valdivia in 1850, was soon followed by others. Chilean governments have often made generous offers to Teutonic colonizers. Much of the Araucano Indian frontier, south of Biobío, has been opened up by Germans, who now own large estates and are very influential in Chilean affairs.

The rich central valleys of Chile, for three hundred years so recklessly cultivated by the native "aristocrats," are today declining, whereas the colder southern "Germanic" regions are developing prodigiously. As the Chilean writer Mariano Picón-Salas remarks, southern Chile, with its lakes and mountain meadows, now looks like a very industrious Switzerland. The wilderness of a few decades ago now produces large crops of cereals. Around Tenuco have been built up beautiful orchards and gardens, and German knowledge of horticulture has caused Chilean fruits to compete in size and beauty with those of California. From there come "the largest cabbages in all Chile"; there "raspberries and currants flower and throw off their scent as in a northern spring . . . ; there grows the conifer, made into paper as in Switzerland; the elm offers red parchment bark for the curing of hides . . ."

After thus praising the able use made of the region's resources, Picón-Salas mourns that already Chile is two regions, its nationality divided, that the Germans, strongly welded in clubs and associations, keep their language, have their own schools. They drink their Valvidian beer, sing their Turnverein songs and shout *"Deutsch ist die Saar."* Picón-Salas is perhaps too pessimistic, for many have been assimilated, and most—though in any international crisis naturally very pro-German—feel themselves to be loyal Chileans.

Fewer Germans live in Perú, though since the World War they have been increasing there and are very strong in retail business lines. 60 percent of the business of Arequipa is run by Germans who are all fanatic Nazis. The German hardware merchant is found in every corner of the country, as also in Uruguay, Bolivia, Ecuador and Paraguay. German estates are scattered through Colombia and Venezuela.

The sons of Hitler make their presence felt strongly in Salvador and Guatemala, exercising a dominance there unequalled by any other resident foreigner. They are numerous and prosperous in Costa Rica, active in Nicaragua and Honduras, less so in Panamá, and are but a light sprinkling through the rest of the Caribbean.

Since Hitler has come to power, German colonization of the Americas has become more determined. Efforts to plant Germans in strategic points are constantly made, often in conjunction with trade negotiations. Trujillo, the dictator of the Dominican Republic, recently sent a special secret mission, consisting of Ernesto Bonethy and Alredo Ricart, to Germany. *La Voz*, Spanish daily of New York, subsequently published a report of a deal with the Dictator to settle the frontier near Haiti with Nazis, the initial colony to consist of 40,000. This, if true, appears to be in connection with a gold-washing concern which will set up modern equipment in private partnership with the Dictator. Trujillo has given special facilities to German doctors sent by Hitler to study tropical diseases and to several German secret agents. He has also made the teaching of German, instead of English, compulsory in the public schools.

2

The German immigrant turns to lines where he can crowd out competition. Hardware stores almost invariably are in German hands; so are music stores and fine printing and engraving establishments. The paint and chemical industries attract him. He is engaged in the sale of machinery, tractors, harvesters—as the Casa Miller in Lima or Emmel Hermanos in Arequipa, or Siemens in México. Germans deal in electrical machinery, motors and supplies. Fashionable jewelry stores everywhere—as La Perla in México or Zettel and Kohler in Lima—are German-owned. In México, Central America, Argentina, Brazil, Chile and elsewhere, he has large hotels. I have also stayed at German hostelries in such out-of-the-way corners as Chilapa, México (Hotel Central), and in Quezaltenango, Guatemala. Many of the best restaurants—such as Tio Hopfer, Schultz's and Bellinghausen in México—are run by Germans.

Coffee-growing is a specialty of his. Good-sized estates are found in southern México, all through Central America, in Venezuela, Colombia, Ecuador, above all, in Brazil. In the last-named he is interested, along with the Japanese, in promoting cotton-growing which rapidly is rivalling that in our own South and has forced Brazil to seek new markets and new ties. In Perú Emmel Hermanos have large cotton plantations in the Majes and Camaná valleys. The Gildermeister Casa Grande in Chicama and the Miller estates elsewhere in Perú are fine, large sugar plantations. The former, with 100,000 acres under cultivation, is the most powerful sugar concern in all South America, turning out 43 percent of all Perú's sugar. The United States has aided German and Italian sugar concerns by greatly increasing Perú's sales quota in this country. Gildermeisters also have big sugar plantations in Chile—the Uña del Mar estate, for instance.

In the Urabas Gulf region of Colombia, the German banana business imitates the methods used by the United Fruit. In Yucatán, Germans have henequén plantations, and German capital has just taken over a Salvador finca of 1,000,000 henequén plants.

Most breweries have been started by Germans. In México, Perú, Brazil and elsewhere they own textile factories, though generally the French and Spanish are more active in this line. In Cerro de Pasco, 15,000 feet up in the Andes, sits a German dye factory, its products in part based on new discoveries of Indian secrets. German and native capital in the Compañía de Papeles y Cartones has just put up a new paper factory in Chile, utilizing $500,000 worth of German machinery.

It has been hard for the Germans to get a foothold in raw-product industries, so monopolized by the English and Americans. But following the war, there was a flight of much German capital to Latin America, and the Hitler regime now makes consistent efforts, through securing concessions and by purchase, to gain control of needed war materials.

Not long after the war, the Krupps acquired land in Llanquihue province in Chile to build a large steel and munitions plant, and Germans were settled in the vicinity. More recently the Gildermeisters—so strong in Perú—have embarked on Chilean nitrate production. Hugo Stinnes bought large oil tracts in Nequén province, Argentina. The Thyssen interests are said to have acquired important concessions in Puerto Pinasco, Paraguay.

Now, since the Hitler drive, in Brazil the Germans have gotten hold of copper mines in Parahyba, nickel mines in Goyaz, oil in Riacho Dolce, in Alagoas, a million and a quarter acres of presumptive oil land in Matto Grosso, and are acquiring 13,000,000 tons of iron ore.[1] They have a railroad monopoly and a private port in the state of Espiritu Santo.

The Germans have oil ports in Colombia, have secured 88,000 square kilometers of oil land, and their new commercial treaty with that country, signed May, 1937, besides giving signal advantages, makes generous conditions for acquiring additional oil lands. Any amount of Colombian currency may be bought with Aski marks for such investment. The Germans also actively negotiated to get hold of the Mexican government's output and royalty shares.

---

[1] The worth of Brazilian oil reserves is much disputed, though the geological formation would seem to favor its presence. A British commercial paper published in Brazil recently reported that successful test boring had been reported in Minas Geraes, near Juiz de Fora and in Santa Catharina and in the Rio Bonito district. Encouraging reports have been received from Matto Grosso relative to an area between Corumbá and Campo Grande, and from Tucum and Boa Esperança in the state of São Paulo. In any case large outlays will be needed for commercial operations.

Now, since expropriation, considerable quantities have been contracted for refining in Germany.

The ramified German banking system, from México to Argentina, facilitates every type of credit operation. The *Deutsche-Sudamerikanische Bank* has branches in Argentina, Brazil, Chile, Paraguay and México. The *Deutsche-Ueberseeische Bank* has six branches in Brazil, six in Chile, three in Argentina, two in Perú, one in Uruguay. Smaller German concerns are found in all the countries.

3

The large colonies of Germans, their business foothold, the large investments, their fine banking system, have all aided the Reich's commercial expansion. A long-established retail system—as in the case of the Japanese—provides an immediate outlet for goods at a minimum promotion cost. German-owned plantations use German electric motors, pumps, tractors and farm-machinery. Hundreds of thousands of German immigrants use German wares. German intimacy with local businessmen makes it easier to sell them goods.

Since the World War, German trade, through the barter system, State subsidies and the use of Aski marks, has in most places steadily increased. During the depression, it jumped by leaps and bounds and even more in the past few years. Sixteen bilateral treaties have been made.

In Brazil Germany has pushed the United States down to second place, especially after the August, 1936, agreement—by which surplus cotton and coffee were exchanged for chemicals, and hides for hardware—made the Hull reciprocity treaty "a mere scrap of paper." In 1936 we sold Brazil 22.1 percent of her total imports; in 1937, 23 percent, a slight increase, though less than in 1934. But Germany forged ahead more last year; and England—though having the largest capital investment there—was nosed out by Argentina, thus dropping to fourth place.

The Santos coffee-growers recently arranged with the Hamburg business group to dispose of 700,000 sacks of coffee for 800,000 Aski marks and coal. The Brazilian government, according to *A Noite* (May 1, 1938), has placed a preliminary order of $5,000,000 in Germany for twenty-five locomotives and 1,000 cars to be used on the newly electricized Central do Brazil railway—a 3,150 mile line through the richest, most populated part of the country.

In all countries British trade has slumped. Though the British still maintain a slight lead in several countries, especially Argentina and Uruguay, even in those German trade has increased. Germany's trade exceeds Britain's in Ecuador, Perú, Venezuela, Chile, Colombia and Brazil.

In Argentina and Uruguay Germany has increased her sales in many lines, especially in cutlery and farm-machinery. The Solingen industries have more than recovered their old market. For a time Germany sold more even than the United States, but in recent Argentine import trade expansion, Germany has been left in third place; the United States now sells almost as much as England, largely because of orders for bombing planes and armaments. Last year we sold more airplanes to Argentina than to China or Japan. But this year we are losing out again. Germany, however, provides the planes and technicians for the Argentine Aeroposta line, serving the southern half of the country. In May the Argentine government announced the probable revival of the quota system. This will at once restore Germany to second place in the market, and push the United States down to fourth place.

In Chile, as before the World War, imports from Germany for quite some years have outstripped those from England, which has thus dropped to third place, behind the United States, which went into second place last year. German and American sales in February of this year were $4,250,000 and $4,400,000 respectively, not much of a lead on our part, but our sales seem to be improving, in the face of decline for us in most of the continent. German and Italian expansion in Chile, new favoritism showed those two nations, plus Chile's proposals to nationalize the copper industry, largely American-owned, the numerous penalties being put upon American investors, may partly explain Roosevelt's determination to pay President Alessandri a courtesy visit this year.

Chile does not place the same severe restrictions on monetary exchange with Germany and Italy as it does with most other countries. More German than British auto cars are sold. The Germans have developed the cheap Opel car, which is gaining ground in many countries, and is far more economical in price and operation-cost than any British or American car. They are now about to turn out a still lower-priced Volks car.

The British have also lost out to the Germans as purveyors to the government-owned railroads. The Chilean government—which runs the most efficient system and best-equipped trains in South America, far surpassing, for instance, the British services in Argentina—believes that the German railways are the best, the most up-to-date in the world and prefer to get equipment from that source. The Chilean lines are now putting on up-to-the-minute streamlined trains, and the Talca-Chillán section is to be relaid entirely with 20 meter heavy steel rails from Germany. In 1937 Chile bought over $3,000,000 of German equipment. An initial order for $5,000,000 was placed early this year in the Reich for equipment in line with the mammoth modernization program being carried out. This program will require still heavier purchases in the Reich.

This year the government-owned Chilean air lines decided to equip throughout with JU-86 Junkers. American bids were lower, but the Chilean authorities believe the Junkers to be superior craft.

In June General Diego Aracena was reported (after first inspecting planes in the United States) to have spent 16,-000,000 pesos in Germany for new hydroplanes for a new commercial and national defense line between Santiago and the far southern province of Magallanes.

And so, German sales to Chile may soon again exceed those of the United States.

German trade with Perú has also increased, and the Reich's economic position there is rapidly strengthening. Long-established commercial houses, such as Klinge, Osechle, Eheder, Emmel and others have flourished greatly since the Hitler trade-drive. With the aid of the German Transatlantic Bank, they are digging in to a privileged position, with wide economic control. The German houses have monopolies over much of Perú's production.

Adjacent to the German-owned port of Chicama large quantities of contraband goods from Germany and Japan are shipped in. With the connivance of high officials, duties are evaded and the goods do not figure in the trade statistics. Secret shipments of war-materials and food-supplies are sent out to the same two countries by this and other secret routes.

Such practices in Perú and many other countries make it impossible to ascertain exactly the trade figures in Latin America for the Fascist powers and Japan. It makes it impossible to determine exactly what munitions are being received. The year I was in Perú, enormous quantities of Japanese goods were imported, but the official trade figures reported no Japanese trade at all. Countries have learned not only to falsify their financial statements, their gold funds, but also their trade figures and munitions purchases.

In Ecuador in 1937, Germany's exports increased from $25,000,000 to $31,700,000. Her share of total Ecuadorian imports increased from 21 to 24 percent. This expansion took place even in the face of severe regulations, which put the Aski-mark trade in a very unfavorable position and greatly benefited the United States. Because of American influence, Ecuador, even at the expense of her own exports, limited her own sales to the Reich—of cacao, to only 4,000 tons; Panama hats, to 60,000 Aski marks—in order to halt Germany's growing dominance in the market. Temporarily we registered enormous gains. This year American sales are falling off again.

This April, Germany signed a new favored-nation treaty, allowing unlimited sales of German and Ecuadorian goods. Germany is put on the preferred duty list. At present there is already a great excess of Aski marks, which are sold at heavy discount. Thus German goods are subsidized by Ecuadorian merchants—the result in most countries—a clever means by which foreign countries contribute to the promotion of Germany's foreign trade without cost to the Reich itself. A big expansion of German business with Ecuador may be looked for in 1938, and the probable wiping out of part of the United States' phenomenal gains of last year. Our sales for February of this year were already down 8 percent from the same month last year.

1937 import-trade figures for Colombia show that all important countries increased their sales there with the exception of Germany, which lost 14.9 percent. To offset this, the Germans sought special advantages. Last November 6, the *New York Times* reported that new exchange-control regulations applied to all countries except Germany. The unrestricted purchase of devaluated Aski marks was permitted. This and recent punitive action by Colombia against British trade will probably bring Germany considerable new advantage.

In January, according to the official *Información Económica y Estadística*, German sales represented 22.1 percent of Colombia's total imports, as compared to 39.3 percent sold by the United States, and only 14.9 percent by the United Kingdom.

In Central America as a whole—our home bailiwick—from 1933-36, the Reich increased her export trade 500 percent.

In Nicaragua, for several years the United States has had a favored position, and still dominates, supplying in 1937, 54 percent of all outside purchases. But we have just cancelled our reciprocal treaty, and even before that our trade was declining. Our February, 1938, sales were 47 percent lower than those of the same month a year previous. Nicaragua last year announced that she would buy no more munitions from us, and placed orders in the Reich and in Italy.

Germany exchanges hardware, textiles, cement drums, toys, motors, and medicine for Nicaraguan cotton, coffee, cabinet woods, hides, and medicinal herbs. Her trade there, which is climbing, is 17 percent of the whole as compared to Great Britain's 8 percent. Japan is in fourth place.

This year the Germans have pushed their trade harder than ever, and are guaranteeing purchases by heavy advances of Aski marks on coffee, henequén and sugar through the government-owned mortgage bank, managed by German Consul, Baron von Hundelhausen.

In Salvador German export trade in 1936 almost equalled that of the United States. In that year Germany increased her share in the market from 24 percent to 33.6 percent, while the United States remained almost stationary, providing 38.6 percent of Salvador's imports. In 1937 both countries increased their sales, the United States going ahead considerably. But with our recent slump, Germany is again advancing. She now shares most of the market for light bulbs with Japan, and is displacing us in the sale of office equipment, especially typewriters, adding machines, and other calculating apparatus.

In Guatemala our export trade has steadily gone down; Germany's has increased.

We sold 41.5 percent of Costa Rica's import last year, Germany 23 percent, Japan 8.2 percent, the United Kingdom only 7.2 percent. Costa Rica now turns to Germany for her railroad equipment.

Of late, the Germans have been doing heavy barter-bargaining in Panamá, which has just sent Germany a $300,000 coffee shipment. Trade was practically suspended in 1934 due to exchange difficulties, but recently arrangements were made satisfactory to both parties.

In México Germany has pushed England down to third place. With the new all-time high tariff there which especially hits our goods—though in May it was slightly modified—the oil expropriation, the breaking off of relations with England, the Reich will probably sell more. México has made arrangements to barter oil in part for German machinery, which will also cut into purchases from the United States.

The Germans are trying to crack through the Hull reciprocity set-up in Cuba. On March 11th of this year the Cuban Secretary of State is reported to have announced that negotiations were proving difficult because of Germany's special system of exchange, but an agreement has since been reached, and the Batista dictatorship has decorated German higher-ups, including Goebbels.

The Reich has gained concessions in the Dominican Republic.

There is no doubt that in part German trade has been artificially pumped up. It is hampered by the excessive devotion in the Reich to rearmament and Ersatz self-sufficiency products, which use up so many productive energies as to limit the kinds of goods she has to sell. On the other hand the rearmament program creates a heavy demand for many of the raw materials found in Latin America, and buttresses up her barter system there. That system, plus trade subsidies, plus Aski marks, plus government-controlled purchasing, plus many other factors can play havoc for an indefinite period with all reciprocal trade treaties made by the United States.

4

Few instrumentalities of coercion and propaganda have been neglected. One of the earliest efforts, antedating those of the United States, was to control news distribution. The Wolff service entered into active competition with Reuters and Havas, and before 1914 the Germans had laid down an interoceanic cable to Brazil. During the World War, it was fished up by the Allies and cut.

But those early efforts are child's play compared to the present drive. The German News Agency, government-controlled, has now gotten an advantage over all others through the Hell Service (named appropriately after the inventor). This is a radio teletype monopoly which permits a single broadcast to reach simultaneously every corner of the globe and be automatically recorded, thus reducing costs to almost nil. The only charge for this service, usually known as *Press Schreibfunk*, is the installing of the apparatus, distributed by the electrical firm of Siemens and Halske, which has retail branches in Latin America. Trial use of the apparatus is free for three months, and if adopted, it costs only a few hundred marks.

No private company can compete with this for cheapness and rapidity of distribution, and the United Press and Associated Press (not being government-subsidized), have felt the pinch of this and other European competition for some years now.

The German News Agency—in Latin America, Transocean—broadcasts alternately in French and German, from 7:15 in the morning until half an hour before midnight. The news is world-wide, not merely of events in the Reich. Needless to say, the *Press Schreibfunk* releases are all cleverly colored. Recently Transocean transmitted stories of relief riots in our midwestern cities and an account of the elimination of all unemployment in happy Germany. Recently were sent over releases summarizing an article in the Berlin *Boersen Zeitung*—and such things are not printed without the full consent of the Brazilian authorities—which called the United States "a democracy of noise." It commented on the vast sums being spent by us, especially in Brazil, to attack Germany and spread propaganda. The "idealism" of the United States, it claimed, was purely "practical" to offset Germany's heavy buying of Brazilian instead of American cotton. Much of America's propaganda, it averred, is spread by "Jewish Yankee telegraph agencies and unscrupulous merchants eager to increase dollar earning."

From *Press Schreibfunk* come such statements as: "Even

in South America people are beginning to puzzle their heads over the real aims of the Pan-American solidarity movement that the United States has initiated, and over the deeper meaning of protection offers that started with the leasing of destroyers [to Brazil]."

In all these reports, the French Popular Front government is damned. The reputations of Loyalist Spain, Soviet Russia, England and the United States are systematically blackened. The virtues of Hitler, Mussolini and Franco are extolled. Blessing is given to the Ethiopian conquest and Japan's invasion of China. Some South American dictators look with favor on all such Nazi news propaganda. For them the word "democracy" is synonymous with rat-poison, Bolshevism and atheism.

In Brazil there are fifteen German newspapers to carry on propaganda. The story of the German press in Hispanic America and the secretly owned or subsidized newspapers in the native languages would constitute a chapter in itself. Heavy advertising, as in Perú, effectively throttles all criticism of the Reich. Favorable press comment is also imposed by radio pressure.

In Chile, the Catholic paper *La Unión* is crammed with news of Nazi triumphs, supplied by Transocean.

The use of German news has been fomented also by the gift of printing presses. Thus, through the European Minister-at-large of Panamá, Hitler recently gave the official National Revolutionary Party of that country fine equipment.

Four powerful German-owned radio stations in Rio and other cities coöperate with the Brazilian government. Executive decree obliges all local stations to rebroadcast this material.

The German steamship services have been expanding,

while prominent British lines and several American lines
have gone into bankruptcy. The lead is taken by the Ham-
burg-Amerika and the Hamburg-Sudamerikanische Dampf-
schiffahrts-Gesellschaft, which maintain fine passenger service and many regular cargo lines. The Hamburg-American
line has just installed the fine all-electric *Patria* on the Co-
lombia-Panamá-West Coast run. Completely air-condi-
tioned, it is the most de luxe boat now in South American
trade.

Air service has been promoted. Until recently, fortnightly
trans-Atlantic Zeppelin service was maintained. A mail
plane leaving Rio every Thursday and reaching Berlin every
Sunday, and another plane flying the opposite direction the
same days, carry on regular trans-Atlantic service. Special
passenger and cargo flights brought the number of overseas
flights last year up to nearly a daily schedule.

In Brazil itself, the Syndicato Condor, a subsidiary of
Lufthansa, operates over more than 5,000 miles and has
thirty-nine landing fields. Regular service is maintained
from Brazil to Montevideo and Buenos Aires along the
coast, to Corumbá on the Bolivian border and from Corumbá to Buenos Aires. Another network extends through
the state of Piahuy.

The Condor-Lufthansa maintains a bi-weekly service over
the Andes between Buenos Aires and Santiago de Chile.
In Colombia, the Scadta system, also a Lufthansa subsidiary,
and the oldest successful commercial air company in the
world, maintains daily service on seven routes, and bi-weekly
service to very distant interior points.

The Lloyd Aero Boliviano, also a subsidiary, covers all
eastern Bolivia, the rich Santa Cruz region. This extensive
service connects up with the Brazilian system at Corumbá,
Brazil. Seven regular routes are maintained, the two longest

being about 700 miles between Trinidad and Cobija, and from La Paz to Corumbá, about 800 miles.

The parent company recently organized the Lufthansa Sucursal del Perú, and exploratory work for a new Lima-Berlin route was carried on by Captain Berthold Alisch, to be in charge of the line. During 1934-1937, he made forty trans-Atlantic air crossings to South America in Dornier-Wal flying boats. His assistant will be Richard Mendes, also with extensive experience (on the Bagdad-Athens route).

On May 1, Lufthansa put in a new de luxe service with fine flying boats of large capacity—JU-52 Junker models with three German-built 750 horsepower Hornet engines—to carry seventeen passengers and a 10,000 pound useful load.

These will cut the flying time from Lima to Buenos Aires to twenty-two hours, broken in two daily flights. They also bring Lima within two days of Rio de Janeiro as compared to four days by Pan-American Airways; and they bring Lima but five days from Berlin.

This is worth much pondering. A far western city on the Pacific Coast of South America is now brought closer by air to Berlin than the former city is to many places in the United States. Argentina is now two to three days closer to Berlin than it is to New York; Rio de Janeiro is four days closer; and northern Brazil is now but two days from Berlin.

France expects to put in a fifty-hour passenger service from Paris to Buenos Aires, using Amphibians No. 47, with four Lioret motors.

These are facts that are remaking trade and international relationships faster than fuzzy speeches about the sacred·ness of democracy.

As this is being written, two Lufthansa officials, Paul

Mesmayer and Walter Grotevold are flying to Guayaquil, Ecuador, to make agency arrangements to extend the service another 1,500 miles north to Tumaco, connecting up with the tight network of German lines monopolizing Colombia's traffic.

Thus will have been completed a network of airways throughout South America, which serve most of the countries far more adequately than the Pan-American Airways because of the ramified web of domestic services maintained by the German companies. Germany has extensive air services for all countries except Venezuela.

Its hangars, landing fields and equipment are of the best. Excellent radio and meteorological service is maintained. The planes, marked with swastika, which criss-cross the southern continent have a high record of safety.

5

This general expansion of trade, investments, communications, aviation, news and propaganda is today part and parcel of the Hitler program for "the spiritual unity of the race," and has political and military significance.

Even before the World War, Berlin had a central bureau for "organization and colonization" in the Americas. The Portuguese and Spanish languages are diligently taught. Men preparing to enter the Latin-American field have to study Hispanic culture and customs, laws, trade regulations and habits. Today they must also acquire fervor for mystic Nazi race doctrines and the spiritual super-state. No longer are they merely commercial promoters but also active agents for the Hitler government.

The Nazi government has added many new frills. In addition to the regular preparation, a special six months' course in "Foreign Political Training" must be taken at an institute founded by Alfred Rosenberg, the great exponent of revived paganism in his war against all non-Aryans and Christians, i.e., against all the base sub-humans, the *Untermenschen*. This institute indoctrinates jurists, economists, commercial agents, scientists. They are taught the National Socialist ideology and the evils of Bolshevism and democracy. They are instructed in foreign affairs, Germanism abroad, racialism, press-relationships, languages, even society manners and sports. They read such books as that of Herr Sanhaber's *Zeitschrift fuer Geopolitik*, and other studies, which expose American business expansion, how our Power interests utilized strikes, punitive taxes, bureaucratic coercion and bribed officials to force native and foreign companies to sell out cheaply. They are taught how to combat British and American methods and propaganda.

Those who, after rigorous selection, are admitted to the course and pass final examinations, are guaranteed posts abroad in the Gestapo or other secret corps, the diplomatic service (which now includes many extra agents), or business firms, obliged to take on such employees.

The Reich is ever behind those chosen. The German press at home and abroad supports them. At least fourteen papers in foreign countries are openly party papers; nearly all other German-language publications are fervently pro-Nazi. Such agents are given material aid, credits, relief in distress, medical care, schooling for their children. They have plenty of German literature for themselves and for distribution; they receive films to show at gatherings. Free vacations are arranged through the agency "Strength Through Joy"—a most solemn Nazi designation, which maintains large excursion boats, easily convertible into airplane carriers.

The work among Germans, naturalized as citizens of other lands, is carried on by the VDA, founded in 1882, but since purged and, under Dr. Hans Steichner, an Austrian, brought to full Nazi bloom. The VDA seeks to prevent further assimilation so that Germans may remain or become—as stated in the last annual report—part of the "super-state racial body." Today, the VDA claims, "racial comrades in foreign states look up to the Reich and its Fuehrer with admiration and deep faith. They feel the blood-unity which is the foundation of the new German life."

All over Latin America, the VDA has formed Bunds of Volksdeutsche Turnvereins and youth organizations and lends them material and spiritual aid. A Bund in Cali, Colombia, on the borders of Panamá, engages in military manoeuvres; other marching Bunds give their eager "Heils!" in Panamá itself. In Rio Grande do Sul alone there are sixty Nazi organizations, affiliated with similar bodies in the Reich. Some of these have recently been suppressed, but recreational and physical culture groups are still numerous. The VDA establishes schools or aids those already existing, supplies them with free Nazi texts, funds and indoctrinates teachers. Speakers are constantly on tour; books, magazines, phonograph records, films, letters are circulated. Radio programs are diffused.

The German Foreign Institute of Stuttgart aids the VDA greatly, with its 45,000 volumes, 800 newspapers, and 400 magazines.

The work in athletics and the Youth movement is aided by Count Schulenberg, director of the foreign section of the Reich Athletes' League. "Naturally," he declares, "the German emblem of honor (sports insignias) for physical capacity is given only to men and women who have become closer spiritually and intellectually to the new Germany." Such decorations serve as bait that gets even the children of non-Nazi Germans. Count Schulenberg maintains a big corps of radio haranguers, who spread Nazi sport and blood doctrines across the far-off ether waves of the Pampas and the Rio Grande do Sul plateau.

Resident German merchants are obliged to donate to the National Socialist Party; the funds then are secretly diverted to local VDA and other propaganda work.

In Brazil, Argentina and elsewhere, second and third generation Germans have been enthusiastically reclaimed as spiritual subjects of the Reich. The belief is held that the Germans will eventually comprise a semi-independent Brazilian state—this was the Antarctic Germany marked on the Greater Fatherland maps even in the Kaiser's day. The Germans were disillusioned during the World War; they are likely to be again.

The overhead generalship for Germany's foreign propaganda work is provided by an independent bureau with cabinet status and not controlled by the Foreign Office. This bureau preaches anti-Bolshevism, denounces democracy and the Jews and—where it can profitably do so—Christianity. Closely tied up with the National Socialist Party and the Gestapo, it carries out the wishes of Nazi higher-ups.

In Latin-American countries with considerable German population, the Reich maintains diplomatic attachés of "Nazi Kultur." These keep the local colonies rigidly in line, oversee many secret activities and are immune from arrest because of their diplomatic status. They report directly to Hitler and have the weight of the Fuehrer in relation to German nationals abroad.

The nerve-center of all this tub-thumping is the dread Gestapo secret service, under the evil-faced, shifty-eyed, jawless Heinrich Himmler. It has large credits for Latin-American activities. Under various guises, Gestapo agents circulate in South America. The head for the West Coast from Panamá to Chile, the organizer of the secret *Der Deutsche Auslandischer Nazi Genossenschaft Bund*, is supposed to be Herr Walter Scharpp, former German consul in Colón. Many a business and professional man, also members of the working class, are paid or voluntary Gestapo agents who keep close tab on the activities of all Germans abroad and denounce those not wholeheartedly pro-Nazi. They likewise report on anti-Nazi propaganda to enable the Hitler regime to bring pressure, official, economic or otherwise to halt it. Since the various German-Japanese-Italian pacts, there is considerable indication that the secret agents of all three governments frequently work together in Latin America.

Such "espionage in México forms a wide network," the 1937 CTM report declares, "with numerous responsible agents and a multitude of gratuitous and voluntary agents."

Hitler agents bomb and break up anti-Nazi German meetings, plays and newspapers. Four such Nazis were convicted early this year of such criminal activities in Buenos Aires.

Thus the struggle for Latin America is not merely for commerce, trade and resources, but of ideology. The battle, first of all, has been for the bodies and souls of all Germans abroad.

Except for the Jews, the outward conversion has been well-nigh complete, although the anti-Nazi daily *Argentinisches Tageblatt* still publishes.

Hitler agents recently tried to fire the building where it is published. That it continues to survive is in large part due to the support of German Jews in Buenos Aires.

The business-power of German merchants everywhere has left little alternative to the so-called Aryan Germans than to seize the Hitler life-line "of indissoluble community of blood and destiny" or perish. Those not becoming "coördinated" face a boycott by all their fellow-citizens. The few who have openly resisted have lost their passports, have been stripped of citizenship and academic degrees, and have been publicly denounced as traitors.

6

The effort to control Germans abroad, body and soul, has included the customary tragic purge of the Jews. Most Jewish firms to the south had their intimate commercial relations with the mother-country. Severance brought them ruin. Local boycotts even terrorized native merchants into not dealing with Jews. Jewish employees were discharged. All the weight of Colonel Ulrich Fleischauer's *Weltdienst*, an anti-Semitic propaganda service of vast ramifications throughout the world, was put behind this effort.

Shortly before this anti-Semitic drive, the League of Nations appointed James G. McDonald, former head of the Foreign Policy Association, as a commissioner to persuade the Latin-American governments to take in uprooted German-Jewish exiles and provide them with professional employment. Accompanied by Dr. Samuel Guy Inman, head of Protestant Missionary work in Latin America, he made a complete tour, and his efforts were gratifyingly successful.

But the Nazi anti-Jewish crusade soon influenced Hispanic officials to persecute all Jews. The Germans staged a continent-wide campaign. Millions of pieces of anti-Semitic literature have been and are being distributed. German merchants have forced newspapers to run Jew-baiting articles. Writers are subsidized. In Argentina, Hugo Wast wrote his infamous *Oro* (Gold), which reproduces the false Zion protocols and calls for the complete "extermination" of the Jews. The Nazis have circulated it from Argentina to México.

Personally I have gathered proof in México of how German merchants actively promoted anti-Jewish persecutions and subsidized newspapers. Mexican under-officials, with pro-Nazi leanings, arrest and deport Jews. Serious anti-Semitic legislation already has been passed. A bill, which would wipe out all small Jewish businessmen and restrict Jewish residence to prescribed zones, almost became a law.

Various prominent papers constantly attack the Jews. In May a pro-Nazi afternoon daily came out with a broad headline "Eighteen Thousand Jews in the Capital Dedicate Themselves to Illegal Activities," and reported that 25 percent of the Jews were to be driven out.

The government at once warned newspapers not to publish anti-Semitic propaganda, based on false reports of official discrimination. "To publish such material is to encourage the rumors and untruths launched by foreign groups in opposition"—a direct slap at the German-Nazi elements. The government specifically denied that any laws would be dictated to eliminate Jews or other racial groups from México.

Ecuador recently ordered all Jews to leave the country. Outside pressure got this order rescinded, but the Jews have suffered much molestation.

Brazil, following the Vargas pro-Nazi coup, also took punitive action to deport Jews wholesale, a course temporarily halted by friendly under-cover American diplomatic pressure. Jews, regardless of nationality, are now forbidden to enter Paraguay.

In Chile, Brazil, Argentina and México, native Nazi movements—secretly subsidized, it is claimed, by the Germans—have taken up the Semitic witch-hunt. Though the Reich itself has persecuted Catholics, in Latin America Nazi agents have cleverly linked up anti-Semitism with religious prejudices, making a Catholic crusade to save the church. Hymns of hate against the Jews as enemies of the Catholic faith are printed on the back of colorful prints of the Virgin.

Hispanic America is a more extreme melting pot than is the United States, but in racial matters, however bitter political disputes, it has had a long tradition of complete tolerance. The German poison has changed all this. The long hairy arm of ignorant Nazi race-hatred reaches out across the Atlantic to persecute a great people that in Germany alone has made more noble and worthy contributions to world culture than all the Nordic Germans have ever made since time began.

7

Inevitably these efforts have led the Germans to attempt also to persuade the respective governments and populations to embrace Naziism. To this end, short-wave broadcasts from the Charlottenburg district in Berlin and elsewhere are sent out in Portuguese and Spanish.

The Germans have developed a narrow beam broadcasting technique which hashes up all other transmission and rides supreme on the air waves, despite even troublesome tropical static.

At Zeesen they have eleven 100,000-watt short-wave broadcasting stations, with a fifteen angle directional beam. These stations are five times the strength of the World

Wide Broadcasting station of Boston, handling our official propaganda, and twice as strong as the G. E. short-wave station. The German stations are twice as strong as anything in England. Their special short-wave technique in addition surpasses all others, and their programs can be directed at will.

Goebbels, too wise to clutter up the radio merely with Nazi glorification, provides classic and popular music and other entertainment. Latin-American artists are used extensively. Visiting Latin Americans are utilized to tell their impressions of the Reich. Much of this propaganda and the program material is prepared by the Reichrundfunk organization.

The work goes on steadily, with little fanfare. German broadcasts fill the air sixteen hours a day in Central America, Chile, Brazil, in all South America. The radio programs published, for instance in the Guatemalan papers, are about ninety percent Berlin broadcasts. For December 31, 1937, I find the trade item that 8,800 additional German radio receiving sets had been received in Guatemala. These sets are sold very cheaply or are given away, and are so manufactured as to receive only German broadcasts and to exclude all others.

The Germans are also turning out phonograph records by thousands, especially designed for local radio use, and which have an up-to-the-minute touch.

The Reich also seeks to control native stations, as already described in Brazil.

Germany has not been able to cut deeply into the movie field. The Latin Americans, if Spanish-speaking films are not available, prefer them in English, a better-known tongue. But the Germans do send out many "educational" films to be shown in private gatherings and loaned free to movies, schools and public meetings.

Recently, however, moved by the new possibilities in Spain, the Reich government-financed film industry has created the Hispanic Film Corporation, using Spanish actors, to turn out films that will cut into the southern market. *The Barber of Seville* is now being shot. Ufa is preparing *Andalusian Nights,* full of Nazi propaganda.

Great pressure is brought on the native intellectual groups. They are flattered socially and writers are influenced or secretly subsidized to flaunt the Nazi banner. A large amount of free space stuff is sent out along with illustrative material. Articles, filled with hazy mysticism, invoking recondite philosophy to aid the swastika cause, are translated and edged into magazines, even into worthy educational journals—the very sort of nebulous phraseology which so enchants a very prevalent type of lyrical Latin mind, improperly considering itself cultured.

Many free scholarships are extended to young people to study in Germany, transportation and expenses paid. Recently a Congress of Ibero-American students was held in Berlin. Military and naval officers are invited in large numbers to the German training schools. Scarcely a month passes without one or more large groups leaving Brazil to study in the Reich. Nearly all the countries are similarly favored. These students go back as Nazi addicts, enamored of the goosestep and the *Heil Hitler!* swastika flag-saluting rigmarole. The Napoleonic complex, all too strong in southern officers, is swelled to the bursting point.

The Hispanic Institute in Berlin collects books and materials on Latin America and ships out literature to the various libraries and universities. It invites southern scientists and others to lecture, sets up cultural contacts, exchanges data, entertains visiting celebrities. This was even true before Hitler came to power. When President-elect Calles visited Berlin, he was treated with the highest pomp, and a big military parade was held in his honor. In New York and Washington officially he was almost ignored. It was Berlin that gave Manuel Gamio an honorary doctorate for his epochal three-volume study in social anthropology on the Valle de Teotihuacán. Hitler has increased the extravagant amount of attentions bestowed upon visiting Latin notables; they are showered with decorations, honors, degrees.

Few American professors are found in large Indo-American Universities (moves are now being made to rectify this), but numerous Germans, many of them of renown, are on the faculties of most of the prominent institutions. Often their salaries are paid in Berlin, and their service in Brazilian, Argentine, Chilean or Peruvian schools counts for seniority and pension rating in the German school system itself. Germans maintain the best private schools in Latin America, their tuition kept low to attract a large native attendance. The instruction is excellent and this, plus cheap schooling, helps to wipe away any distaste of Nazi saluting. German schools in the single Brazilian State of Rio Grande do Sul number 2,845.

Recently, though, the teaching of Portuguese was made compulsory in all schools in that state. All teachers there must now be Brazilian citizens, unless special exception is obtained from the government. Nor can schools longer be subsidized by foreign governments or even foreign associations.

In the state of Santa Catharina a new law makes Portuguese the chief school language and forbids the display of emblems other than the Brazilian flag in educational plants. All teachers must be Brazilian by birth.

April 19th, President Vargas signed a dictatorial decree forbidding public demonstrations and political activities by foreigners, or the use of uniforms and special emblems. Financial aid to organizations within Brazil from foreign governments was made illegal. Schools, newspapers and propaganda bureaus were strictly regulated.

May 7th, Vargas created by dictatorial decree an "immigration and colonization council," and forbade foreign languages to be taught to minors under fourteen. Foreign language newspapers, books and magazines are prohibited in rural regions. The provisions smack of Brazilian-style Naziism.

Part and parcel of the Nazi secret service and the various Kultur drives, the German firms aid valiantly. Their warehouses store the leaflets and books sent out to the New World, many of them from the Fichte Bund in Hamburg. Such business houses have been accused by high Chilean and Brazilian officials of providing arms and credits to Nazi groups.[2]

Everywhere, many native business firms are whipped into line.

The Brazilian Integralistas, or Green Shirts, though decidedly a native manifestation, led by Plinio Salgado, were favored, before being outlawed, by constant fairly open

[2] Consider the Nazi activities of the Stahlunion, Herman Stoltz, the powerful Hasenclever, Egon Renner and Van Hartt of Rio Grande do Sul. Members of the firm of Wiedman, Machner and Company of Porto Alegre, and Herr Schnitze of the Deutsch Morzen in Santa Catharina are said to be Nazi agents. In Perú the powerful Hamburg house, Federica Emmel, S.A., with headquarters in Arequipa and branches throughout southern Perú and all Bolivia, agents for the Krupps of Magdeburg, Grusonwerk, and Diesel-Deutz motors, push the Nazi cause even among the Indians. In Panamá, Hans Herman Heildelk and Ernest Neuman, the German consul, owners of the Boyd steamship agency, have been cited as doing secret Nazi work. Neuman also owns the largest hardware stores in partnership with Fritz Kohpcke, also said to be active.

German aid. That aid has since continued. Employees of German firms were required to join. The Green Shirt program, full of imitative phraseology, depended largely upon Nazi and Fascist ideology. Brazilian opposition Congressmen, before representative government was abolished, charged that the Integralistas had received money and aid from German sources. German agents have been arrested and similarly charged. Germany certainly was selling arms to minority groups. Etzberger Brothers arranged to send recalcitrant Governor Flores da Cunha, of Rio Grande do Sul, the German stronghold, $1,000,000 worth of arms.

At one time, the Integralistas claimed 25 percent of the army chiefs and 90 percent of the navy.

The violent suppression of all political elements except the Green Shirts largely made possible the Vargas coup of last year. Vargas climbed into absolute dictatorship with their aid, adopted their program, absorbed some of their leaders. High Integralista Nazis were given important government posts. The Integralista leader, General Gôes Monteiro became Vargas' chief of staff.

The organization was then ordered disbanded except for cultural purposes. The new corporate state created by Vargas was to be supreme, undisputed even by those who had aided him. Vargas thereafter ruled in the ornate Guanabara Palace in Rio with bayonets, an absolute despot, albeit a shaky one.

Having thus divided the Nazi movement by his coup, Vargas has increasingly suppressed the remnants that did not fit into his personal Fascist-governing plans. The recent attempted coup (May, 1938)—in alliance with naval officers, German bank employees and financial interests, and German and Italian agents—shows that the Integralistas still have strength, or at least ambitions. Arms used in the Integralista revolt were of German origin. The Reich Kultur attaché, H. H. von Cassel, has been under a cloud, and in May left the country hurriedly. Brazilian officials have charged that local German firms supplied money and are now producing documents, dating back before the Vargas coup, showing definite German aid and generalship in the movement. It is well to remember that prior to last year, Vargas himself was definitely allied with the movement, sent it telegrams of congratulation, reviewed its demonstrations with the Nazi salute. The police should know whereof they speak.

But the Vargas government, if almost completely Fascist, Nazi and totalitarian in its methods, is following a distinctly nationalistic policy—of late influenced by secret American diplomacy—that is putting a decided crimp in many German activities. Regulations concerning schools, control over the teaching personnel, and the teaching of Portuguese, the suppression of the marching Bunds—such acts reveal that Vargas' Fascism is now Brazilian, not a foreign-controlled brand.

But his victory is not in the slightest a victory of democracy or popular government. In fact the minority Nazi group, the Integralistas, probably has far more popular following than Vargas' own bayonet-supported dictatorship. As the *Manchester Guardian* put it, the revolt was a "Fascist uprising against a semi-Fascist dictatorship," and the London *News Chronicle* remarked that Vargas had put down the Green Shirts, but "we have seen no statement as to the color of Dr. Vargas' shirt, but it seems there is no reason to doubt that he has one and that it has a color."

But the irritations over German activities have grown acute, and the investigations into the May "pajama revolt" have put Germany on the spot. So uneasy became the situation that in June Germans began leaving the country, and on July 12, the Reich declared it would throw as much of its Brazilian business as it could elsewhere. Brazil is now throwing railway supply orders to the United States. We are now once more exporting more than Germany.

The Germans know that Vargas, for all his brutal methods, sits on a very shaky seat, and is universally hated in his own country. They know that the series of revolts ever since he seized power marks universal discontent with his regime. They do not believe that his dictatorship can last much longer. Having found him vacillating in his relations to Germany, they hope for a regime even more economically dependent upon Berlin in which they will have larger undisturbed influence. Part of Germany's world plans depend upon this.

The hint is given in the *Boersen Zeitung* of Berlin, May 13th, following the Integralista revolt:

"It is to be hoped that the Vargas regime will learn from these experiences that in the long run it is impossible to rule merely with force against the people's will. It is doubtful how long bayonets will serve their purpose.

"The internal weakness of the Vargas regime, which must support itself increasingly with the use of bayonets, has been exploited by its great northern neighbor. This North American influence is as unpopular as the previous dollar diplomacy. To camouflage this dependence on North America charges are made of alleged interference by other powers."

It would be amusing if our State Department continues to support the present tyranny, and the Nazis now become advocates of democracy. The Brazilian story and German participation therein are not yet finished.

In Chile, the Nazi movement, according to Congressman Meza of Santiago, was subsidized by the Germans. The

Nazis, led by Jorge González von Marees, were allowed to parade and to terrorize all others. At one time, encouraged by former Dictator Ibáñez (for a time last year ironically become a Communist—Popular Front hero) and later by Alessandri, the Nazis were able to put 10,000 disciplined and armed marchers on the streets of Santiago. Since then they have been discouraged, and in March, 1937, polled only 18,000 votes, as compared to the 37 percent of the total polled by the Socialist ex-President Marmaduke Grove.

In Argentina, though in foreign affairs the government follows English, to some extent Italian, lead, President Justo coerced all democratic organizations but for the most part allowed Nazi and Fascist groups a free hand. President Ortiz follows the same pattern.

Of late non-governmental elements have made such a noise against Nazi propaganda that all the newspapers have taken up the cry.

"The Nazi machine has transferred its terrorism to America," asserts *La Critica*, recently temporarily suppressed by the government, itself semi-Fascist.

Organizations have been formed to boycott German and Japanese goods. Congressman Enrique Dickman has announced he will demand an investigation of all foreign organizations and schools. The German marching song, *Horst Wessel*, but not *Deutschland Ueber Alles*, has been prohibited, and for international labor day this year—May 1st —to prevent violence, the government prohibited the Luna Park meeting of Nazi Germans and forbade the carrying of foreign flags. German schools have been ordered closed in La Pampa territory.

In México, the Gold Shirts' secret organization was born of a conference with Nazi agents in Mexicali, and at one time, according to local newspaper editors, was subsidized by German firms. Prominent Mexicans have charged that German companies are assessed for National Socialist funds, which are diverted to fomenting propaganda and the various local pro-Nazi groups.

At present the principal activities of this nature center in the local so-called Brown House on Uruguay Street, headquarters for the native National Socialist Party and the Nazi *Jugend*. Also for the secret propaganda agency, *Deutsche Volksgemanschaft*, false-fronted by a charity organization. Relations are said to be maintained with Nazi agents in the United States.

Close Nazi relations, it has been charged, are maintained with the reactionary General Ramon Yocupicio, governor of Sonora. Baron Ernst von Merk, with a record of Gestapo activities elsewhere, is the right hand man of General Saturnino Cedillo, known for his reactionary opinions and Napoleonic ambitions, and is said to have arranged secret shipments of arms to Cedillo, who revolted in May. Other Nazi arms shipments have come in via Guatemala and the United States.

Various Nazi agents have been unmasked in México along with their relations with such organizations as the Mexican Nationalist Union (a new front for the Gold Shirts), the Nationalist Youth, and a wing of the Anti-Reëlection Party. Following an anti-Hitler editorial in *Mexican Life*, an American magazine, Nazis carried on a campaign to shut off its German and native advertising.

8

What does this all add up to? Is the struggle for markets, for trade, a sufficient explanation? Is it merely the need for raw supplies, the need to dispose of war materials?

Why then the intensive effort not merely to add Germans abroad to the Reich's great "spiritual" empire, but to convert native governments and peoples to Naziism?

Obviously the stakes are much larger than mere commercial interest. Today international trade is the handmaiden of future war and conquest. This explains in part the determination to sell Latin America airplanes, war vessels, submarines, cannon, munitions. The elephantine expansion of German munitions industry reinforces this determination, and sales have been made to nearly every country. Krupp and Rhine Metall Borig wares are exchanged for raw materials. New German arms companies have been founded in Brazil.

In Chile, British Vickers still has a good hold, but the Germans have been cutting in and have sold many supplies, including bombing planes. They are said to be turning out two cruisers for Venezuela. They have sold Ecuador considerable ammunition. Brazil and Argentina have bought German munitions.

Dictator Trujillo of the Dominican Republic, according to former Washington Minister, Dr. Angel Morales, has recently got a large secret arms shipment from the Reich. Secret shipments have gone into Nicaragua and Guatemala.

The sale of munitions is the opening wedge for military and naval experts, who thus get a foothold in the native defense institutions. Still more war supplies can then be sold and political influence is gained.

General Knudt, of World War fame, long led Bolivian forces during the Chaco conflict. The late Captain Röhm, formerly head of Hitler's S.A., was also prominent there. A Reich military mission instructs the Ecuadorian army. Germans built up the Chilean army and a special mission is training the Chilean flying forces. Sixty-five German and Italian planes were purchased in 1937, and still heavier purchases are projected. Argentina's army is largely German-trained. German officers are thick as fleas in Brazil. Germans have trained México's cavalry and installed machinery for her national munitions works, which turn out rifles, machine-guns, artillery, cartridges, shells and bombs. In May, 1938, a German shipment of arms, arranged by Baron von Rosenthal, of 1,500 machine-guns and 1,500,000 rounds of ammunition, arrived at Vera Cruz.

In Perú, the influence is largely financial: a mission of former Reich officials determine the country's fiscal, currency and statistical matters. Perú is said to have a secret understanding with Germany, and the German firm of Gildermeister—and one of the Gildermeisters is the diplomatic envoy to the Reich—owns the important private port of Chicama, which appoints through political pull even its own customs agents and excludes all outsiders. What comes in and goes out through that port is not known to the outside world. The Gildermeister estate also has a powerful radio station which receives messages and transmits directly to Berlin. The station is always heavily guarded by armed Germans.

9

The whole Teutonic Latin-American crusade, carried on in such grandiose scale and so successfully, apparently has for its goal an ambitious achievement of world power. Latin America is today definitely planned as part of Germany's proposed defense line. On events there may hinge her success in any conflict on the continent of Europe.

Following the 1885 Congo Congress, Germany began a dizzy period of colonial expansion. As her navy grew, she became more arrogant, wanted colonies in the Americas. Her battleships prowled Central American and South American coasts. In the guise of collecting debts, she played her guns on defenseless cities.

The Venezuelans have not forgotten the *Panther's* 1902 attack on Maracaibo, behind which lie rich oil fields, in which the Germans smashed the aged San Carlos fort, defiled the chapel, stole the bells, and arrogantly threw pennies to the soldiers they had defeated.

Bunau-Varilla, who negotiated the Panama Canal Treaty, claimed that German influence in Colombia blocked our demands. Germany wanted the future canal herself.

Nicaraguans remember the apology their government had to give to a German cruiser because a Nicaraguan slapped his father-in-law, the German consul.

Since those days the Germans have learned much. In the New World they now play the game of Machiavelli rather than that of the iron shard. Former aggressiveness has been replaced by more cunning manoeuvres for position and influence.

The outcome may spell the fate of the British empire, for from Argentina come British bully beef and the wheat essential for survival. Argentina and Brazil are keystones in the arch of the British colonial system. For England, Venezuelan and Mexican oil is rapidly becoming a matter of life and death. In case of war, the Roumanian wheat and oil fields and the oil supply of the Near East could be cut off. England must depend for the large part of her raw materials at such a moment on the Western Hemisphere.

During the last war, England fought two naval battles (lost the first, won the second) off the coast of South America. She could win any such battle today.

What then can Germany do without a fleet to strike in

South American waters? The answer is that, though Germany is rushing to completion a mammoth naval program, she apparently does not intend to be entirely dependent upon one or two naval battles but now seeks definite New World allies. Even if they do not openly join with her in any struggle, they can withhold supplies from Germany's enemies. Germany is going the limit to preserve or create pro-Nazi regimes in Latin America, but may, as in Spain, eventually intervene in the name of neutrality and the sacred Monroe Doctrine.

Strong-arm German influence once established, many possibilities would arise in war-time. In the last war, little Salvador, already German-dominated, refused to declare war on the Central powers, remained neutral even at the price of an American blockade of her ports. Honduras was coerced into declaring war on Germany, but was so furious she at once gave resident Germans every facility. México, smarting from our Pershing expedition, openly pro-German, gave great aid in divers ways to the Central Powers.

For another war, Germany is far better prepared to the south than before. The equivalent of strong Nazi regimes exist in several countries. If she cannot control Latin-American war-supplies and food she can perhaps plunge Latin America into conflicts which will cut off such exports. She can try to promote internal revolution. The present German policy to the south is but one of many bricks laid one on another in a daring gamble for world power.

With every Nazi-Fascist victory, diplomatic or military, the prestige of Hitler and Mussolini in Latin America increases. Most of the numerous dictators there, themselves petty Hitlers, believe today that Germany is the coming World Power whom they should favor and whose form of government they should emulate.

CHAPTER

III

The Black Shirts March

Eᴀʀʟʏ this year, the semi-official *Corriere Diplomatico e Consulare* boasted that "seven Latin-American countries are proceeding decisively toward stabilization upon the principles laid down by Premier Mussolini's Fascism."

"No one can possibly doubt," recently wrote Luigi Federzone, President of the Italian Senate and long head of the Black Shirt phalanxes, on returning from a 'vacation' in South America, "that the Brazilians in their accomplishment [the coup of Vargas] profited by the experiences of Fascism in founding itself in Italy." This appeared in Mussolini's own paper, *Il Popolo d'Italia* of Milan.

"It is a fact," continued Federzone, "that the Italian Fascist organization, the Italian press and the Italian support of Brazil have contributed to creating the new state of affairs."

Virginio Gayde, the head of Italy's propaganda machine, even before Vargas' establishment of a "corporate" state in Brazil, declared that Italy and Fascism would soon have new recruits among American nations.

Dr. Nicolà Pende, of the University of Rome and Chief of Fascist Action for Italians in South America, envisions a great cultural league to which already, he claims, half a million Latin-American intellectuals adhere. In articles, entitled "For the Cultural Empire of Fascism," a call has been sent out over a continent and a half for a great cultural congress to be held in Buenos Aires. This, declares Pende, "by the unanimous vote of the Latin Nations" will place Rome "at the head of the Latin cultural world."

Mussolini, Gayde and Pende have a great field to cultivate even if they restrict their activities merely to Italian New World colonists. Of all European countries, during the past seventy-five years, Italy has sent more of her sons to western shores, perhaps some five million in all. In three-quarters of a century, two million Italians—predominantly from northern Italy—have flooded into Argentina. 56 percent of all foreigners there are Italian. Next to New York, Buenos Aires is probably the largest Italian city in the world. Few leading families are without an admixture of Italian blood. Probably a third of the population can trace Italian heritage. The Italian speech of the newcomers has made Argentine Spanish the most corrupted on the continent, more divergent from the pure Castilian than that of any other Hispanic country.

Over a million Italians people southern Brazil. It has been estimated that at least 35 percent of the country's 46,000,000 inhabitants have some Italian blood. São Paulo, today a great industrial center of over a million inhabitants, is almost entirely Italian. It ranks with the great Italian-peopled cities of the world, along with Rome, Naples and New York.

Italians are a big element in Uruguay. Paraguay is very dominated by Italian capital and steamship companies. The name of its President from 1928-31, Dr. José Guggiari, attests to the long-standing immigration of Italians into the very heart of the continent.

Chile has frequently invited Italian immigrants and has given them land-grants.

They comprise the largest European group in Perú. Italian influence there dates far back. Lima's fire department is run by volunteers, mostly Italians. In May of this year was celebrated the seventy-second anniversary of fire company "Roma No. 1." In the sixties, this company helped fight off the Spaniards from Callao, and its members won citations for bravery. In 1879, during the Perú-Chilean War of the Pacific, "Roma No. 1," with 1,500 volunteers marched to war and creditably won more citations. Over the years the Italian colony has gained the affection and trust of the Peruvian people. Today it enjoys large economic privileges. Over $100,000,000 Italian capital is invested there.

For more than a generation, Italians have had influence in Venezuela. There are many in Ecuador and Colombia.

Further north, while there are many influential Italians, they do not bulk so large in numbers or importance. In Honduras, for instance, the last time I was there, the leading hotel in Tegucigalpa was run by an Italian ex-aviator, but they cannot be said to be numerous in Central America, México or the Caribbean.

The wealthy, far southern, temperate-zone part of the continent is their stronghold. There they exercise an influence that may someday change the destinies of the nations.

While the mass of Italian immigrants have been poverty-stricken settlers and proletarians, many have become prosperous farmers and small businessmen. Others have become wealthy rapidly. Large Italian companies now reach out to invest in the New World, and powerful economic control now radiates from Italy across the seas.

The strongest Italian banking concern in the field is the *Banca Comerciale Italiana*, with agents or branches in Argentina, Brazil, Chile, Colombia, Ecuador, Perú and Uruguay. In Argentina, the *Banco de Italia y Rio de la Plata* and the *Nuevo Banco Italiano*, with head offices in Buenos Aires, each has over a dozen branches scattered across the Pampas. The *Banco Italiano* of Valparaiso is in less dominating position, but the *Banco Italiano* of Lima is one of the two powerful institutions of the country, maintains branches throughout Perú, owns great sugar and cotton estates, as in Ica, and is the principal financial agent of the government.

The leading Italian bank in Brazil is the *Banco Italo-Brasileiro*, with headquarters in São Paulo, but Italian capital is strong in numbers of institutions.

Everywhere in agriculture, the Italians are strong. They have built up the great wine-growing industry of Argentina —the annual output being 150,000,000 gallons—and in Mendoza maintain the largest *bodegas* to be found anywhere in the world. They are predominate in the Peruvian and Chilean wine industries. In Chile are produced the finest wines in South America, the peer of many a European favorite.

In Brazil, Perú and Colombia, they own sugar and cotton plantations. Many are engaged in the quebracho industry in Paraguay and the Argentine Chaco. In Brazil, Argentina and Uruguay, they are active in the dairy industry, turn out cheeses and sausages. In Perú, Brazil and Argentina, they have gone into lumbering.

They have mills and factories for flour, spaghetti, crackers and biscuits, chocolate (in Perú, the Torino and Lomellini factories), shoes, leather, drugs, wall-paper, paper, beer, soap, candles, perfumes, textiles, crockery and fine chinaware. Italians are strong distributing agents for farm machinery, some of it manufactured in Italy, much of it from Germany.

2

The large Italian population has given Italy a broader base than any other country for a strong steamship service. The finest, swiftest and cheapest passenger liners in the South American trade are Italian. Some are the most luxurious palace-boats afloat anywhere. *Cosulich* of Trieste has a general passenger service to South America and cargo service from Brazil and the Plata River. The *Lloyd Sabaudo* sends boats from Genoa to Rio, Santos, Montevideo and Buenos Aires. The *Navigazione Generale Italiana* has a regular de luxe service out of Genoa and Nice to Brazil, also to the Guianas, Colombia, and the west coast. The *Navigazione Libera Triestina* covers Central America. The *Transatlantica Italiana* limits itself to Brazil and Argentina. *La Veloce* handles Central American, Caribbean and west coast trade.

The Italians have made many mass and single air flights to South America. General efforts toward regular commercial service to and in South America—in charge of Umberto Klinger, head of Italian civil air-service—has led to the recent inauguration of a trans-Atlantic route. Bruno Mussolini's flight early this year was partly to promote this purpose. Trial flights for the service were made with the Savoia Machetti bombing type of sea-plane. General Pellegrini was sent over to celebrate the necessary contracts with private and governmental agencies in Brazil, Uruguay and Argentina. The new line flies via Gibraltar and Dakar, to Natal and Rio de Janeiro in Brazil, then to Montevideo and Buenos Aires.

Despite the fine air, steamship, banking services, the large Italian colonies in the various countries are not so well-organized for retail trade as are the Germans, or, as in some countries, the Japanese. The colonists do not provide the immediate commercial outlet so important in the building up of trade by the other two dictatorial powers. However, the strenuous efforts of Mussolini's government, if not resulting in commercial gains comparable to those of Germany and Japan, have shown slight increases in various countries, and in some cases, where juicy contracts for munitions were obtained, large increases.

Very favorable trade treaties have been arranged with almost all the countries. Mussolini, in greater financial straits than Japan or Germany, has not been able to utilize the direct barter weapon to the same extent. But through friendliness and diplomacy, the Italian government has secured notable concessions everywhere. At the time Roosevelt was in Buenos Aires to talk neutrality and establish the principle of non-intervention and to denounce forced conquest, Chile signed a treaty with Mussolini's government, which also recognized the latter's forced conquest of Ethiopia. Italy and Germany have been allowed to unfreeze excess credits in Chile, something the United States and England have not obtained.

A new trade treaty, made with Argentina in 1933, has increased Italian trade and good-will. Relations with Brazil are tops. In Perú, the best commercial arrangements of all have been granted.

In Cuba, the Italians have just cracked through the American reciprocity set-up and the differential tariff which gives such an advantage to American goods. Agreeing to buy definite quantities of sugar, tobacco, coffee and liquors, Italy has gotten all handicaps set aside and the removal of all quota restrictions on Italian goods. Italian (and British) autos at times have outsold American cars in Brazil and

Argentina, despite American assembly plants on the ground.

Recent developments in México are likely to bring in Italy as a heavy purchaser of Mexican oil, which will prove a lever for corresponding trade concessions.

3

If commercial gains for Italy have been only moderate, her propaganda gains have exceeded those of any other nation. Her first drive—as later that of the Nazis with Germans— was to convert the Italian settlers to Fascism. This was more difficult than in the case of the Germans, for many Italian immigrants are definitely proletarian. Many had taken an active part in the Argentine and Uruguayan labor movements. But little by little, propaganda and pressure has worked. Recalcitrant Italians were cut off from their Fascist fellows. Large Italian firms boycotted all non-Fascists; they were thrown out of their jobs, their passports rescinded. By and large everywhere, the resident Italians have mostly been whipped into line or into silence.

The second propaganda advance was to convert the Latin-American governments and populations to the Fascist creed. The customary instruments were utilized.

Besides the various Italian-language papers, many Spanish- and Portuguese-language papers were brought into line. One of the largest afternoon Buenos Aires dailies is now Italian-controlled. The four leading dailies of Lima, Perú, have intimate relations with the *Banco Italiano* and are subsidized by heavy Italian advertising. Above all, *El Comercio*, the predilect organ of the wealthy Civilista land-holding class and the Catholic hierarchy, supports Fascism wholeheartedly. Co-owner Carlos Miro Quesado has gone to Italy to study the corporate system in order to help implant it further in Perú and there heads an official Italian propaganda bureau for half a dozen South American countries. The columns of the paper overflow with lyric praise for Mussolini and glorify the Italian campaigns in Ethiopia and Spain.

The Rome propaganda office maintains a free press-service for Latin America, and does not require, in fact prefers, that the source of information be not divulged. Thus poorer papers, particularly in the interiors, run this material as though from their special correspondents abroad. It exalts Mussolini, Japan, Germany, Franco, belittles the Soviet Union, the United States and Great Britain.

Short-wave broadcasts are sent out daily from three powerful short-wave stations in Rome. A new station, even more powerful than those of Zeesen, Germany, will have been completed by the time this book goes to press. With Argentina and other countries, two-way broadcasting has been arranged. This has permitted the making of arrangements with many local stations to re-broadcast Italian propaganda. The Italian government is a heavy purchaser of radio time over local South American stations. Also, Mussolini has given Panamá a powerful radio station.

The *Instituto Interuniversitario Italiano*, founded in 1923, actively promoted cultural relations and has branches in many of the southern countries. Many Italian professors are sent forth, salaries paid by the Black Shirt government. It aids generally in the exchange of knowledge, and helps students and professors visiting Italy. They are given letters of introduction to influential people.

For all the countries, numerous scholarships, plus free transportation, are maintained at the military, naval, aviation and other Italian schools and universities. Annually, known Fascist sympathizers from each country are invited to Rome at government expense, where they are fêted by Mussolini personally.

One of the latest Argentineans to go to Italy for aviation study is Jorge Ortiz, the son of the newly elected President.

In Perú have been organized Balilla, or children's Black Shirt marching groups, and special imitative Fascist women's corps. These and other efforts, as well as most youth propaganda, have been carried on by the Italian school, Antonio Raimundi, by the Italian Sports Circle, the Italian Social Club and various other such centers. Numerous lectures in behalf of Fascism are given in the National Catholic University and the Italian Art Museum, especially by the Italian Minister and the Papal Nuncio. One of the most active supporters of Fascism in the Catholic University is Alberto Benavides Canseco, Professor of International Law and brother-in-law of the Dictator-President.

At this writing, while an Italian mission runs the Peruvian army and police, the head of its Chief of Staff, Colonel Jorge Vargas, is studying in the military college in Rome. When the Peruvian cadets recently paraded in Panamá, officialdom and the press there hailed them as occupying the brave advanced post of Fascism in Latin America.

The sending of Italian emissaries of prominence to Hispanic America began long before the Fascists came into power. At one time Italy sent even so prominent a man as Orlando to drum up trade and influence. But since Mussolini came in, the effort has been intensified. Prominent Italian statesmen and others are constantly en route to the southern lands. We have already noted the voyage of Federzone, long touted as the most important man, next to Mussolini, in the whole Black Shirt movement—an impassioned, mystical and fanatic Fascist and the original founder of the Nationalist *Sempre Pronto* Blue Shirts. In Buenos Aires he was officially made "the guest of the nation," and was fêted as have been few visitors.

In 1934 the flight of Balbo's great air-squadron to Rio, the greatest and longest mass flight of military planes in history, had a terrific effect on Brazilian official mind. Other less heralded flights have been made. The most recent has been that of Bruno Mussolini, with two companion planes. The Italian authorities described this as "a propaganda flight."

Bruno's plane was donated to the Brazilian government with elaborate ceremony. Italian Ambassador Lojacono, in his presentation speech, told Brazilian Secretary of War, Enrico Caspar, that the gift was "a friendly gesture to a sister Latin nation."

When the United States promoted the Pan-American aviation congress in Lima, with the obvious purpose of shutting out Europeans and selling American planes, our government aided the private commercial firms selling bombing planes—part of our general program of peace—by sending down the air-craft carrier *Ranger* at tax-payers' expense, with a fine squadron of seventy-eight army wingers, and army fliers, also at tax-payers' expense. But we had no monopoly of the show. The Germans came along with Focke Wolf, Hotha, Klein, Junkers and Heinkel planes. Italy, enjoying special government invitation, showed up with a whole load of planes aboard the *Gloria Stella* to pay tribute to Jorge Chavez, an early Peruvian aviator killed in Italy. They brought a whole assortment: Caproni, Caproni Ghible and Fiats.

Waiting until the American planes were sailing over in perfect, sober formation, forty of Italy's most daring aviators dashed in and recklessly performed thrillers over the

City of Kings, stealing the show. They sold six more bombers, the Americans none.

The Italians then flew on with the rest to Chile, Argentina, Uruguay and Brazil, calling forth a delirium of enthusiasm.

The propaganda by the Italians has been facilitated by common Latin culture and institutions. Though the Germans have piped low about anti-Catholicism in Latin America, the persecution of the Church in Germany has raised doubts of the Nazi movement; but Rome is Catholic; Mussolini plays ball with the Pope, and Fascism is considered a protector of the religion, a belief heightened among reactionary feudal elements by Italy's armed support of "Christian" Franco in Spain.

Though some feeling against Italy was provoked by the invasion of Ethiopia, success more than offset this; and though Ethiopia was already a Christian nation, the propaganda was spread that Italy was merely invading that dark benighted land of Africa in order to promote Catholicism. The liberal concessions at once given there to the Church and to Catholic missionaries, gave point to the contention. Chile, Brazil, Perú, Salvador, Guatemala, among others, have recognized Italy's conquest of Ethiopia. Recently Uruguay joined the parade, and its foreign minister, in reply to criticism, has justified the act on the ground that it is not a violation of the Pan-American pact by which all the New World nations agreed not to recognize territorial conquest, since that pact applies only to America. To continue to refuse to recognize Italian victory would cause Uruguay to seem hostile to Italy with whom she has the closest relationship.

The collapse of the League of Nations also has promoted Italian purposes to the south. For many years, the Latin-

American countries, worried by our marine interventions in Nicaragua and Haiti, hastened for the most part to join the League. Invariably rather than call on us in settling their numerous disputes, they invoked the aid of the European assemblage. But with the Japanese invasion of Manchuria and the failure of the League to do more than give a little slap on the wrist, the Latin-American countries have been steadily losing faith in Woodrow Wilson's stepchild. Now they have none at all. Some, such as Salvador and Guatemala, under the influence of the Fascist powers and Japan, left the League long ago with blatant denunciations; others have merely quietly folded up their tents. Recent defections are Chile and Venezuela, both much under German and Italian influence.

A third force bad for the Fascist cause in South America has been dissipated. The cultural leadership of Spain and Portugal is a very important factor in the southern countries. With the abdication of King Alfonso of Spain and the rise of the Republic, a wave of liberal sentiment led by resident Spaniards swept over Latin America. Many resident Italians temporarily broke away from the Fascist whiplash and began celebrating the end of monarchies and dictatorships.

The South American dictators became alarmed. So did the big land-holding classes. So did the Church. For them, the Franco revolt was a God-send. Also for the Italians. Italian aid to Franco greatly strengthened Mussolini's influence with all the feudal dictators of Latin America.

Very early after Mussolini's coup, imitative Fascist organizations sprang up spontaneously here and there in many Hispanic countries. One of the first was in México in 1923, led by Saenz de Sicilia. Others succeeded it and still exist. In Argentina a strong Fascist group, aided by wealthy Italians, was organized with official aid when Dictator Uriburú expelled the Soviet Commercial Agency in 1931. It was known as the Legión Cívica and has about 150,000 members. Seven other small Fascist organizations eventually appeared, now welded into the Guardia Argentina. The Guardia is pledged at any critical moment to act with the Legión Cívica.

Uriburú's dictatorship promoted these bands and itself was promoted as a semi-Fascist experiment and with Fascist coöperation. His successor, puppet President Justo, removed elected governor after governor, by sending in for the most part Fascist Interventors. Gradually thereafter Justo eased control into the hands of the traditional Conservative Party.

Ortiz, the recent President, was candidate on the Concordia ticket, made up of Conservatives, renegade Fascists and renegade members (of which he was one) of the Radical Civic Party, and took power without having a majority of the popular vote. Fascists are rarely molested in Argentina, though democratic groups have few rights.

In Chile, the Fascists and Nazis were openly abetted by Dictator Ibáñez and later by Dictator Alessandri.

Federzone and others have openly testified to Italian assistance to the Green Shirt Integralistas of Brazil. Italian employees have been obliged to join, and the Italian banker in Brazil, Count Matarazzo, along with such German industrialists as Hasenclever, Von Regan and Hartt, and others, have been charged with handling Integralista financing.

Following the recent unsuccessful Integralista Palace coup, Cesare Riselli was arrested, allegedly bearing documents from the Italian government, urging "energetic support" of the revolt.

4

As is true of the other rapidly arming powers, the expansion of war industries has made Italy put forth strenuous efforts to sell munitions, war vessels and airplanes, particularly the latter. The selling of such products necessitates the sending of experts, which increases economic and political influence and insures further orders.

Italian munitions are found in nearly all the countries, including those of Central America. Heavy shipments of Italian artillery and machine-guns were sent to Perú last December and have been distributed among the garrisons of Fort Santa Catalina, Barbones Arsenal, and the frontier barracks along the Ecuadorian border, where a boundary dispute simmers.

This February twenty officers and sailors left Venezuela for Spezia to bring back the two war vessels purchased there, the *General Urdanata*, and *General Soublette*, paid for with Venezuelan oil. It is said other orders have been arranged. The Italians recently offered Chile two 10,000 ton cruisers in exchange for nitrates. Italy has sold numbers of war-vessels to Brazil, and last February delivered three Italian-built submarines. The Italians are now training the Bolivian army. Of late they are said to have sold Paraguay river gunboats, munitions, fifty-four war planes.

Most of the countries going in for armaments have bought many Italian planes. Half a dozen years ago Italy sent aviation attachés to the more important countries to promote sales and give official support to private Italian companies. No less a person than De Pinedo was sent as attaché to Buenos Aires and persuaded the government there to buy many flying craft. Balbo's squadron of twenty-one planes was sold to Brazil. About the time the United States proposed to lease war vessels to Brazil, Chile cabled an order to its Aracena mission then in Rome studying aircraft to buy large quantities. Orders were placed for Junker bombers and Italian army-type Bredda and amphibian planes. When the Italian air mission visited Chile last year, sixty planes were reported sold.

The greatest success has been in Perú. Since the aviation demonstrations over Lima, the Italians have been favored in every way. They have been erecting at Las Palmas aviation field, just south of Lima, the big Caproni assembly plant, now under the management of Adlo Bert, a famous World War flier. It has an announced capacity of fifty war planes annually, though informed persons claim it can, if necessary, turn out 300. Also, using the German engineer Von Stach Galzheim, the Italians have been building a gigantic modern hangar for the government, the largest in all South America. The steel for these plants comes from Germany. Perú's aviation budget has steadily climbed from 1,648,466 gold *soles* in 1932 to nearly 6,000,000 in 1935.

Perú has refused to liquidate all of the 2,000,000 *soles* of her debt to the United Aircraft Company (already cut down from 3,600,000 *soles*), or all its $800,000 owed the Electric Boat Company, or $1,500,000 owed an American dock-works concern, or its guano loan, or its $85,000,000 foreign debt, but at the same time is spending money for Italian planes. This is the tactic of England, of France, of Italy, of the whole world with reference to their debts. Anyway, today Perú has a large air fleet, claimed by some to number 500 war planes, nearly all of Italian make and under Italian control, and within less than a day's flying time from the Panama Canal.

"We believe," says F. Pardo de Zela, Peruvian Consul

General in the United States, "that the Italian Air Force is one of the most efficient in the world. It is . . . natural and logic [sic] that our officers and pilots, who handle airplanes of Italian make, should be trained by Italian instructors and pilots."

And so Italians now train the Peruvian pilots and are part of the inner organization of the country's air force. Italian officers are in charge of the Peruvian army and even of the Peruvian police force and Civil Guards, numerous as the army.

Recently E. Olguín, an Aprista leader, nephew of the Bishop of Arequipa—according to the Sub-Secretary of the Party—was arrested and taken to Lima where he was tortured by officers of the Italian mission by having an electrical apparatus thrust up his urinal canal. According to unverified reports of other released prisoners, the Fascist mission has introduced other modernistic Black Shirt instruments of torture into the prisons.

On parade days school-children are obliged to give the Fascist salute. Many have refused, and as a result they or their parents have suffered. The University students have been far from docile. Last year, when General Camoratta, Chief of the Italian Police Mission, came to speak at the institution, the students threw him into the patio pond, then ran him off the campus. The affair was hushed up, though fifteen students were arrested and deported.

Long ago, the present President-dictator of Perú, who rules by force and not by law, a rather dull and ponderous militarist, was Minister to Italy where he had intimate relations with Mussolini, both before and after the latter's seizure of power. Later when Minister to Spain, Benavides declared that "the peoples can be saved only by men identified with Fascist doctrines."

Today, Perú, in which there is such a large Italian colony, where Italian investments total over $100,000,000, where the Italians are the bankers of the government, has largely been integrated into the Fascist column.

The two centers of power in Perú, where its immediate destinies are decided, are the Palace fronting the Plaza de Armas, the residence of Dictator Benavides, and the *Banco Italiano*, on Carrera and San Pedro streets, an institution run by Gino Salochi, a man known as "the viceroy of Perú." In a few short years, the *Banco Italiano* has seen its petty capital multiplied many times. It now enjoys special discount privileges with the Central Reserve Bank and is the favored financial agent of the government.

The Italians recently sold $300,000 worth of munitions (practically a gift) to Nicaragua, and the Secretary of the Italian Legation in Costa Rica flew to Managua when they were delivered by the steamer *Leme* in January of this year. This has given the Italians a strong influence there. To Guatemala Italy has sold Bredda machine-guns, anti-aircraft guns and artillery. According to Dr. Angel Morales, former Dominican Minister to Washington, Trujillo, the dictator of that country, recently bought four Italian bombers manned with Italian pilots. Salvador has bought four Italian bombers, paid for with coffee, and two officers, Julio Sosa and Francisco Ponce, and the mechanic Belisario Salazar, are studying aviation, air-tactics and Italian motors in Rome.

General Ubico, the ruthless dictator of Guatemala, is very partial to the Italians and is constantly seen with the Italian minister to whom the local Mussolini constantly turns for advice on all important matters. Ubico has shrugged at the alleged shipments of Italian and Nazi arms through to anti-governmental factions in México. Guatemala and Italy do not charge each other consular fees on such key products as coffee, macaroni and wines.

In Chile, Italian General Longo is the big-shot in the air force, directing a corps of Italian instructors. When the Chilean poet, Vicente Huidolro, wrote a biting poem, *Fuera de Aqui* (*Get Out of Here*), he was brutally beaten up. Recently a public pro-Loyalist lecture on Spain was prohibited at the request of the Italian Embassy.

Argentina has long admitted Italian influence in its political life. Many of Argentina's leading men are of Italian or partial Italian descent. The Fascists make the most of that. They hold memorial services for prominent Argentineans, hailing them as the new type of man Fascism is producing.

The present Minister of Foreign Affairs, José Maria Cantilo, himself part Italian, for five years Argentine Ambassador in Rome, has been chosen with a special eye to the cultivation of Fascist friendship.

The real foreign influence in Argentina, of course, is Great Britain. No important step is taken without consultation with the British minister. Now Great Britain's overtures to Italy, the apparent rapprochement, has swung Argentina further in that direction than before and makes her more comfortable in her dual friendship with the two countries.

The various dictators and large sectors of the South American populations are strongly influenced by Fascism and the practices of the Fascist State. Few high officials of the south have failed at one time or another to sing high praises of Mussolini and Hitler. Dr. Manuel Fresno, long governor of Buenos Aires province, dictator of a fourth of the country's inhabitants, has referred to Mussolini and Hitler as "the saviors of Europe." Archbishop João Becker of Porto Alegre has stated: "I pray to God that in the present international controversy [the conquest of Ethiopia] intrepid Italy, land of genius, of science, of art, be not humiliated. I likewise pray to God to protect Fascist Rome, the Pope's Rome, the seat of Christianity."

In Cuba, the Italians have been very busy, increasing their embassy and consular staffs. Dictator Batista has been hobnobbing with them of late, and Mussolini has sent him his autographed picture. Italian influence is said to be responsible for the arbitrary closing of numerous Spanish clubs on the island, most of which are very pro-Loyalist and had been sending funds, food and hospital supplies home to the Peninsula.

Italian influence, strong in Brazil, overwhelming in Perú, important in Argentina, and potent in at least four other countries, is an expanding force, and in conjunction with Nazi propaganda and influence, and the strong efforts of Japan, may well bring the European struggles to American shores.

Mussolini, before he came into power, declared that the achievement of Italy's true greatness eventually would require the destruction of the British Empire and its monopoly of the major part of the resources of the world. The Latin-American drive by the Fascists obeys the law of struggle Italy has set for herself in compassing her expansion. If Italy does not have such grandiose ambitions in South America as does Germany, she realizes, as Fascist leaders have said repeatedly, that it cannot be ignored in any world struggle. In that struggle, Italy expects her sons in exile to carry their part of the burden. She expects certain Latin-American countries to come to her aid. She expects, like Germany, to be able to cut England's life-line of supplies.

CHAPTER

IV

The British Lion Retreats

MARCH 14, 1931, Great Britain, trying to turn the tide of depression and recapture its share of the Latin-American market, staged one of its greatest acts of commercial showmanship—the Empire Trade Exhibition in Buenos Aires, at a cost of $5,000,000. Not exactly Shakespearean, nevertheless this grandstand play had for its major actor a Prince of Royal blood and many of the glittering trappings that formerly delighted the Elizabethan bard, ever so interested in Spanish settings.

When Baldwin ousted the Duke of Windsor from the throne of England, he not only lost for the Empire a King, but also its star salesman, the man who made the Argentine exposition such a huge success. The Duke, closely linked with British Big Business, often put on trained-seal acts to promote trade and investment abroad.

Nothing he ever did was more adroitly arranged than the 1931 Argentine tour, part of one of the most intensive selling campaigns ever promoted by any nation.

The Prince already had much experience in such promotion work and had already gone on numerous similar patriotic expeditions. He had spent much time studying sales methods and the needs of British commerce. Some of his intimate companions—frequently they accompanied him on his various trade tours—were large industrialists vitally interested in foreign markets.

Right after the war, His Royal Highness toured the Dominions, to give them a chance to thank him for his brave services at the front and to thank them for their contribution to the enormous territorial expansion of the Empire by war and to the saving of the world for democracy. This tour —as others—was arranged with a canny eye to sales-promotion. Though this was never allowed to intrude openly, Bonar Law once let slip, "For sheer commercial brilliance, the Prince easily overshadows even His Majesty."

The Prince himself, wont to give talks on salesmanship, once said that the chief requisite was personality. "When a lot of men come to sell you something, you will be much more likely to buy it from the fellow you look upon as a friend."

And so he made several trips to Canada, the first time in 1919 on the new *Renown*. In Newfoundland, ex-soldiers broke through the police lines to pump his hand. In Toronto he ran after a wounded veteran's cap, blown off by the wind, and 50,000 people became hysterical with joy. In Australia and New Zealand, he mixed with "vulgar" merchants, danced with shop-keepers' daughters, trod the sheep-ways. In the British West Indies he sampled rum and ate bananas.

His trip to India was not quite so happy. The Hindus waved black strike banners under his nose and promptly assassinated the fifty-three Pharsi merchants who risked greeting him. But he hobnobbed with the wealthy Indian industrialists and rajas, the people who really count and are likely to take more British goods.

He tried a foreign expedition by visiting Japan in 1922 and won the salaams of even the Geisha girls. He came back to England to dedicate the Wembly trade exposition, of which he was President, then visited British Africa. In 1925 he made another foreign expedition, this time to Argentina. He was whirled through Buenos Aires behind four black high-stepping horses, and a delirious populace smothered him with roses and daffodils. President Alvear, though he had been stressing economic independence a little too strongly, received him with great éclat. The Prince liked the gay life of the capital, the warm hospitality of its people, and promised to return on some other auspicious occasion.

Now thoroughly trade-conscious, His Royal Highness, back in England, advised British industrialists how to improve their methods. At Mansion House he told the leading manufacturers of the Empire that they had to jack up their sales forces by imitating American and German methods. They burst into cheers.

In various lectures, he tried to take the curse of commonness off the sales profession. He held it up as a privileged gentleman's occupation. Salesmen he indicated were not a pariah class devoid of culture. Youth could be trained for salesmanship "without loss of general culture." In fact culture could be made useful in commerce. The public schools and universities should lead the way "by recognizing the need of commerce as well as industry for the best type of intellectual and moral leader."

Just prior to his 1931 trip to Argentina, he spoke at Guildhall to the Incorporated Sales Managers' Association. He made an earnest plea for higher wages for salesmen. Employers engaged "in the struggle for world trade" had to wake up to the need for "a more adequate and more appropriately educated staff." Otherwise British trade would die.

"We have got to realize," he continued, "that the world

markets of today are not those of the times of Queen Victoria or even those of King Edward. . . . A goodly share of the best brains . . . must be concentrated on the difficult, complex but interesting job of fighting competition."

In preparing for his Argentine trip, His Royal Highness followed his customary procedure. He read copiously about the Pampas country. He consulted with British manufacturers and visited their plants to learn just what England could sell, what she could buy. He learned the tango and Spanish.

For the next act of the drama, the curtain rises in Spain. The Prince made a preliminary trip there as a publicity stunt to build up greater expectation in South America. Also, Empire salesmen are well aware of the great cultural influence of Spain on the New World. To take the curse off his Protestantism, His Royal Highness could do no better than visit the land of His Most Catholic Highness, King Alfonso, whose wife is a stately blond Englishwoman, and visit Catholic shrines.

The Royal Party flew to Paris and took the Sud Express for Madrid. A wreck helped out. The Royal Party floundered through mud and rain to help valiantly in rescuing and comforting the passengers. In the same rain, His Highness autoed over winding slippery roads to Santander. The party boarded the Oropesa, which took them to Coruña.

The mayor of that sparkling little northwest port presented the Prince with a casket of earth from the Battlefield of Elvina, which all Hispanic Americans know saw the Tommies of England battling to save Spain against her enemies, a generosity that has since vanished. On the battlefield itself, His Royal Highness unveiled a monument to Sir John Moore, who died on that sacred soil. Next the Prince examined the skull of St. James in the Santiago de

Compostela cathedral and the precious vial of the Virgin
Mother's Holy Milk. In Vigo he tendered silver cups to
the international horseshow and the Yacht Club. Both
were very much in the Argentine news, for leading Pampas
breeders were exhibiting their pedigreed stock. Several Argentine entries were to compete in the international regatta.

All of these doings were cabled extensively through Reuters and other agencies to South America. The large Argentine dailies maintain offices in Madrid, and *La Nación's*
bureau on Conde de Peñalver was generous with its cable
space. The crowds, the homage, the military parades, the
abnegation of the Prince during the wreck, the disappointed masses that awaited the arrival of the train that
never arrived, the expression of reverence on His Highness'
face as he entered the Santiago cathedral—all was detailed.

And so, the Prince and his party reboarded the *Oropesa*
—no battleship for good-will, as has been the style with
Hoover and Roosevelt, but a fairly dinky merchant ship—
to make the final crossing to the Plata. On board the
Oropesa was a neat little Humber car (not the usual smart
Vauxhall the Prince customarily used), which given high
transportation and tariff costs, is more within the purse of
the Argentineans.

And so His Royal Highness cast the dazzle of his presence over British wares on display in Buenos Aires and
made the exposition an unusual success.

2

This and similar special efforts, which still continue, have
been prompted by the steady decline of Britain's economic
strength and trade. Although England's financial position
in Latin America is still almost as strong as that of the

United States (in the far south, much stronger), she has faced severe set-backs in the battle for the market.

British influence to the south dates back more than a century. England was the mid-wife of Latin-American independence, though Napoleon was the cause of premature birth. The Napoleonic invasions shook the authority of Spain and Portugal in the New World, but it was England that provided the intrigue, encouragement and often the funds for Western Hemisphere revolt, which began in earnest about the time the United States and England were at war in 1812.

The independence movements were the culmination of several centuries of fierce struggle with Spain for British imperial supremacy. The raids of the English buccaneers have filled history with romance. Their efforts predicated, centuries later, the visit of the Prince of Wales to Argentina—part of the same long persistent pursuit of commercial advantage.

England was a friend of the revolutionists who finally carved out independence from Spain. As early as 1789, the first great continental patriot, Francisco Miranda, presented to William Pitt a plan endorsed by revolutionary representatives from México, Chile, Perú, Argentina, Venezuela and Colombia, offering England an alliance, commercial privileges and territorial guarantees. Subsequently when Miranda disembarked in Ocumare and Coro to free Spain's colonies, he did so under the protection of British guns. Miranda carried a banner showing the British Goddess of the Seas with her foot on the Spanish lion. England also befriended Bolívar, the great liberator, and British aides were usually by his side. Loans were made to revolutionary movements in a dozen countries.

England won the gratitude of the republics. Besides giv-

ing tangible aid, Canning warned off all other European
colony grabbers, took a stand against Spain's re-conquest
of the best dominions, loaned the new Republics money
to get started, made favorable trade agreements before
other countries could get on the ground. New British firms
were immediately planted throughout the two continents.

"Don't let Johnny Bull get ahead of you," were the
secret instructions to our first representative in México.
Johnny Bull, however, was already on the ground. British
capitalists had snapped up at bargain prices the rich mines,
dilapidated after years of revolt, and were already shipping
in new machinery. The Empire's vital interests were being
pushed hard.

In Perú as early as 1822, England loaned £148,000 to
cover previous assistance to the new government by new
British merchants in Callao. The following year, British
capitalists came to the rescue with 1,200,000 Peruvian
pounds, and three years later they granted £616,000. Various conversion loans during the century swelled the totals,
along with trade and development.

The first British loan to Argentina was granted during
the administration of President Rodríguez (1820-24). Other
loans followed.

England has over a century of financial experience in
Latin America. At first she made many of the blunders that
American capital was to make a hundred years later, but
having the field largely to herself for so long, she was able
to retrieve ill-considered bonanza loaning by taking liens
on the natural resources of the various countries. Thus in
Perú, she reached out to control the valuable guano deposits, and in 1893, the Grace-Donoughmore contract arranged
for the surrender of all British financial claims in return for
66 years usufruct on the Peruvian railway, free navigation

rights on Lake Titicaca, and other compensations—all consolidated under the new Peruvian Corporation, which to this day plays such a prominent role in the country's economic life.

Thus England gradually built up a sound capital investment that today, despite many reverses, the rapid invasion of American capital and the competition of other European and Oriental nations, totals at least $6,000,000,000.

Her great stronghold is Argentina. Her investment there totals over $2,000,000,000, three times that of American capital. There Britain holds the citadel of financial power against all comers, is still the predominant outside influence, not only in finance and business, but in politics and foreign policy. Argentina is the base which has enabled British capital to reach out partly to control the economies of adjacent countries. British capital is the backbone of so-called Argentine imperialism, which has played such a dirty back-stage role in the Chaco War, has meddled in Paraguay, Uruguay, Bolivia and elsewhere on the continent.

Recently Viscount Davidson declared, "Perhaps it is not appreciated sufficiently that in time of peace, no less than in time of war, Argentine international trade is possible because up and down the trade routes of the world are to be found the ships of the British Navy. . . . The comradeship of the Argentine and British Navies is part of past and present-day history."

In Brazil, also, British investments, totalling nearly a billion and a half dollars, exceed ours nearly three-fold. Her next great stronghold is México. Prior to recent oil confiscations, she was a close runner-up to us, with an investment of nearly a billion dollars. Chile claims $700,000,000 of British money. In Cuba, British investments have declined fifty percent and now total less than $200,000,000. In little Uruguay, very much under British influence, $200,000,000 has been invested, well over twice the amount of American capital there.

In the whole of Latin America, the total American capital investment perhaps exceeds that of the British, but the latter still holds a more basic position, since a larger part of their investments is in resources and public utilities rather than in relatively worthless government paper. Thus in Perú, the United States theoretically has the larger investment, but so much of it is in scandalous defaulted bonds that in reality our investors are second in the running.

For the better part of a century, British banking dominated Latin America, and is still more extensive than that of any other foreign power. The great Anglo-South American bank and its wealthy subsidiary in Brazil, the British Bank of South America, through ramified banking services in Spain and Portugal, long controlled much of the Spanish and Portuguese financial activities in the New World. A depression merger has seen these two institutions absorbed by the powerful Bank of London and South America, an institution founded in 1862. It has twenty-five branches in Argentina alone, sixteen in Brazil, seven in Chile, six in Paraguay, five in Uruguay, four in Colombia. It operates in Ecuador, Guatemala, Salvador, Nicaragua, Venezuela and Perú, and in the British West Indies.

Grace Brothers and Company (partly American) operates in Perú. Huth and Company is very strong in Chile. The National Bank, Ltd., Glyn, Mills and Co., and Lazard Brothers have important relations with the New World.

Strong Canadian banks, much of their capital controlled in England, buttress the Empire's position to the south. The powerful Bank of Montreal recently had difficulties in its chosen field of México; but the Royal Bank of Canada is ramified throughout the continent. It operates in Argentina, Brazil and Uruguay, has six branches in Colombia. It is influential in Venezuela, Perú and Panamá. It formerly maintained 52 branches in Puerto Rico, the Dominican Republic, Haiti and Cuba, and in Martinique and Guadeloupe, but now has only thirty-five. It has also retired from Costa Rica. The Bank of Nova Scotia operates in Cuba, the Dominican Republic and Puerto Rico; the Canadian Bank of Commerce in Brazil and Cuba.

3

British communications have kept pace with these financial and commercial developments. Fine steamship lines are maintained, though they suffered greatly as a result of the war and some (such as the Nelson Steam Navigation Company, the British and Argentine Steam Navigation Company, the MacIver Line) have since gone into bankruptcy, merged or withdrawn, as a result of Italian, German, American and Japanese competition.

The Booth Steamship Company largely dominates the Portuguese-Brazilian field. Its boats touch all Brazilian ports. Large liners sail out of Liverpool and New York to Pará, then steam over 1,000 miles up the Amazon. Some even go to Iquitos in Perú.

The Pacific Steam Navigation Company, with twenty-five vessels, largely restricts its operations to the west coast of South America. Its *Reina del Pacifico*, on the London-Callao run, is still the largest, though no longer the most sumptuous, vessel in South American Pacific waters. Houlder Brothers, the big Lamport and Holt Line, the powerful Royal Mail Steam Packet Company, the Blue Star Line, the Canadian National Steamships, and others, serve Brazil and Argentina. The Royal Mail, Leyland Line, and Elders and Fyffes are particularly active in Colombia and Central America. The Cuban Line touches at Havana and Vera Cruz. Numerous regular cargo services are maintained, including one direct from India to Buenos Aires.

Many local companies are dominated by British capital, as for instance the Argentine Navigation Company (the wealthy Nicolas Miahanovich interests), which ply to Paraguay; the Sud Atlantica, which serves Patagonia and Porto Alegre; the Uruguayan Navigation Company, which plies between Buenos Aires and Montevideo; and the Colombia Railways and Navigation Company.

English cable service, until the World War, had almost a monopoly. The Western Telegraph Company and the West Coast of America Telegraph Company, associated with Cable and Wireless, Ltd., have a network of cables around all coasts. Direct cables extend from England to Cuba and Brazil. Direct wireless telephone connections are maintained between England and Brazil by Radiobras.

In Latin-American air-service, England is today far behind the United States, Germany, Italy and France. Some local companies operate, but England has never attempted the trans-Atlantic flights to South America so common to German and Italian companies and aviators, nor has it staged any mass military flights.

Recently Lord Forbes and Lord Beaverbrook toured the Antilles and returned to England to point out that the island of Trinidad was the true focal point for a complete South American air-service. Lord Forbes said it would be unpardonable to let the Dutch go ahead with their plans for a South American system from their "ridiculous island of Curaçao," and Lord Beaverbrook remarked that it would be an "eternal dishonor" for England to ignore her air opportunities in Latin America.

The two Lords are apparently unaware, says the *Latin-American World* of London, that England can't operate in Trinidad, the Caribbean or northern South America due to a "disgraceful agreement" made by the Ministry of Civil Aviation with Pan-American Airways, which restricts British operation to the south trans-Atlantic route via Natal and Rio, Montevideo and Buenos Aires.

However England hopes to enter the air field in South America in a big way next year or so. All the imperial air-services have been coördinated and equipment standardized. Airplane plants have been heavily subsidized to turn out new monoplane designs, and new "shadow factories" are under construction.

That at the Specke Airdrome will be one of the largest factories in the world, capable of bringing out forty Bristol Blenheim bombers daily. The operation of the plant will be turned over to Rootes Securities, Ltd.

Canadian capital, on the other hand, has shown some initiative in the aviation battle to the south. The Canadian Car and Foundry Company made a contract with México in April, 1938, to build and operate on a fifty-fifty basis an airplane manufacturing plant at the military aviation works of the Mexican government.

Of the first fifty planes turned out, forty will be Grumman military planes of the type used in the American Navy. Ten will be training ships. Later Burnell troop transport-planes, and new fighting-type planes will be built. The first two years' production will be absorbed by México, after which export markets will be sought. Costs will be 30 to 40 percent less than in the United States.

The British have led in railroading. The trans-Andean

companies have built the great route over the Andes, connecting Buenos Aires with Santiago, Chile, which passes through a tunnel ten thousand feet above the sea. British capital controls most of Argentina's 26,000 miles of railroads, and most of those of Bolivia and Paraguay. It was the initiative of the half-mad American, Henry Meiggs, that built the great central railway of Perú, which crosses the Andes at a height of 16,000 feet, but the railroad today is controlled by the British-Peruvian Corporation.

Most Brazilian railways are government-owned, but the British have the Great Western, more than 1,000 miles long, the Leopoldina Railway (nearly 2,000 miles), the Mogyana Railways (nearly 2,000 miles), the Paulista Railway (nearly 1,500 miles) and a number of shorter lines.

British railroading is strong in Colombia and Ecuador. In Uruguay, the British own all but about 160 miles; in Venezuela, all but about 170 miles. In Salvador they own the Acajutla-Santa Ana line, have interests in Costa Rica. The Queen's Own, between Mexico City and Vera Cruz, is a beautiful piece of engineering and competent electrization. In Cuba the important United Railways of Havana and Regla, 1,369 miles, running east to Cienfuegos and Santa Clara, are British.

The street-car systems from Mexico City south to Argentina are largely in British or Canadian hands. Though many light and power companies, since the war, have been wrested away by the American and Foreign Power Company, the British are still strong in the field. The big Canadian-Belgian International controls the central systems in México, Argentina, Brazil and elsewhere. The Brazilian Traction Light and Power Company, Ltd., has six subsidiaries in Brazil, serving 8,000 square miles of the richest regions, with light and power, gas and tramlines.

Heavy British investments have gone into mines in Chile, México, Brazil, Perú and elsewhere. In oil the British have been successful explorers and developers. The Royal Dutch Shell has large investments in México, Venezuela and Colombia. In México, this company has been largely besting the American concerns. Ten years or so ago, American capital exported over 60 percent of México's oil. Last year British interests controlled 60 percent of production, and new arrangements—had not recent governmental expropriation upset the apple-cart—would have put them in a still more commanding position.

4

England has not neglected the news field, which is an adjunct of commercial penetration, a purveyor of good-will and sympathetic interest between the two cultures. Reuters long held the preëminent position and, up until 1916 (when the United Press, and shortly the Associated Press and Hearst's International entered the field), even had a monopoly on all United States news, which had to be relayed to London to be sent out.

Now the American services dominate; the French Havas service is probably as powerful as Reuters; the Italians have a free press service; and the Germans are making the biggest inroads of all.

Recently England has felt obliged to set up a free news service, government subsidized, in imitation of the Italians and Germans. The news and its propaganda-coloring from British sources is far less inimical to the United States than that from other countries. The British rarely invoke the fears of Latin America toward so-called American imperialism. Occasionally they truthfully stress the fact that the

South American countries most closely linked commercially with England came through the depression with the least disaster, for trade barriers were never raised appreciably.[1]

England has at last also fallen into line in the propaganda scramble and March 14th, the BBC, the government broadcasting company, inaugurated short-wave programs in Spanish and Portuguese, with an appropriate address by Sir John Keith, Director General of the concern.

The far-reaching Latin-American Society of Great Britain, quite appropriately is headed by Lionel N. de Rothschild. Its annual dinners held at Hyde Park Hotel are usually attended by a member of the Royal Family, cabinet members, Hispanic diplomats and big manufacturers. A recent one was attended by the Duke of Kent, the Secretary of the Department of Overseas Trade, and the Lord Chancellor. The Brazilian Ambassador was one of the speakers.

"The Royal Family," said Mr. Rothschild, proposing a toast, "has always helped to foster good relations between this country and South America."

Cultural and trade relations are also promoted by the Ibero-American Institute of Great Britain.

And in 1931, the Crown Prince's trade journey was paral-

---

[1] In Brazil, the advertising agency G. Street and Company, publishes *Wileman's Brazilian Review,* "a weekly journal of Trade, Finance and Economics," and handles much of the Empire advertising in South America. Ravenscroft operates in Argentina. Other publications, such as *The West Coast Leader, The Anglo-Brazilian Chronicle, The Anglo-Brazilian Graphic, The Review of the River Plata, The South American Journal, The South Pacific Mail, The Buenos Aires Herald, The Standard, Britannica, The Times of Argentina, The Times of Brazil, The Sun,* tie the British colonials together and exercise influence in the various countries.

In England itself are printed quite a number of specialized magazines, such as the *Brazilian Press,* the *Chilean Review, Latin-American World, Tropical Life,* etc.

leled by the trip of Philip Guedalla, who led an Oxford and Cambridge party to Argentina to promote greater knowledge of that country and stimulate ties based not merely on trade.

The last year or so, the British have also organized cultural societies, such as the Anglo-Brazilian Cultural Association in Rio, which provides English books, brings lecturers and promotes the exchange of professors.

The number of British residents in the various South American countries is not large. Almost everywhere they are outnumbered by the Germans, and in Brazil, Chile, Argentina and Perú also by the Italians; in Perú, Brazil, México, Panamá even by the Japanese. But the English groups have been long established. Everywhere are to be found staid British clubs with long traditions, with their bars and restaurants, their excellent libraries and reading rooms where it is lèse-majesté even to say hello to a friend. They have cricket fields and in a number of countries have taught the natives the game.

The British do not mix to the extent that other nationalities do, but they know their way about, have entrée to the best society and the highest official circles, and newcomers are soon put through the proper ropes. British-club balls are important social events to which it is an honor to be invited.

But, according to Sir Malcolm Robertson, Ambassador to Argentina, British residents must now do much more.

"In Argentina," he said early this year, "there is a large patriotic British community, but frankly I believe that not even those Britishers are sufficiently in contact with the Argentine people. They live apart, and I have heard criticisms of those who mixed with Argentineans that 'they have become natives.'"

He praises the Argentineans highly and recommends that the British residents all become "natives" as soon as possible. As a further argument he reminds his compatriots, "It is lamentable, but we cannot get by without Argentine wheat and meat."

5

In recent years the British have not had an easy time in South America. Before the World War, they were in a far superior position, especially in the southern continent, though in the Caribbean, México and Central America, United States investments and trade had cut in heavily, and we were just beginning to reach further south. In South America, the British even then were also beset by the Germans. In Chile, even before 1914, German sales had outdistanced those of England.

The World War cut Europe off from South America except for the moving of absolutely essential supplies. The vast market fell into American hands. Then the aggressive post-war policy of the United States, the sudden dizzy expansion of our financial empire, brought us the overwhelming share of the market almost everywhere south. American investments soon equalled or surpassed those of England in all except the far south of the continent and in Brazil. Our golden loans buttressed up all our trade gains and set a current of goods moving toward tropical waters. England staged considerable come-back, but even by 1920, for her, new recession set in.

In 1929 our prosperity bubble burst. The loans we had poured out went into default. England, also hard hit by depression and the decline in purchasing power due to the collapse of South American governments, nevertheless recovered more quickly at home, and her long experience, established markets, financial investments and intimate contacts served to regain for her temporarily some of her loss. This general effort was symbolized by the famous visit of the Crown Prince in 1931. This period, however, also saw the eager trade rivalry of Italy, Germany and Japan, the last an entirely new factor.

These past few years, British trade has been slipping again badly. The inroads of the Fascist powers have been far more at the expense of England than of the United States, though we are far from occupying the privileged position we gained shortly after the World War. In exports to Brazil, England has dropped down to fourth place. Whereas the American share of Brazilian import trade between 1934 and 1936 declined from 23.4 percent to 21.9 percent, the British share declined from 18.2 to 10.93 percent. In Argentina, though England still leads all comers, her exportations continue to decline, having dropped from 20.4 percent in 1936 to 18.9 percent in 1937. Both German exports (third place) and American exports increased. Last year we cornered 16.4 percent of the market, nearly equalling England's total, though this increase does not seem permanent.

Alarmed by her decline in her long monopolized market, England has been bringing renewed pressure. Late in May at a British Chamber of Commerce luncheon, the British Ambassador warned Argentina she could not expect Britain to continue to be her best customer unless more British goods were bought. Shortly after, the government announced it would likely return to a quota system, which would equalize imports and exports from each foreign country. This will at once give England at least 28 percent of the market, will greatly increase German sales to Argentina, and will push the United States down automatically into fourth place.

But nearly everywhere, except in Argentina and Uruguay, German exports to Latin America now surpass England's. In several countries Japanese sales also top those of the United Kingdom.

This is in part due to the more specialized nature of British exports. The rapid expansion of the Japanese textile industry, on the basis of low labor costs, greater efficiency and barter, has cut heavily into British sales in Latin America. England has sought desperately to secure quotas in the various countries against Japanese cotton and woolen goods, here and there with some success, although, as in the case of Perú, convenient means have been promptly found to violate such agreements.

England—though her merchants are more organized, divide up the ground so as to avoid competition, and work in close harmony with the government—follows the old laissez faire principles and has not resorted to barter, special currencies, and other cutthroat devices utilized by the Fascist powers. As a result she has seen treaty after treaty go by the boards. Colombia has just denounced the Clarendon-Mosquera favored-nation treaty, which had served to channelize Anglo-Colombian trade relations without interruption for seventy-two years. In May, Colombia, to the consternation of England, arbitrarily cut off all import licenses for British textiles, a step which aroused a storm in the House of Commons for proper protection of the Lancashire mills.

Thus the new barter competition by the Fascist countries and Japan is but half the story. The various Hispanic countries themselves are demanding not merely favored-nation clauses, which they consider an old-fashioned idea, but definite promises to buy determined quantities of goods at determined prices. They insist on special privileges for certain key exports. Thus Colombia now demands of England a reduction of import duties on coffee, bananas and other products to the same level as those imposed on the same goods from British colonies.

England, to set up defenses against Japanese and German inroads on her empire, reverted in part to the old Colbert system of Empire protection, to her own trade acts of two centuries ago, thus making all British possessions a sort of closed-in world. But if this temporarily consolidated the economic network of the Empire, it has had grave political repercussions. Such acts long ago caused her to lose the thirteen colonies; such a system was the cause of the hardening of the arteries of the Spanish Empire, one of the causes of its dissolution. This closed-door economic system has in some instances played havoc with British trade outside the Empire.

6

In her struggle for trade, England has been playing the armament game along with all other world powers. Latin America knows more of Basil Zarahof and the Rothschilds than does the United States. England has been doing her best to outdistance the United States, Italy, Germany, Japan and Czechoslovakia in arming the Latin-American countries. Vickers is still strong in Chile, Bolivia and Argentina. Previously right after the World War, English munitions agents, by inflaming the Tacna-Arica controversy, sold a whole fleet to Chile—the battleship *Canada*, four light destroyers and six submarines (the last built for her in the United States by the Electric Boat Company). Last year

English munitions concerns drew up a comprehensive plan for again building up the Chilean navy and simultaneously fostered much of the wild talk in Chilean papers against the imperialistic pretensions of Argentina, played up a typical boundary dispute. As a result Chile ordered two cruisers and an indeterminate number of destroyers.

England provided much of Bolivia's munitions for the terrible Chaco War, and through Argentina, much of those of Paraguay.

At this writing, two Englishmen are in jail in Bolivia for fraud in connection with such sales. The British also share Brazilian naval rearmament orders with the United States and Italy.

England's strong foothold in Argentina has given her quite an edge on other armament countries. In 1930, she sent a loaded air-craft carrier to Buenos Aires for demonstration purposes, but in aviation there the sales-laurels go mostly to Italian and American companies. In naval influence, however, England is still king of the roost.

Last year seven war vessels for that country slid off the English ways, the last being the $2,000,000 destroyer *Misiones*, turned out at Birkenhead. Eight more vessels: seven destroyers, of the British H. class, and a 7,000-ton training ship have been ordered to be delivered by May of this year.

But in armaments the Germans, Italians, Japanese and Americans have in most places cut in heavily, taking the lead.

7

For England, the products of Latin America are of vital importance over and beyond any question of mere commercial prosperity. During the World War, she sent over more actual funds to Argentina for supplies than even to the United States. In a new European war, especially with Italy blockading the Mediterranean, England's Roumanian and Mesopotamian oil supplies would be cut off. She would have no access to the Ukrainian and Roumanian wheat fields. For this reason the British recently have promoted oil production in the New World at a great pace. The recent expropriation of oil properties in México— where British output had at last so greatly outdistanced that of American companies—was a real blow below the belt.

England has big tin reserves in the Malay peninsula, but wishes to have those in Bolivia also accessible, for tin and wolfram and vanadium (Bolivia and Perú) are absolutely essential for producing the steels used in battleships and armaments. Though the need of the United States, which has practically no tin, drove American capital into Bolivia, England still controls the refineries. We still get most of our Bolivian tin from across the Atlantic. The price is set in London.

Argentina, Uruguay, Venezuela and Brazil are mainstay countries for wheat, cattle and other food supplies. Argentina exports three-fourths of the total world export of corn.

All this has led to great English influence in Latin-American political affairs. Today her influence, though her need for a market and above all for the raw materials of Latin America is imperative as never before, is not as great as when the American republics gained their freedom from Spain. In those days the Hispanic countries did not put much stock in the Monroe Doctrine. They knew that their real safeguard—or destruction—depended on the British fleet, and they were far more interested in Canning's promises to guarantee New World autonomy than in those uttered by James Monroe. For nearly a century England was called in by preference to arbitrate most disputes. The existence of Uruguay, the Belgium of South America, as a buffer state between Brazil and Argentina, the two claimants, was due to British diplomacy.

But since those days, British influence with South American countries has sadly declined. This is in part due to the inroads of the Fascist countries, partly due to the loss of prestige and commercial efficiency and to the unreliability of English diplomacy; partly it is due to the United States. British diplomatic manoeuvres on the continent of Europe of late have revealed her hypocrisy and double-dealing as never before in history. Her weakness in the Spanish imbroglio, the manner in which she has played second-fiddle to the Fascist powers, her backing down in the Ethiopian dispute, her mangling of the League of Nations to suit her own selfish interests of the moment—these and similar actions have lost for England much of the respect she once commanded in Latin America. The Hispano-American countries believe that she has connived in every recent aggression against small nations and cannot be depended upon in any crisis.

The purposes of Germany and Italy are at least clear. And it is easily to be seen that England no longer even exercises the balance of power in Europe. That role has been taken over by Mussolini.

The Latin-American countries also have been incensed and injured by British Empire trade tactics. They are also a bit amused now by England's stodgy commercial practices, her easy-going complacency that since she has always had such a big slice of Latin-American commerce, she will continue to have it.

The recent attitude of England in the oil-expropriation in México did not add to England's prestige. Whatever the merits of her case, her conduct was peculiarly abusive in contrast to the generosity and understanding of the United States. The British notes to México were musty, dishonest, full of legal evasions, uncomprehending. If England had a good case, she certainly was not able even to state it intelligently. Her last note in the second week in May recited México's failure to pay her debts, and pettily demanded the immediate payment of 300,000 pesos on claims.

México, though not legally obligated to pay at that moment, handed the British minister a check, took England to task for writing insulting notes criticizing the internal affairs of México, and broke off relations. México was irritated; and beyond México, Latin America was amused. Folk there know England does not dare send warships to Vera Cruz. They know that Italy, Germany, France and other European countries owe England money, but that she has not only not sent them abusive notes but has not dared even try to collect it. They know that England, with far greater resources than México, owes billions to the United States which she makes no effort to pay. Perhaps England, in picking on weaker México, is merely showing bad temper and bad conscience for her own cowardice in dealing with European affairs and for her own financial double-crossings.

A recent suggestion has been made that we turn over several hundred million dollars of British debt—a drop in the bucket of American claims on England—to the Mexican government and let her pay the English petroleum companies with this paper, the theory being that we do have a chance to get a few dollars out of México and practically no hope at all that England will ever meet her foreign obligations.

8

In more recent years, north of Panamá, and in Colombia and Venezuela, the United States has pushed back British pretensions. The Venezuela-Guiana boundary episode of 1895, during Cleveland's administration, caused him to invoke the Monroe Doctrine and force England out of the habit of direct intervention in countries near and north of Panamá. Gradually England relinquished all claims on inter-oceanic routes at Panamá and Nicaragua (though she squeezed out a new colony, British Honduras, in violation of the Monroe Doctrine), reduced her West Indian fortifications and accepted American diplomatic tutelage— though at first not with too good grace. Eventually it was England which insisted on writing the Monroe Doctrine into the League of Nations covenant, for perhaps she knew cannily that this would make it less possible for us to protest at her sphere-of-influence doctrines in so many parts of the world.

But though Secretary of State Olney, at the time of the British-Venezuela imbroglio, informed England that we were supreme in the Western Hemisphere and that our word was law everywhere on anything to which we gave our attention, British diplomacy is still strong in Argentina and her satellite countries, Uruguay, Paraguay, and now Bolivia. It was the British Minister in Argentina who a few years back put into the Argentine bonnet the bee of "Buy from those who buy from us," thus cornering the bulk of that country's import trade, to the annoyance of our State Department. This, however, proved something of a boomerang when applied elsewhere in countries from which England bought but little. In fact it helped promote the German and Japanese barter systems, and elsewhere United States trade.

When Roosevelt went south to Buenos Aires to propose a species of Western Hemisphere alliances, a neutrality proposal which would clap an embargo on New World goods on warring European countries, in other words, a control of New World resources under American leadership, British interests to the south were menaced as never before in history. England's whole world position was threatened, her national security jeopardized. The American proposal would have cut off supplies to England as effectively perhaps as Mussolini's airplanes in the Mediterranean might do. It would have cut the British life-line.

Naturally this would also have been a fatal blow to the economies of a number of Latin-American countries, so there was little hope that Roosevelt would be successful. But there is no doubt now but that England definitely moved to spike the project. Just prior to Roosevelt's speech, the British minister in Buenos Aires was presiding over an elaborate ceremony bestowing twenty scholarships in England to Argentineans. Through Argentina especially, England stalemated the Roosevelt proposals.

We got no corner on Latin-American resources, nor control over them in possible war-time, nor any workable neutrality pact. Except for words of good-will, some more peace pacts, a promise on our part not to intervene in Indo-American countries (a very important matter), Roosevelt largely failed in Buenos Aires. England can still be assured, unless German and Italian and Japanese efforts in that quarter achieve their full purpose, of a backyard supply of war-materials.

There is little doubt but that Roosevelt's efforts quite frightened the British. He would have accomplished just what the Fascist powers are trying to accomplish by other means. It is pretty patent now that England, in making a new rapprochement with Fascist Italy, not only was taking the Latin-American scene into consideration but that she was moved to take this step in part by American policies, and wished to have an additional lever in preventing us from cutting off British supplies in that quarter by any future treaty arrangements with the southern countries. England knows that Mussolini's victory in Spain will greatly influence Italian influence in the New World. The only other powerful influence in Argentina, besides British and American, is Italian. In view of our recent hard trade drive there, which has played such havoc with England's exports to what was long an almost exclusive British purlieu, Great Britain prefers to share influence there with the Italians whose goods do not so greatly compete, in a desperate effort to forestall the American advance.

In the twenties the European powers, including England, made common cause against American trade in the Latin-American countries. They all tried to crack through the lead we had achieved during the war. Recently there has been a sort of tacit, though very limp, world line-up of the so-called democratic nations. But Tory England does not give a whoop about democracy except as an export slogan for the United States; and now the new shift in England's heart, a new alliance, with mutual concessions and guarantees between England and the Fascist powers, again promises soon to see a joint effort by all concerned to limit American trade and influence to the south.

If anyone thinks England is our friend in the struggle

for Latin America, he is as naïve as some of our statesmen.

England has seen the hand-writing on the wall, even if her Tories are betraying the country, the Empire, and the hopes of free men everywhere. Now, as during the World World, she has just ordered that all her merchant ships in South American trade—particularly those carrying meat and wheat from Argentina—shall be converted so that guns can be mounted on them at an instant's notice.

World affairs today are a shifting battle-line, and the devil takes the hindmost. In Latin America, England doesn't wish to be the hindmost, but despite all her efforts she is slipping badly.

CHAPTER

V

Red Star South

By curious coincidence, the principal constellation in the sky over the Catholic republics of Latin America is the famous Southern Cross. But during the last twenty years, students of international affairs, sweeping their sociological telescopes in that direction, have noted a new red star in the heavens of political events. The Red Star of Communism over South America has waxed and waned according to political circumstances, but in one after another of the twenty countries, the doctrines of Karl Marx and Nicolai Lenin have attracted small groups of intellectuals and some workers and peasants. Communist parties—branches of the world-wide Red International—have been founded.

When the United States bought Alaska, we thought that Russia's imperialistic ambitions in the Western Hemisphere had been forever checked. But in these troubled postwar years, the great sprawling land that already occupies a sixth of the world's surface and stretches across Europe and Asia, has made a new bid for power in the Americas.

Hers is not the old-style imperialism of economic penetration, spheres of influence, political overlordship or territorial conquest, but a new imperialism that seeks to bring under its sway the minds and hearts of the working-class all over the world. Soviet diplomacy has endeavored—not very successfully—to win the Latin-American countries and

133

their governments and promote trade, but the real hope of
Stalin and his cohorts has resided in propaganda—their
Marxist program of universal proletarian loyalty and their
belief that "capitalism is doomed."

This conquest is more feared by southern dictators than
any Fascist, British or American financial or political expansion, for its success would spell finis to old-style military
dictatorships, to the Catholic Church, landed aristocracy,
native capitalists and foreign investors. It would replace
conventional Latin-American militarism with the dictatorship of the working-class, a form of rule which at present
the Communists insist shall be falsely called "democracy."

Unlike imperialist Germany and Italy, the Soviet Union
does not depend on her nationals abroad for the spread
of her particular brand of sociology. In Hispanic America
are found few Russian immigrants. A handful of religious
sects, long-bearded and isolated, know that at home, today
as under the Tsars, their members would be persecuted for
lack of conformity to the official political church. A few
white Russians, ex-princes and princesses, counts and no-
accounts, the old aristocracy and Tsarist military officers,
run restaurants and tea-rooms, don smocks and play in
balalaika orchestras, sell automobiles, perfumes and cos-
metics and otherwise painfully adjust themselves to forced
exile.

Only Argentina and Brazil have considerable Russian
population, in good part Jewish and proletarian. Buenos
Aires boasts a Russian daily, a Russian theater, Russian
synagogue and a bulbous-shaped Greek Catholic temple.
There are over a hundred thousand Russians in Brazil.

But the Soviet power abroad resides, not in ex-patriates,
but in the Communist movement—the Third International,
usually known as the Comintern. Soviet might in world

affairs is interwoven with foreign Communist parties, expected to follow without question the lead of Russia in international policy. Every Communist, up to a certain point, is thus an agent for the Soviet government; Russia, not his own country, is the Communist's spiritual fatherland, his utopia, his dream, his anxiety and hope. To Soviet Russia he gives his emotional loyalty, not to the Fascist or democratic or capitalist nations of which he is a citizen. His own government he wishes to overthrow, peacefully or otherwise, in order to establish the rule of the working class. The Comintern—dominated and assisted by the leaders of the Soviet State—is a militant propaganda instrument paralleling Soviet policies.

All Communist Parties and their members, from Hyde Park to Union Square, from Toronto to Buenos Aires, from Canton to Melbourne and Capetown and Valparaiso, must adhere faithfully and unquestioningly to the Party Line established by the Comintern in Moscow, or suffer expulsion. Party tactics support Russia in world affairs.

At times rapid international changes have necessitated quick shifts in Soviet policies, and the Communist Party Line has temporarily lagged—especially during the period when the Soviet Foreign Office returned to the traditional game of European power-politics and back-scenes intrigue. At other times, the Soviet Union has found it convenient to take one position while having the various Comintern units throughout the world, for purposes of threat or conciliation, assume an entirely different attitude.

In the New World, Soviet diplomacy has not fared well. As early as 1919 Moscow sent over Borodin—later so famous in the Canton military academy as the power behind the throne in Kuomintang and Chinese affairs—as a secret agent to México. Provided with confiscated jewels, he traveled under an assumed name with a Mexican diplomatic passport. Ostensibly he came to buy Mexican henequén for the harvesters of the Ukrainian wheat fields, but his real mission was to provoke trouble and precipitate armed American intervention. At that time it was feared England would soon attack the Soviet Union, that the United States would back her up. Our troops were on Siberian soil. The Bolsheviks hoped to divert our energies into the armed conquest of México.

Borodin had a number of mishaps, bought no henequén and caused no intervention, but he did found—with the help of Rabindranath Roy, an exiled Hindu nationalist who later became Borodin's aid in China—the first Communist Party in México.

2

Actual Soviet relations were established with México soon after President Plutarco Elías Calles came into office in 1924. From the start they got off on a bad foot. Leaders of the official Mexican labor party were refused permission to visit the Soviet Union. Soviet Foreign Minister Tchitcherin made the tactless statement that México would now provide the Soviets a base in the Americas. This elicited the tart statement from Calles that the Soviet Legation would have to respect international law and México's sovereignty.

Thus the first minister, Petskovsky—a big-bearded revolutionist with tobacco-gnarled teeth, for seven years held in a Tzarist Siberian prison and a personal friend of Lenin—arrived in a very frigid atmosphere.

But in this truculent period, the Bolsheviks romantically believed that with a wave of the wand myriad Communist legions would spring full-armed into a great world-revolution. Petskovsky promptly attacked the Mexican Regional Confederation of Labor (CROM), the official labor organization, the head of which, Luis N. Morones, was a member of Calles' cabinet.

This made Petskovsky as popular with the Mexican authorities as a mouthful of scalding coffee. From then on, Morones and the CROM waged incessant warfare against the Legation, the Communists and the Soviet government.

Petskovsky did not content himself with public denunciations. The Soviet Legation became the active center for the most radical anti-government forces and of the local Communist Party. Following Petskovsky's arrival, the official Communist paper, the weekly *El Machete*, blossomed out with an illustrated format four times its previous size and was widely circulated. Communist membership, heretofore insignificant, began to climb. Comintern organizers, some of them American Communists, appeared on the scene. Branches of Soviet Red Aid and the Young Communists were launched. The National Peasants' League, under Ursulo Galván, was organized and affiliated with the Moscow Fromintern. Friends of Soviet Russia, the Anti-Imperialist League, the whole series of false-front organizations, utilized by the Communists, were promoted and flourished.

Soviet around-the-world cyclists toured México and were given a big ovation. Soviet scientists lectured. One scientific expedition combed the country for new plants to be acclimated in Russia. A commercial attaché, M. Truskonov, appeared with a lively blond wife and began pushing Amkino films, toys, embroideries, fine woods, and other Soviet products, and bought lead, zinc, sugar, sisal, etc.

Mexican Communists, labor and peasant leaders, artists

and intellectuals were given free trips to Moscow to be trained in propaganda and organization methods. Among the painters were Xavier Guerrero, Diego Rivera (who painted the walls of the Soviet soldiers' club) and somewhat later, David Siqueiros, who had led the Jalisco miners to seize the mining properties of that state. Presently open Soviet aid to striking Mexican railway workers made local ill-feeling explosive.

The CROM had long been trying to persuade the railway brotherhoods to affiliate with the more conservative government labor organization. Unsuccessful, the CROM had organized a dissident minority federation of 5,000 workers. When the brotherhoods called a nation-wide strike, Morones, head of the CROM and the governmental Labor Department, declared the walk-out illegal and used CROM railway federation members to keep the trains moving. At this ill-timed juncture the Soviet railway workers in Moscow donated 50,000 pesos to the strike fund.

Mexican officials knew that no foreign exchange was granted without the definite approval of the Soviet government. Such approval depended on reports from the local Soviet Minister in México. The Mexican government was furious, seeing red in more ways than one.

After 1926 and after the arrival of Ambassador Morrow, the Mexican government grew increasingly conservative, and by 1928 Provisional President Portes Gil began to suppress labor and peasant organizations and, above all, the Communists. Leaders were jailed, sent to Islas Maria penal islands without trial, or assassinated. Among those killed, right on the streets of Mexico City, was Julio Antonio Mella, the Cuban student leader.

In spite of this the Mexican Communist Party, backed by the Soviet Legation and aided by Communist organizers from the United States, promoted the new left trade-union organization, the Unitarian Trade Union Confederation (CSUM). Portes Gil smashed this in turn, and ruthlessly.

Petskovsky was supplanted by Madame Kollontay, a famous revolutionist back in Tsarist days, previously Minister to Norway, and author of the book, *Red Love*. Though a very cultured, charming and unaggressive woman who apparently followed merely a passive non-intervention role, she was openly snubbed by Mexican officialdom, and before she left the Soviet Legation was raided and guests arrested, in imitation of the London Arcos raid. No official apology was ever tendered, and when, soon after, she was transferred back to Oslo, she was not accorded the customary protocol leave-taking.

She was succeeded by Dr. Makar, a Jewish medico, who had been a physician with the red armies of the Ukraine.

By this time Soviet policy was in a transition stage. Socialistic nationalism had greatly replaced revolutionary crusading. Seeking now to placate the other nations of the world and secure recognition, Russia desired to squelch the belief that she was spreading secret propaganda in foreign lands.

But the Communist parties everywhere retained a militant barricades psychology. Even the most liberal persons were venomously attacked as "Social Fascists"; and so the Soviet authorities, wherever it became expedient, disavowed the extremist tactics it had so recently abetted and threw the Communist parties to the wolves. Makar would scarcely let a Mexican Communist step inside the Legation.

But despite Makar's conciliatory attitude, friction with México multiplied. The Mexican government was suppressing the Communists ever more determinedly. More peasant leaders were assassinated. Every act of the local

Communists was blamed on the Soviet Legation and the Soviet government.

Towards the end of 1929, the Comintern ordered that direct action be taken in all countries in protest against the persecution of Mexican Communists. Wild demonstrations were staged before the Mexican legations and consulates. The bill of the Mexican Foreign Office for new window-panes went up. When President Ortiz Rubio in 1929 toured the United States, our own Communists met his train everywhere with red banners, placards and hoots, and scuffled mightily with the police. Mexican patience evaporated.

Makar was not even given his walking papers; he was ordered, via a general press-release, handed to American correspondents, by Mexican Foreign Minister Genero Estrada, to get out of the country on the first boat. Taken quite by surprise, Makar procrastinated, and when he finally belatedly did reach Vera Cruz to embark, he was placed under arrest for five hours, his baggage confiscated and shipped back to Mexico City.

The Soviet assistant commercial attaché, who remained to wind up business matters involving millions of dollars, was arrested, held incommunicado, physically abused and finally deported. A representative sent down by Amtorg, the Soviet trading agency in New York City, was also arrested. As he was an American citizen, Morrow secured his release, but he was at once deported. So ended direct Soviet diplomacy in México.

Under President Lázaro Cárdenas, who came into office in 1934, all organizations, Communist, Fascist, liberal, reactionary, were once more allowed full democratic rights. The Communist Party revived under the leadership of Hernan Laborde, whom the Soviets had so aided during the railway strike and later had sent to Moscow for instructions.

The CROM, the official Calles' labor group, was now supplanted by the far more radical CTM (Mexican Labor Confederation), with a membership of 900,000, led by Lombardo Toledano. Just before founding this body, Lombardo and other labor men journeyed in a body to the Soviet Union. However, Lombardo denies being a Communist, declares labor must follow a Mexican pattern. Though in many respects he largely has adhered to the Communist Party Line and for a time coöperated in a Popular Front including the Communist Party, he has been growing cool toward the more radical sect. In May, 1937, the CTM at his instigation expelled disobedient unions under the Communist Party influence, with a combined membership of 300,000, until they mended their ways, and the new Party of the Mexican Revolution, organized in March, 1938, of which Lombardo is one of the principal ramrods, has established the principle that no Communist is eligible for membership.

Even so, today the Communists are stronger in México than any other Hispanic country. On April 18, 1938, the police raided the Mexico City headquarters of the Party and reportedly found a large collection of arms and dynamite.

3

The other Soviet diplomatic venture to the south was in Uruguay. This was equally ill-starred.

Recognition was bought with cold cash. In 1925 a Soviet commercial and propaganda mission toured Latin America, offering to make enormous purchases of hides, sugar, metals and other raw materials in return for recognition. Argentina, Chile and Brazil hastily made a pact not to recognize the Soviet Union until all should agree. But Uruguay, in return for the purchase of about a million dollars' worth of meat, hides, etc., tendered recognition. Arrangements were made with Russia to take her oil and lumber in return for chilled beef.

From the Soviet Legation in Montevideo, the base for Comintern agents, much propaganda went out. Secret propagandists appeared in all countries, especially in those which, hard hit by depression, suffered governmental overturns. Disorder made it possible for the Comintern to gather new recruits more rapidly.

These multiple efforts bore fruit in the *Confederación Latino Americano*, affiliated with the Moscow Red International. In Montevideo in 1931 it held an international congress, largely manipulated by the Soviet Legation there. Nearly all Hispanic countries were represented. From far-off México came a delegation headed by David Siqueiros. Not merely political romance flourished in the sessions. To his wife's dismay, Siqueiros went back to México in the company of one of the Uruguayan delegates, the poetess Blanca Rosa Blum. This congress represented the strongest general movement to date of Communist and Soviet influence in Latin America.

In 1926 a South American Soviet trading agency was set up in Buenos Aires, the Iuyamtorg corporation, under Mr. Kraevsky. As did the commercial attaché in México, the Soviet representative in Buenos Aires introduced Soviet goods, handicrafts, movies, fine woods, novelties, embroideries, toys, bicycles, etc., to help pay for Russia's heavy imports of raw materials: metals, cattle, hides, tallow, oranges, grapes, lemons, vegetable oils, etc. Direct steamship service was established between Russia and Montevideo and Buenos Aires. Soviet purchases were used as an argument to try to persuade other South American countries to extend recognition.

These efforts lasted five years. In 1931, under General Uriburú's new dictatorship, the Iuyamtorg offices were raided and closed, the police charging that it had been the center for a Communist plot. A strong Fascist party was immediately organized.

Iuyamtorg moved to Montevideo, but there also a dictatorial coup soon occurred. The new pasha, General Gabriel Terra, soon broke off relations with the Soviets by demanding that they make purchases of a certain kind and amount in Uruguay. In December, 1935, the Soviet representatives departed; the following month, Iuyamtorg hastily liquidated its affairs.

The Soviet government now has no representative in all Latin America.

Apparently it has given up active efforts in that direction, and more and more has withdrawn inside its own borders, troubled by so-called Trotsky plots and vast "wrecking" activities by haters of the regime, protests which it drowns with the firing-squad.

The Soviet government does send out short-wave broadcasts in Spanish. It has six powerful broadcasting stations, and the Moscow station of 500,000 watts is ten times more powerful than any station in the United States, and five times as powerful as the strongest station anywhere else in the world.

But the Russian programs are largely for consumption in Spain, and do not seem to be designed with any special intention of reaching Latin America.

4

If the Soviet government itself is now largely quiescent in Latin America, the Comintern still operates and still sends out secret agents. American Communists have been utilized in México, Cuba, Puerto Rico and Haiti; German, Italian and American Communists in Brazil; Italian and other Communists in Argentina, Uruguay and Perú. All in all, the Communist parties to the south, what with such reactionary regimes, military dictatorships and the suppression of all civil liberties, have not had an easy row to hoe, even though such oppressions increase Communist prestige. In most countries Nazi and Fascist groups are much stronger and wage incessant warfare.

Nor do the Communists by any means control even a near majority of left labor and peasant elements. Nationalist and anti-imperialist movements have arisen to dispute Communist control over the masses. In México, the official National Revolutionary Party has often reiterated its opposition to Communism. The labor federation is affiliated with Amsterdam. In Cuba, the Agrarian Party, Young Cuba, Autenticos and the A.B.C. movements have had far more influence than the Communists.

Quite some years ago in Perú, Communist ideology was promoted by a truly brilliant polemicist, the crippled Mariategui, editor of the magazine Amauta. Even his opponents admit that his book Seven Essays on Peruvian Reality is one of the most powerful pieces of economic writing in the Spanish language.

But the heirs of Mariategui have fallen apart. Revolutionary sentiment in Perú now follows the leadership of the more glib Haya de la Torre, who has welded a huge following into APRA (American Popular Revolutionary Alliance), a nationalistic union of the proletariat, peasants, middle class and even native capitalists on an anti-imperialistic program to bring about a democratic, semi-Marxian, semi-Fascist regime.

Over ten years ago the Communists smelled out this heresy, and throughout the continent the Comintern circulated in vast quantities a virulent attack on Haya de la Torre and Aprismo by the Cuban Communist, Julio Antonio Mella. For years the Communist kept up a bitter barrage on the APRA movement, within and without Perú. The most savage abuse was heaped upon Haya de la Torre. The Communists even coöperated with reactionary elements to undermine him. At other times they hotly accused him of treason for not calling revolt against Dictator Oscar Benavides, at the time of the Leticia trouble, though with patriotic sentiments aroused in the country, no more inappropriate moment for such an action could possibly have been chosen.

Now the Communists soft-pedal all their earlier frantic accusations and seek a Popular Front with Haya de la Torre's group, which is outlawed by the Benavides dictatorship. On the other hand, the Communist leaders who shouted so loud for the overthrow of that government and so criticized the APRA's stand, are today holding plump bureaucratic jobs. APRA continues to have the real support of the Peruvian masses.

In these later days, the Communists all over the continent are also faced by the bitter hatred of Trotskyite seceders. In México these are led by the exiled Trotsky in person, allied with the expelled Communist painter, Diego Rivera, Francisco Zamora, a columnist on one of the conservative dailies, and Fritz Bach, an émigré German. Elsewhere also small virulent Trotsky factions have arisen to take issue with the Communists. The mutual hatred of the two sects is revealed by their constant venomous name-calling. Note the following hash of nonsense from *The Communist International*, the official Comintern organ:

"Only the contemptible counter-revolutionary Trotsky-ites who are trying to pin the activities of the Cuban people to the 'Left' flag, and to ingratiate themselves with the imperialists, can spread defeatist theories that the victory of the Cuban revolution is impossible without a simultaneous proletarian revolution in the U.S.A."

5

The dictatorial regimes that exist almost everywhere to the south make it difficult to ascertain with much exactitude the actual present-day strength of organized Communism. The various dictators make it more confusing by labeling all their opponents, even the most reactionary, as "Communists." Thus, as Dr. Samuel Guy Inman, head of Protestant missionary work in Latin America, has pointed out, when former President Alessandri, a decided reactionary, was in exile, he was called a "Communist." When he got back into power, he called those who had temporarily ousted him "Communists."

Following the Buenos Aires Pan-American conference, attended by President Roosevelt to discuss neutrality and non-intervention, all the delegates except those of México and the United States held a secret session to discuss means of combating Communism, and incidentally all liberalism and democracy. Guatemala, Salvador and Honduras made an anti-Communist pact long before Japan, Italy and Germany. Many southern governments have agreements with their neighbors not to harbor any Communist exiles. All oppositionists are conveniently labeled "Communist."

Latin America, not highly industrialized, does not have, except in a few places, a large proletariat in the "Communist" sense. Except in a few countries, its peasants, mostly negro and Indian, are kept down in ignorance and poverty, and know little of economics or politics, however much at times they may be stirred up by demagogues. Most Latin-American Communists are urban intellectuals, excited by new doctrines from over the sea, but without deep roots in the labor or popular forces in their countries. Their Communism is often academic rather than representing actual mass force. Manuel Seone, an outstanding leader of the Peruvian APRA, has analyzed this very capably in his booklet, *Creole Communism*.

The strongest movement exists in México, but even there it does not have more than a few thousand dues-paying members. Even so it does have much labor union influence and was strong enough in May, 1937, to precipitate the secession of 300,000 workers from the Lombardo Toledano Confederation, the CTM. Laborde, the Communist head, was at once ordered to New York to confer with Earl Browder, American Communist leader, then was told to go back and beg pardon, for his act had violated the new Comintern tactic of the Popular Front.

Earl Browder has also journeyed to México to attempt to try to organize a People's Front and spoke at what was described as a mass-meeting on June 29, 1937.

"The beginnings of the People's Front is that solid foundation which enables General Cárdenas to take over your railroads for the Mexican people."

This was, of course, a most presumptuous statement. The railroads were taken over as part of the Six-Year Plan, which was enunciated at a time when the Communist Party was outlawed in México.

Browder's statement was also premature in that in May of this year a popular front of the middle-class, workers, peasants and the army was effected, but the Communists were excluded from it because of previous disruptive tactics.

The Communists in México publish *El Machete, Ruta, Rumbo, Pro-Patria*; and the Communist-controlled artists' and writers' league, LEAR, headed by Mancisidor, who journeyed to Moscow in 1936, publishes the militant *Frente a Frente*. The Workers' University, jointly supported by the Government and the CTM, publishes *Futuro* and the processed weekly, *Mexican Labor News*, both of which while insisting they are non-Communist, on various issues follow the Party Line. The two publications enjoy postal franking privileges.

In Cuba the Communists, though entirely suppressed during the Machado regime, kept an underground organization going, also a youth organization and the Anti-Imperialist League. An adult organizer of the Communist student associations in the United States, using the name Simon, spent a year or so in Cuba doing organization work. Other American Communist agents are secretly at work there now.

Under the more democratic rule of President Grau San Martin (1933-34), the Communists came into the open and surged into control of the powerful Cuban Labor Confederation. Convinced that the moment had come for them to seize power, the Communists made bitter attacks on the Grau government, called numerous strikes, seized factories and estates. The Grau government retaliated, staining its record by a brutal army massacre of Communists out parading with the ashes of the martyred Mella.

The Communist harassing of the liberal Grau government merely helped bring about its downfall and aided the victory of the harsh military dictatorship of Batista. Grau was helplessly crushed by the hostility of the American government and American capital desiring a more conservative regime, by the militarists scheming to betray him, and by the Communists wishing to seize all American property.

The Cuban Communists, driven underground again by Batista and smarting from their failure, bitter toward other factions, boycotted the March, 1935, general strike, which otherwise would likely have ousted Batista and brought in a more liberal and democratic regime. The stupidity of Communist leadership at that time lost for the Communist Party much of its hold on labor and the masses.

Shortly after, *The Communist International* admitted that since even before the fall of Machado in 1933, the Communists had blundered woefully and continuously in Cuba. Yet as late as the middle of 1935, the Communists were still calling Grau San Martin, "a cowardly deserter," "a bourgeois Fascist," "a paid agent of Gringo imperialism" and even viler names. They were calling Guiteras and Trotskyites "wolves of the same gang" (*Red Flag*, October 5, 1934), though Guiteras, the leader of the Young Cuba movement, was never a Trotskyite. They continued their abuse of him in ever shriller crescendo.

But after the failure of the 1935 strike, the Communists veered around and sought the friendship of both Guiteras and Grau. "*The first and most important condition,*" declared *The Communist International*, "is that the broad masses of the people of Cuba should be united against imperialism, against the menace of intervention and blockade, for national freedom and the national independence of Cuba." This was precisely the program of the Grau government (as of APRA in Perú) which the Communists had so bitterly denounced and had helped put under the sod. The Communists, after 1935, decided that they would no longer call the various democratic groups "Fascist," but should choose allies among them in order that, when they again got into power or at some other opportunity, they could steal away their mass following, i.e., repeat their same old blunders. It is not surprising that Grau and others have spurned Communist approaches.

Today anyone in Cuba known to be a Communist is in danger of jail or the firing squad. The movement is entirely underground. Several tiny clandestine papers are published, such as *La Bandera Roja*, Red Flag.

The Dominicans, apart from exiles in New York, have scarcely heard of Communism; and in Haiti, despite secret Comintern organization work, there are only a few Communist intellectuals, some of whom have spent varying terms in jail. In Central America and Colombia, Communist agitators have been active in banana strikes.

In a recent strike in Costa Rica, President Jiménez recognized the Communist Party as having the right to bargain for the workers. According to the head of the company, the strike-leaders were not Communists, because his manager "could buy them off." But certainly the strongest Communist group in all Central America centers in Costa Rica. A strong, probably Communist-controlled, League Against War and Fascism there, has conducted boycotts against Japanese and Nazi goods.

The story that the 2,000 or so persons, massacred a few years ago by Dictator Martínez of Salvador, were Communists, is poppycock. Those assassinated were ignorant Indian serfs on the large native- and German-owned coffee *fincas* and in adjacent villages who had never heard of Communism but had been stirred up by political skulduggery. In Salvador only a half dozen intellectuals and several leaders of the small clandestine labor movement profess sympathy for Soviet doctrines.

In Nicaragua there are no Communists, but elsewhere extreme Left-Wingers in 1928 hotly denounced General César Augusto Sandino for his failure to enunciate a radical economic program, instead of sticking to his one-track war against American marine invasions. They were against "imperialism" but denounced everybody against imperialism who did not adhere to their doctrines, and even more particularly those who did not follow their peculiar Party Line, at the moment rigid as a prison's stark wall. They attacked Sandino still more savagely when he laid down his arms after the marines withdrew and supported President Sacasa, though previously he had publicly promised time and again to do just that.

Today the Communists hail the martyred Sandino as a great, if not quite kosher, leader and try to corral his memory as part of the faith.

There is a considerable movement in Ecuador, supported by leading writers, mostly in Guayaquil, who write books on the oppression of the Indians and advocate agrarian communalism. In Colombia are published two Communist organs, *El Soviet* and *El Bolshevique*. No political parties are allowed in Venezuela, but there seems to be a considerable underground movement, long schooled in secret propaganda since the days of the ruthless dictator, Juan Vicente Gómez.

There are some Bolivian Communist intellectuals, such as Tristan Marof, mostly in exile. Economic distress since the Chaco War has increased popular discontent, making an unstable political situation, held in check only by the iron dictatorship of Germán Busch. His semi-Fascist government, late in April, 1938, passed a law outlawing all "Communist, Anarchist and Bolshevik" organizations. Those holding such ideas and propagating them were made subject to from two to five years' imprisonment. The law applies to all radio-station owners, editors, publishers, theater or movie managers that permit the diffusion of extremist ideas. Editorial houses publishing extremist works will be fined 5,000 pesos, and the editions will be confiscated.

In Perú all "international" organizations are forbidden, though ironically President Oscar Benavides himself is pretty much under the thumb of the Japanese and Italians, and school-children are frequently required to give the Fascist salute. When I was there in 1934, some democratic rights still existed. There were then a mere handful of Communists in Lima, led by a simple, uneducated worker, Espelucín. In the south flourished a stronger group which pretty well controlled the railway workers and had just carried on a successful strike. The movement is now illegal, though ironically, most of the Communist leaders, as we have mentioned, are holding down soft jobs in the pseudo-Fascist Italian-influenced dictatorship of Oscar Benavides.

Most Peruvian radical sentiment is embodied in the Peruvian APRA, led by Haya de la Torre.

In Chile, the lenient military dictatorship of President Alessandri allows almost complete democratic expression. During the series of revolutions resulting from world depression, the temporary regime of Marmaduke Grove was labeled by the outside press as "Communist," though actually he is a Socialist. In any event there is a well-established Communist Party, led largely by lawyers, intellectuals and politicians, but having some following among mine and nitrate workers. *La Bandera Roja* and *La Opinión* are the principal publications. Communist deputies sit in Congress, a larger percentage in fact than in any country except Russia.

6

In the Communist "Third Conference of Latin-American Parties" held in Uruguay in the autumn of 1934, the program was laid down to bring tactics into line with the new orders from Moscow for Popular Front alliances. This explains the somersaults in Cuban and Peruvian policy. In the latter, they somersaulted right into jobs in the present reactionary regime. The same Popular Front trend also explains the curious developments now going on in Chile.

There the Communists have succeeded in creating a broad Popular Front. One of its leaders, Senator Elias Lafette, returning from Moscow, recently passed through New York and gave many addresses to the local Hispanic colony. The Popular Front is opposing the conservative candidate, Ross Santa María, being imposed by President Alessandri.

Among the new idols of the Communists of the Popular Front has been ex-Dictator Carlos Ibáñez, who, when previously in office, promoted industrialization with foreign capital, made many secret unsavory concessions to American interests, promoted a Fascist movement, put down strikes with the army, jailed all opponents, including Communists, and destroyed the liberty of the press as never before in Chilean history. Astonishingly enough he was recently the Communist white hope for getting rid of the Alessandri regime. But if he gains power again, the Communists will probably enjoy far less freedom than they now do under conservative Alessandri. They will merely have helped create another Brazil.

The Socialists, however, blocked the candidacy of Ibáñez, who has since announced himself as an independent aspirant. The Popular Front has postulated a colorless politician, Pedro Aguirre Cerda. A wealthy plantation-owner, he has not been particularly pronounced for his views, except for being a politician opposed to Alessandri. Ironically enough the Popular Front is supported by the native Chilean Nazi Party! The real struggle, of course, is between the candidate of the present Executive and the former Dictator Ibáñez.

The activities of the Popular Front in Chile reveal little but an appetite to get ahead politically. But it is the big rallying cry at the moment all over the world for the Communists. The faithful consider it lèse-majesté to breathe a word of criticism of the new set-up. It follows the Party Line. It is holy.

In Brazil, Argentina, Paraguay and Bolivia, Communists are outlawed and plenty maltreated. In Buenos Aires there is considerable Communist sentiment and a large underground movement. At one time, four Communist magazines were published, but now only secret *hojas*. Arrests are made frequently. On April 17th of this year, the police rounded up twenty-nine leaders in Buenos Aires.

"There are no Communists in Buenos Aires Province," declares Governor Manuel Fresno, the worshipper of Mussolini and Hitler, in this year's annual message to the legislature. "There is no other flag than that of Argentina within the provincial limits, and only one Argentine sentiment rules the hearts of our citizens."

In Brazil—though Dictator Vargas for a long time called everyone who opposed him, from bankers to ditch diggers, "Communists," and though Comintern agents have worked there assiduously—there was, when some civil liberties were allowed, but little evidence of a movement. Before 1930, a National Alliance was formed of the Tenientes (under army officers), the Travailistas (Socialists, later supporting the dictatorship), the Alliance Liberale ("a party of the bourgeoisie and landlords"—so the Communists themselves describe it—"closely connected with the U.S.A."). The Communists supported the National Alliance, trying to be the little tail to wag the dog. Getulio Vargas was thus assisted in seizing power, and though the Communists are today jailed and murdered, the country gone Brazilian-Fascist, that early effort of the alliance is still hailed as a great tactical Communist achievement. Regardless of the sinister consequences, it obeyed the New Party Line, even before the New Party Line had been adopted, therefore is sacrosanct.

The unsuccessful revolt of Carlos Prestes several years ago, though labeled by Vargas and the foreign press as "Communist," was merely a liberal wing in the army, and few of its leaders knew anything about Communism. The little tail, though, was still wagging and controlled a few proletarian elements in São Paulo, who bravely met the firing squads.

However, the Communist underground movement in Brazil, if not large, is well-disciplined, and now, thanks to Vargas' arbitrary rule, is growing. After all, the average factory wage in that great Roosevelt democracy known as Brazil is less than $12 a month!

Though General Terra seized Uruguay by armed force, overthrowing one of the most enlightened regimes ever existing in Latin America, once he had terrorized all opponents into quiescence, he gradually loosened up on the bit, and now allows all parties to function.

In spite of the activities of the Soviet Legation there

prior to this coup, the Communists were never able to elect more than two Congressmen, and in the national elections just celebrated—in which the two leading candidates were close family relatives of Dictator Terra, the Communists participated but cut no ice.

7

All told, Soviet efforts in Hispanic America, diplomatic, economic, and political, have resulted mostly in failure. The tendency in most of the countries is at present frankly Fascistic and pro-Nazi. The various dictatorial regimes have great sympathy, open or secret, for Hitler and Mussolini. All are pro-Franco except Costa Rica, México, and to a certain extent Colombia.

However, from a long range view, the opportunities of Communism are sufficiently large. The best Bolshevist allies are the ruthless and oppressive governments, which suppress all freedom and democracy and thereby foster clandestine intrigue, secret plots and terrorism. The dictatorships force even conservative and liberal groups to line up together with the Communists in a united front. The inevitable fall of such dictatorships is likely to bring periods of disorder in which extremist doctrines will have their day.

Dictatorship, the prevalent land monopoly and harsh serfdom, low wages, suppression of legitimate labor organizations, illiteracy, the prohibition of all civil liberties, suppression of the free—such conditions give point, justification and opportunities to Communist propagandists. Economic and political injustices are sowing the dragon-teeth that will likely really leap into Comintern warriors.

The masses to the south are rapidly awakening and stirring. If they do not find freedom, if they do not find more generous leadership to right immemorial wrongs, in-evitably they will turn to Communist guidance. Communist doctrines if intelligently modified undoubtedly can be made to appeal to the Indian minorities which for centuries have lived under a system of land communalism. The general world trend toward collectivism and greater governmental control gives more plausibility to the neat Communist program.

Probably the impending struggles for freedom in the southern countries will follow nationalist lines and be in accord with the deep, vital traditional forces of Latin America, rather than obey imperialist coercion, the pene-tration of foreign capital, or the acceptance or stereotyped doctrines from abroad, Communist, Democratic or Fascist. The Communists know this and are rapidly hastening to adopt the nationalistic slogans that a few years ago they ridiculed and denounced. Hence the present defeat of the Communist movement should not cause its potentialities to be too greatly discounted.

Already it has pricked military dictatorships and pseudo-Fascist regimes into life. If nothing else, it will serve as a force which will still further provoke more such reactionary governments into existence. Such reactionary tyrannies, the Communists have already helped to create or perpetuate in Cuba and Perú and Brazil; they are paving the way for the same thing now in Chile. In this direction, or in any future break-up of the present semi-feudal militaristic regimes that at present weight down the life of South America, the Communists will undoubtedly find a chance to play a more important part than at present.

But the trend of Latin America economically is at pres-ent toward a type of State-Capitalism of semi-Fascist na-tionalist character. In some countries the trend is toward laissez-faire capitalism, though with extensive State-controls. Only in México is there a definite semi-Socialistic current, but decidedly nationalistic in spirit, and very much cut to a Mexican, not Communist, pattern.

On the whole the Communists have been too dominated by rigid theories and outside controls to gain the general confidence of the southern countries. Their pigeon-hole doctrines airily shove aside the deep racial and cultural conflicts of the south as though these were quite non-existent. Nor have the Communists ever understood the peasant and land problem of the southern countries, the dual heritage of Spanish and Indian law. And the southern peoples have suffered too many centuries, and are suffering now, from dictatorships, to be enamored of any program that does not heavily stress the innate rights and dignity of the individual man.

CHAPTER

VI

Franco Invades Latin America

Peace or War in the Western Hemisphere was not decided in the Buenos Aires Pan-American conference called by Roosevelt. To a far greater extent it is being decided on the battle-fields of Spain—and the answer is more likely war than peace. A good part of the fate of the Western Hemisphere in the near future is being fought out at Madrid and Teruel and Lérida. Generalissimo Franco's promise of success in the Spanish struggle has already helped to consolidate the existing Black League in Latin America. It has opened the doors of the continent more than ever to the already very successful drive of the German-Italian-Japanese combination for the markets, political resources and control of that area.

Fascism is at our doors in bloody earnest. The strengthening of the Fascist alliances through Latin America, and the interalliances of reactionary Fascist-like governments there, far from providing stable and free rule, are increasing economic and political problems, introducing unstable stress. New iron-might, instead of creating security, is likely to convert the southern continent into a shambles.

Then it will be too late to seek other solutions, and not all our good-will messages to the dictatorial and high-handed regimes of Hispanic America will longer hide the fact that democracy is dead to the south and that we have bartered our national security for a good-neighbor policy based in part upon a myth and a fraud.

The good-neighbor policy in Latin America became nearly an empty shell when our government under the guise of false neutrality allied itself, in effect, with Italy and Germany, in creating a policy that has penalized the popularly elected government in Spain and aided the Franco rebels. In doing this we have greatly abetted the Fascist invasion of Latin America.

Spain has been the first big trench in the battle for our own continent. Spain, in its own right, quite apart from its Nazi-Fascist backers, has great influence on Hispanic America. So has Portugal on Brazil. Those mother countries have far greater cultural importance for New World lands than England for us.

In Spain are some forty institutions concerned with cultural relations with the western countries.

Bonds with the Old World are also reinforced in the New by large numbers of Spanish and Portuguese immigrants, who exert considerable and constant influence. The promise of Franco victory in Spain has already promoted dictatorial reaction in Hispanic America, just as the submission of Portugal to Nazi influence already has had its evil effects on Brazil. Our own policy toward the Spanish struggle has definitely aided the Italian and German drive to the south.

The immigrants from the mother countries, speaking the same language, are scarcely foreigners. In New York the very large Spanish colony is made up largely of poor people; they have been heart and soul with the Spanish government, the Loyalists. They have starved in order to send funds and hospital supplies back home to aid in the fight. But in the southern lands, the Spanish colonies are dominated by wealthy and reactionary members, even when, as in Cuba, there are also large numbers of small businessmen, farm-hands and workers. To the south, the Spanish and Portuguese immigrants have found the road to material success much easier than in the United States. Many have become wealthy merchants, bankers, great baronial landowners ruling thousands of serfs; and in most countries, Spanish and Portuguese, rather than native ecclesiastics, have seized the high lucrative post in the Church. As a result, these influential immigrants have used their large economic power to swing official support, already very disposed, more decidedly to Franco. Those Spaniards, who felt otherwise, with the help of the various governments have been terrorized into silence.

Nowhere did Franco receive more sympathy than from the dictatorships to the south of us, for mostly those governments are semi-feudal tyrannies based on military force, very similar to that which Franco strives to establish on the Peninsula.

Nor has Franco disdained to cultivate this rich field further, for it has given him tangible aid. Numerous special agents have been sent out. Even before the Aragón drive began, Father Pedro Ibáñez and Walls Taberner, two Franco representatives on "a cultural tour" to contact local reactionary elements and organize more systematic propaganda for the rebel side, returned to Salamanca to report to the Spanish Fuehrer on conditions in Argentina, Chile, Perú, Uruguay and Brazil. General Gonzáles Marín has been touring Central American and other countries, organizing the Spanish residents into pro-Franco units. In Santo Domingo a government-encouraged Franco bureau puts out expensive glossy print propaganda in favor of the rebels. There are 4,000,000 Spanish residents in Latin America, and their adhesion means important support in money, ammunition, supplies, as well as serving to influence the various governments in favor of the Franco cause.

To Cuba went Manuel Villanueva, also a personal emissary of Franco, who has organized 5,000 pro-Franco Falangistas, who hold numerous meetings in dark shirts with the gold insignia of a sheaf of five arrows. They have enlisted the support of a leading daily, owned by a reactionary Spanish family. It is claimed that their meetings are attended by Fascist diplomats, and at a recent banquet in the Marianao Casino, the German Minister was the speaker of honor.

And every German and Italian agent of the many that flood Latin America, has been a spy, informer and assistant of Franco and his cause. An Italian consul was brought into court in México on such charges. Italian espionage in México, headed by Fernando Fiell, tipped off the Franco insurgents as to the course of the *Mar Cantabrico* which was taking airplanes and other munitions from New York and Vera Cruz, with the result that it was intercepted and sunk.

In Chile, the German minister succeeded in having Spanish war-films showing Franco's bombardments of civilians barred from exhibition. Senator Praderas Múñoz declared that it was one more proof of the influence in Chile of insurgent agents.

Italy's aid to Franco and the growing success of the Nazi-Fascist cause in Spain—contrasted to the supineness of the so-called democratic countries, England and France, their abject surrender to the fake neutrality pact, their failure to prevent Italy and Germany from violating it—have led various Latin-American dictators to feel that their best guarantee against any liberal or democratic movement lies in friendliness to Italy and Germany.

As Dr. Raymond Leslie Buell, President of the Foreign Policy Association has stated: "The victory of Germany and Italy in Spain is bound to injure the ideas of liberalism and democracy throughout Latin America."

The Italians are quite aware that in fighting for Franco in Spain, they are not merely seeking Mediterranean hegemony, but are also preserving their stake in Latin America. No less a person than Federzone has stated—misrepresenting the character of the Loyalist government—that the Spanish crisis might have had very bad repercussions in the New World had not insurgent Spain arisen "to nip in the bud the activity of the Communist international, and if Portugal, with which Brazil maintains the closest relations, had not resisted the contagion."

Germany is also already using Spain as a base for many camouflaged trade-drives on Latin America. It has already set up the subsidized Hispanic Film Corporation, expected to capture the vast territory of the Spanish-speaking New World.

The Compañía Hispano-Americana de Electricidad de Barcelona, known as *Chade,* is the descendant of the *Deutsche Ueberseeische Elektrizitat Gesellschaft,* that has wide interests throughout Central and South America. This company has complicated European ownership, but the majority control is still said to be German. Latin-American papers have charged that this concern has actively promoted pro-Franco sentiment in South America, and that it looks upon a Franco victory as necessary for the consolidation of German mining and ship-building interests in Spain and for the further expansion of its own activities throughout our own two continents.

The victory of Loyalist Spain would have a tremendous effect in blocking German and Italian imperialism in South

America, and in freeing the Latin-American people from the incubus of the tyrannical governments that weight them down.

Uruguay, Guatemala, Salvador and Nicaragua—all ruled by petty tyrants who established their sway by force and murder—hastened to recognize Franco; Brazil sent congratulations to him, has refused to permit vessels of the Spanish government to enter Brazilian harbors. The Madrid legations of some Hispanic countries became a foci of Franco spy-rings and cached ammunition to aid the Franco cause to strike a treacherous blow behind the Loyalist lines. Argentina harbors and abets Franco agents. Many of the southern countries have bought arms in the United States to ship to Franco, and have provided him with information that has aided him to intercept supply vessels for the Spanish government. While maintaining relations with the Spanish government, many have sent secret agents to Franco.

The Latin-American dictatorships, by suppressing all news and propaganda in favor of the Loyalists, have sought to create a one-sided public opinion and further buttress Franco's cause. They know that arguments in favor of the elected government of Spain are dangerous for their own improper rule at home. In Brazil the best ticket of admission to a prison cell or death has been to speak or write in favor of Spain's Liberal government or denounce Franco. In Perú Loyalist sympathizers have been jailed. In Cuba, the government forbade all public meetings, articles, collections of funds or hospital supplies for either side, but in practice enforced this only against Loyalist sympathizers. Recently a large group of Cubans and Spaniards were arrested for collecting funds for the Loyalists and charged with conspiracy against the Cuban government, which of course is merely the dictatorship of Fulgencio Batista, who burns 'em alive.

In May his government sent Francisco Navarro Montalvo on a special diplomatic mission to Burgos.

Only in México and Costa Rica, both enjoying free speech, do public sentiment and the official attitude largely coincide, and both are strongly in favor of the cause of Spanish democracy. México, which has its own national arms factories, shipped supplies to Spain, and in fact Costa Rica and México have been the only two countries in the world to take a consistent moral position within the framework of established international law toward the Spanish struggle, and continued to maintain straightforward relations with the legal government, menaced by revolt and subjected to foreign invasion. For those of us who believe also in the triumph of free and democratic institutions in the world, their course, quite aside from the legal principles involved, was heartening.

In Costa Rica, a strong anti-Fascist movement, one wing led by Vicente Saenz, conducted effective boycotts against Japanese and German goods and raised the banner of support boldly in favor of the Loyalists. When the Spanish diplomatic representative there turned pro-Franco, he was arrested and deported.

Elsewhere the governments of the two continents in varying degrees supported Franco, although several temporarily posed as neutral, and many official elements were even in favor of the Loyalists.

From all over the continent, native Nazi and Fascist organizations have sent missions to Franco. One such organization in México named a delegate for the purpose of getting Franco to intercede with Hitler to provide more means for overthrowing the Cárdenas regime there. Atalaya Arboleya, Head of the Argentine Phalanx, the chief of the largest Fascist group in the country, personally visited Franco in company with Franco's own consul in Buenos Aires, Manuel López Meva. These goings and comings are part of the general effort to promote the so-called Black League of Latin America, in which Franco, backed by Italy and Germany, already has a hand.

2

This pro-Franco attitude on the southern continent was to be expected. Despite President Roosevelt's statement that never have the governments of Latin America so represented the will of the people, the fact is that most of them never have less represented the people, never have they been under narrower or more dictatorial rule. The majority of them are brutal, often entirely illegal, dictatorships holding their power by force and terrorism.

Thus, despite our laudatory congratulations to the new President-elect of Argentina, Roberto Ortiz, our praise for his "democratic" government, which for Mr. Hull was such an "inspiration," represents a dull continuation of the brutal military dictatorship that seized power seven years ago. In the elections last year, though Ortiz' party, through the army, controlled the polls and prevented all free campaigning, his opponent polled the majority of the popular votes. Ortiz was put in by gerrymandered election districts and fraud in the electoral college. If he represents democracy, then a flea circus has bigger elephants than Ringling Brothers.

No more brutal regime has ever ruled in the continent than in Brazil. Under Trujillo, Santo Domingo is a chamber of horrors. The Batista regime in Cuba burned my friend

Octavio Seigle alive. Benavides rules Perú by bayonets, having set aside the election that deposed him and his clique. The story of our Western Hemisphere at this moment is not a pretty one, and our State Department is merely hiding its head in the sands when it talks about noble democratic Latin America face to face with a bad Fascist world. This is merely a pretty bed-time story for children and American newspaper editors. The fact is most of Latin America is openly semi-Fascist—naturally a Fascism of its own brand —and ruled by governments that practice the worst features of Hitlerism. Naturally they have been pro-Franco.

Following the special Pan-American conference in Buenos Aires in which Roosevelt talked democracy and peace and everybody agreed to sign peace pacts, Saavedra Lamas, Argentina's Foreign Minister said, "Now, we'll have to arm like hell." And all the Latin nations of the two continents, except México and the United States, thereupon held a behind-the-scenes congress to decide upon common measures to suppress democracy—of course they called it by other names, and all began piling up armaments.

Naturally those governments—though to please the United States they pay lip service to democracy—actually are afraid of democracy or they would not be ruling their people with machine-guns. They are fascinated by Fascist ideas, and look upon Hitler and Mussolini as the saviors of civilization. Those southern regimes have provided fertile ground for Fascist propaganda. With every Fascist victory diplomatic or otherwise on the continent of Europe, the reactionary Latin-American governments grow more open in their favoritism toward Franco and Germany and Italy.

Latin America has been well aware that Spain was not merely suffering a civil war but is the theater of a battle for world power. Franco's victory will mean a victory for Musso-

lini and Hitler. By that victory Fascist influence is being
further cemented on most of Latin America. Thus the
Italian-German drive in Spain has been a struggle not
merely for the control of Europe and the Mediterranean
but for the control of overseas empire and power.

A victory of democratic Spain, i.e., by the popularly
elected government, would send a fresh and virile wave of
liberalism through the dark tyranny-ruled continent to the
south. It would checkmate Hitler and Mussolini in their
designs on Latin America far more than all the present
feverish propaganda being sent out from Washington.

It has been argued that the victory of the Loyalists would
be an opening wedge for Communism in Latin America.
But the Popular government in Spain has no great reason
to be overly grateful to the Soviet Union, is under no obligations to Moscow to allow Russia special privileges in
the Spanish Peninsula, as Franco is obligated to Mussolini
and Hitler.

Russian sales to Spain at the outset of the struggle were
just sufficient to permit a general hue and cry to be raised
that Loyalist Spain was Communist, though the Communist Party in Spain at that time had a smaller membership
than the Communist Party in the United States, and Russia
was exercising a right provided for by long-established and
universally accepted international law. Equally, commentators should have shouted that Mussolini was Communist
when the Soviet government sold him oil and supplies to
help him carry on the conquest of Ethiopia.

In any case, the Spanish government represented that
chosen by the Spanish people.

The Russian arms that Loyalist Spain received in the
early part of the struggle were paid for with cold cash. The
Soviet government, however, soon joined the treacherous

neutrality pact which largely prevented the Spanish government from getting necessary outside supplies but which gave a free hand to the Italians, Germans and Franco-Moorish revolters.

From the standpoint of established international law and respect for a friendly government, for a time the Soviet attitude was more decent than that of England and the United States.

Then Soviet Russia left Spain in the lurch, and thereafter became one of so many false neutrals who caused Loyalist and democratic Spain to be steam-rollered by the Fascist Powers in a gamble of imperialist expansion.

3

Sumner Welles of our State Department has taken American journalists severely to task for calling Brazil Fascist and thus endangering American friendship in that quarter. It is a sad day when a high member of our State Department converts himself into a voluntary propagandist for a regime as brutal, as anti-American, as that of Vargas in Brazil. Vargas himself claims he is not a Fascist. To prove it, he suppressed the Integralista Party along with all other parties, Congress, State and local governments and all civil rights.

In fact, he is not Fascist, he has merely taken over and written into the new constitution the program of the Fascist party there; he has appointed Fascist-Nazi leaders to high posts. He is not Fascist; he is just a dictator who uses totalitarian methods. He is not Fascist. He merely declares one minute that he is running a corporative state, and the next that he believes in democracy. He merely doesn't permit democracy to be practiced. Actually he is a dictator with more absolute power in Brazil—for the moment—than

Mussolini in Italy or Stalin in Russia. The difference is that Vargas' power, if he can shoot and kill at will, is hollow and not at all endorsed by the masses. He heads a constantly unstable regime, bound to grow constantly more unstable.

Benavides of Perú is little more than a Mussolini puppet. He never sets foot in public without the Italian Minister at his elbow. Nor does Ubico of Guatemala.

This whole Fascist invasion of Latin America has been carried out swiftly and brilliantly. It is aided by the reactionary anti-democratic regimes that exist there, some of them owing their control to previous American loans. With large munition supplies to export, the Fascist nations gain a definite foothold in the military establishments of the southern countries. No one but a blind man can fail to see that the Hitler-Mussolini drive in Spain has been the spearhead of a drive, among other things, to control also Latin America so rich in raw materials necessary for war and one of the world's greatest markets.

The role of the United States in all this is an unhappy one. We have been manoeuvred into a policy of friendship for Latin-American dictatorships but not the Latin-American peoples. This is false friendship. It rests on no sound basis. It is, in short, a colossal fraud. Our slogans of friendship could well be marked "Made in Germany and Italy." We could not improve the chances of the Japanese-Fascist-German combination in Latin America better than we are doing by many of our acts. Our government has, in part, been playing the Fascist game in Spain, and it is in part playing it in Latin America.

Our Spanish neutrality law, tied to England's petticoats, definitely favored the Franco Fascists and placed a penalty on the Loyalists.

Prior to January, 1937, the United States throughout its

history had permitted the sale of arms to friendly governments engaged in suppressing revolt. The only justification
for a change in this venerable policy would be to prevent
arms from getting to either side. Obviously our State Department is, instead, helping the Nazi-Fascist rebels, not the
democratically elected government. We are helping Germany and Italy. The justification, given by Senator Nye,
when pushing the original bill at the behest of the State
Department, was that the neutrality pact engineered by
England should be backed by the United States. The falsity
of that pact is long since apparent. But our State Department, still a little tail to English diplomacy, has smothered
all change, thus giving further basis for the growing belief
in many American circles that in many matters it is essen-
tially Fascist-minded. Mr. Hull states that to change the
act to a more moral basis and in accordance with long-ex-
isting practices of international law, would expose us to
risks.

The neutrality act has never been applied to the Orient,
where there is actually a war and where there is far more
justification and far more risk of entanglement. Could it be
that we have more powerful private interests involved in
the Orient, such as those of the Standard Oil Company?
Yet in México Mr. Hull showed no particular tenderness
toward the interests of the Standard Oil. Obviously his
policy is not at all consistent, and—to say the kindest thing
of it—is highly opportunistic.

He has been very nasty toward journalists criticising his
policies. His assistant, Mr. Sumner Welles, has taken them
to task on various occasions—with a father-knows-best air.
But in the Spain-Germany-Italy business, the two Washington statesmen are definitely endangering the American position, especially in the New World. To assist Italy and Ger-

many in Spain is greatly to assist them in Latin America, where presumably we are trying to offset their influence. Here is a whip, we say to the Fascist Powers, and then pretend they won't use it on us.

Our embargo, as Dr. Buell has pointed out, "has turned out to be an instrument of intervention against the Loyalist government." We are not neutral. We are taking sides. We are taking sides with Germany and Italy. We are not neutral. We are not impartial. We are definitely aiding Franco to assault the established government. We have assumed responsibility for helping to put down the people's government in Spain.

If weak democratic governments cannot get arms from the so-called democratic Powers, a premium is put on Fascist revolt everywhere, not merely in Europe but in America itself. If the so-called democratic Powers, out of fear of Communism, thus betray such democratic governments, then they will be driven, as was Spain, in trying to get arms where they can, and that means Soviet Russia. We drive them into the arms of Communism, the very thing which, at bottom, we claim to be trying to avoid. Instead of that we aid Fascist uprisings. This is a short-sighted and perverted policy.

The test of the State Department's sincerity will soon arise in South America. If the tyrannical semi-Fascist governments of Brazil, or Perú, or Argentina, or Guatemala, face revolt, will our government prevent them from receiving arms, while allowing other countries to provide arms to the democratic forces? We know the answer beforehand. The State Department will back the existing South American despotisms to the hilt, as it is in fact doing at the present moment. As Buell concludes, the present policy toward Spain "injures not only the sense of justice, but the interests of the American people." The matter is even worse than that.

We protested sharply to México for transshipment of American airplanes and war-supplies to the Spanish government, forced her to stop. But we have never once protested to Canada, Germany,[1] Italy, Panamá and other Latin-American countries, some of which have been transshipping American war supplies to Franco. The State Department has hastened to O.K. such supplies, which might easily have reached Franco, yet it has quibbled over every shipment that might possibly be suspected of reaching the Spanish government.

Mr. Hull has claimed that he has been as impartial in the Spanish crisis as a cigar-store wooden Indian. He protested, nevertheless, against the cruel bombings of noncombatants in cities. His protest might have had some moral validity if the policy he supports did not directly aid the bombing of those cities by Italian and German planes. But then we Americans are early taught to keep our morals for Sunday school and not let them interfere with what we actually do on week-days.

This muddleheaded undercover policy has brought war

[1] Secretary Hull, recently nettled into grossly insulting one of our leading correspondents and columnists at a press conference, has been obliged to go to great lengths to show that the United States has sold Germany only airplane engines for commercial purposes and that these were transshipped to South Africa. The Loyalists and British labor leaders have claimed that American munitions were transshipped from Germany to Franco. However that may be, Hull's argument rested on the naïve theory that commercial airplane engines can never be used for war purposes. At this moment of writing, American aviators, at the behest of the State Department, are under arrest for flying commercial planes to México, claimed to be for transshipment to Spain, the argument being that such planes can easily be transformed into military or scout planes. The obvious answer to this muddled business is that our State Department does not mind Franco using American scout planes, but the Loyalists must not do so.

closer to our shores. By supporting Spanish Fascism and abetting and flattering the semi-Fascist dictatorships to the south, we shall likely reap what our State Department, in the false name of democracy and friendship, is now sowing —namely, war or ignominy. Democracy down there at present is merely a whistle-britches echo.

Franco's victory will be merely the stepping stone to more ambitious schemes, of which it is merely a prelude.

And thus the battle by Germany and Italy to seat the puppet Franco in power in Spain has been also a battle to control the whole Latin world and its rich resources. It has been a battle for the American continent, not merely for Spain. Franco is merely the cheap tool of a scheme of imperial aggrandizement. That scheme casts its dark shadow across the Americans. It lies at our doorstep.

CHAPTER

VII

The Good-Will Racket

No portion of the globe has endured the unasked good-will ministrations of righteous Americans more than Latin America. The efforts to help and to save Latin America range from those of the Communist Anti-Imperialist League to the representatives of the Power Trust. Liberals, missionaries, concessionaires, newspapermen, bankers, sugar-growers, airplane companies, radio corporations, Presidents of the United States, Chambers of Commerce, Rotary Clubs, students, women, pacifists, labor leaders, socialists, agents of the Society for the Prevention of Cruelty to Animals, committees on coöperation, on cultural relations, for world peace, scientists, geographers, philosophers, doctors, educators, tax experts, sound money men, bond-holders, patent-medicine venders, etc., have flooded Latin America with saccharine words of friendship and this country with the true facts about our neighbors.

While our golden tide of loans and investments, to the tune of six billion dollars, poured into the laps of ebullient southland politicians and dictators, official Latin America beamed back at us fulsomely. But now that the golden stream has dried at its source, now that the awakening southern peoples have been forced by depression into defiant economic nationalism, their officials, despite our new good-will, do not so often go out of their way to sing our praises—nor writers, politicians and radicals to attack us for "imperialism."

In their earlier frequent tirades about the "Yankee peril," the latter rarely stopped to distinguish between all Americans and the bankers and public utility pyramiders whose money helped corrupt the political life of the regions to the south of us. Despite all our earlier dollar generosity and old-style good-will—for even those days we had the same slogans—we were distrusted, feared, even hated. Our pre-Roosevelt declarations of friendship, laid on laughably thick at times, though not so much as now, brought us little in real dividends of non-official cordiality. We poured our fountain of benevolence into a desert of ingratitude. Now that the good-neighbor policy of Roosevelt makes deeds apparently correspond more closely to our protestations, in many quarters we are really reaping considerable friendliness rather than merely voluble protestations.

As a nation we began to grow really Latin-American conscious twenty years ago, shortly before we entered the World War. Even earlier than that our government promoted the Pan-American Union of the sovereign republics of the Western Hemisphere, with the American Secretary of State as honorary President—a sort of bureau of colonial control, constantly advocating friendship and understanding, but well-permeated with smug Anglo-Saxon superiority and commercialism.

It still operates as an arm of our control. Though ostensibly a free association of the twenty-one American nations, the headquarters are in Washington, in a building donated by Carnegie, its director has always been an American (from the United States), and it is very much under the thumb of the State Department. Despite its many worthy side-issue achievements, its promotion of many excellent cultural relationships, it still remains, in organization and spirit, basically a bureau of colonial control.

Cleveland and Olney, toward the end of the last century, had arrogantly told England, in connection with the Venezuela-Guiana boundary dispute, that the United States, in whatever matter it chose to concern itself, was supreme on this continent. At the beginning of this century, Teddy Roosevelt sent an ultimatum to Germany, backed by fleet mobilization, not to collect debts in South America by force. In 1907 Root made his good-will tour to allay feeling aroused by the Platt Amendment, which had chained Cuba to our will, our annexation of Puerto Rico, and our "rape of Panamá." In 1909 President Taft shook hands with Dictator Porfirio Díaz on the El Paso International bridge. President Wilson denounced Shylock loans and marine interventions and perpetrated both.

By 1928 Coolidge felt Latin America sufficiently important to attend the Havana Pan-American Congress in person. And to stop anti-American feeling regarding marine intervention in Nicaragua and Haiti, Lindbergh was roped into the good-will game by swinging around the Caribbean circle, to add his reputation and medals to the splendor of that reunion in the troubled household of tyrant Machado. Lindbergh reaped official flattery, many impressive demonstrations, a fortune in gifts, and considerable popular condemnation. Pershing visited Panamá, and because of a secret navy scheme to force that country to cede more territory, his car was stoned. Hoover anticipated his own administration with a good-will tour on a battleship that took in every important country except México. There, unfortunately, Congressmen impolitely denounced his jaunt as a cloak for marine intervention in Nicaragua, and in Argentina both popular and official reception was cool, very cool.

Official American interest in Latin America has been active since 1809; but general popular interest had to await upon certain other less official developments. It was diverted to Europe by the World War, but reasserted itself immediately after, when, tired of worrying about the Old World and its ingratitude and desirous of affirming our new-found international financial supremacy, we turned to Latin America as a field for fresh endeavor. Earlier everywhere there, except in lower South America, the war had thrown to us without an effort vast trade and investment monopolies.

Two significant factors made possible this extensive new interest: the development of communications, especially cable and telephone service, under American capital control; and a prompt shift in the news-distribution to Latin America from London to New York, which thereafter inevitably caused the publishing of a larger body of Hispano-American news in the United States itself. Distribution of news thus became an integral part of American economic expansion southwards and thus focused more attention upon southern affairs.

This was soon followed by our wild-cat loan period, and every bond-salesman became a glib authority upon the saltpetre of Chile, the hardwood jungles of Brazil, the succulency of Argentine pampas grass. It takes a lot of cultural pap and romance to sell billions of dollars of shaky bonds.

Prior to the World War the foreign news peddled in Latin America and news from Latin America were purveyed chiefly by Reuters. Even the Associated Press derived its information about that part of the world via the British Isles—just as today most of our Bolivian tin comes by the same round-about route. London, with its 150,000 miles of radiating submarine cables, was the natural news-feeding point. Second was Paris, from which Havas, the great French government-subsidized agency, sent out its continent-wide dispatches. Germany, looming up with its Wolff service, laid down a cable via the Azores and Liberia to Pernambuco, Brazil.

These agencies, all aided by their respective governments, were active in furthering trade interests. The news they peddled warred upon competitor nations, and all focused their guns on the United States, which threatened to be the new invader of the field. The information that emanated from the Rue de la Paix was heavily larded with stories of American official graft, scandals, lynchings, our barbarism in general. The fact that the United States is predominantly a Protestant land was not overlooked in influencing opinion in Catholic countries.

The first American challenge to this European news control began before the war with a vast cable battle. American service penetrated México, Central America and the West Indies. Our cable lines gradually crept along the west coast of South America to Chile, then across the Andes to Argentina and Uruguay. Finally Brazil was penetrated and the network rounded out. From 1914 to 1928 this cable system was expanded more than 13,000 miles. Ultimately it was mostly concentrated in the hands of the International Telephone and Telegraph Company.

This gave the first real opening for American news agencies, a process soon hastened by the World War. Censorship had played havoc with Latin-American confidence in European agencies. Every item became auxiliary propaganda for winning the war, and the news became even more biased when, in 1916, the German cable was fished up near Brazil and cut.

In that year the United Press established its first office in South America and ere long was supplying a hundred newspapers with "impartial" American reports. Roy Howard, then head of this organization, speaking before the Pittsburgh Press Club declared: [quoted in the *American Mercury* by Genaro Arbaiza] "While America has been sound asleep, England, Germany and France have been making international hay." The various European agencies had all been "furthering the interests of their particular countries." The American news agencies "should have years ago begun trail blazing for our commercial control. . . ." These should be "valued assistants of our diplomats. . . . Uncle Sam has had his press-agents behind his show instead of ahead of it."

Thus, American-delivered news, like that provided from Europe, was to be the handmaiden of American commercialism and diplomacy rather than a vestal of the Goddess Truth.

The Associated Press and International News jumped into the field and established relations with over eighty papers. Other services became active: North American Newspaper Alliance, King and Bell features, Pan-American News Service, the Spanish-American Press Syndicate. International News Reel photos soon stared from Latin-American drug-store windows.

In 1917, [as reported by Arbaiza] James Carson of the Associated Press, just returned from a Latin-American tour, informed the Fourth National Foreign Trade Convention that "your European competitors have inaugurated one of the cleverest press campaigns in the history of the trade, and are using publicity in the guise of news throughout a large area in an effort to discredit American merchants. . . . in a dozen . . . ways endeavoring to discredit Americans." He warned that even greater than the German peril was the English peril. But by that time, of course, the Germans had been driven out.

Soon after, Havas practically abandoned the field, and Reuters was to cede its news coverage and services in Latin America to the Associated Press, a deal dividing up the world into spheres between the two companies much as we now divide it up with respect to air-services. New York during the war became the Hispano-American news clearinghouse. The Monroe Doctrine, boasted the head of one large American press association, had been applied to the news. From that time on our good-will efforts could flourish.

But just as good-will those days proved singularly unconvincing to our Latin-American friends, so, subsequent to the war, various difficulties began to arise to challenge, not only our trade supremacy, but our news supremacy. The European agencies fought to recover the lost ground. Today, Havas, utilizing government radio to Brazil, can beat the American services on rapidity of transmission of nearly all world news and can undercut them in price. So can the German service. As a result, the Associated Press, bowing to the inevitable, has arranged with Havas to utilize its news in correspondent papers in certain places to the south. It is there re-slugged A.P. Though our agencies still dominate the field, many of the southern newspapers fearing American influence, propaganda and coloring—especially in various dictatorial countries—having found they can get world news elsewhere, are loath to continue the present high tolls to North American agencies.

Not only are the big pre-war European agencies back on the job, but others are more active than before. PAT (Polish), Canada, Stefani (Italian), Enit (Italian Tourist), Roma (Italian), Transocean (German), Fabra (Spanish, now suspended), Rengo (Japanese), are significant government-subsidized bureaus, not to mention various nationalistic private ones, maintained by commercial, religious, party and other organizations.

All this represents a propaganda and good-will war that cannot be lightly discounted. According to press report, total French foreign propaganda for 1933 cost approximately 102 million francs, and France spends much less than the Fascist countries. We have already considered Hitler's and Mussolini's huge propaganda machines abroad.

Not only has this European competition entered the field, but various Spanish-American countries have set up their own government-subsidized services. In México *Ariel* long served Central America to offset American influence. *Trens* is another semi-official service. The Peruvian Information Service, the National Information Service (Colombia), the Brazilian Telegraphic Union, Cadelp (Perú), Columbus (APRA Revolutionary Party), are some of these organizations. *Antorcha* was a bitter anti-American service run for a time by José Vasconcelos from Paris.

Also, enterprising young Latin-American journalists and others have flocked to New York to establish bureaus, which, if they have not competed on cable news, supply filler material copiously. This, according to their bent, has been openly anti-imperialistic or anti-American. More often such agencies soon become an adjunct of publicity for large American business concerns, handling, in return for generous subsidies, prepared releases setting forth the good-will and prosperity resulting from American commercial activities. A few only were or are honest and impartial.[1]

[1] Among such private efforts that have flourished here at one time or another, or are still active, are: The Consolidated Information Service (critical of America); International Aeronews Service (airmail material for the Caribbean); Inter-American News Service (radical); Latin-American Press Syndicate (open forum attitude); Inter-American Publicity Service

The Latin-American papers can also fill up their pages, as we shall see, by a variety of free propaganda material, prepared by large American business interests and others.

This multiplicity of news sources puts the major American news associations in a difficult position. The European services having no effective competition from within their respective countries, can largely dish up their news as they see fit. But there are many competing American services struggling for a foothold, and this has caused the Latin Americans to demand the truth about the United States as they demand it about no other part of the world.

To compete effectively, the American services have been obliged to carry news which was often very critical. Thus, while our earlier marine activities in Haiti and Santo Domingo raised little anger in Latin America, in more recent times—despite the fact that the news correspondents of our two largest news associations in Nicaragua were the American collector of customs and his assistant—South America received far more information regarding the Sandino struggles than would have been previously possible.

One large American service, trying to provide full and impartial news, soon found itself in conflict with powerful American interests, who saw in every item of this critical nature a thrust at the profit-making game. For the Latin Americans a speech by Senator Borah—head of the Senate Foreign Affairs Committee—was ever gala news; but as late as a half dozen years ago—though one may now laugh—he was considered by American businessmen abroad as a terrible radical, an unpatriotic and dangerous menace, and,

(Central America); HSH (sport news for Cuba), Inter-American Newspaper Syndicate; Radio Service (sport); Plus Ultra; International News Association, Syndicate Service, etc. Sipa carries American business propaganda.

despite his official position, one whose words should not under any circumstances be heard by the tender-minded, American-bossed southern countries. The President of this news agency told me at that time that he had been raked over the coals by influential capitalists for sending anything Borah said—though it was published in the United States—out over the wires to Latin America.

When that same agency once reported a dirty scandal in this country about a certain gyp oil company, at that moment seeking a juicy concession in Colombia, this was considered a horrible betrayal. The company might be accused in the American courts of various and sundry crimes, but it was considered unpatriotic that this news get to Colombia or that the government there be in any way warned of what sort of a noose it was putting about its neck. The agency's correspondent was promptly insulted and excluded from the local American club in Bogotá.

This attempt to provide a service more attractive to Latin America than that of any of its competitors, one based on honesty and liberality of news, soon resulted in even more serious difficulties in many powerful quarters. The agency was molested with exorbitant news-tolls rates by certain American companies having telegraphic and wireless monopolies in various Latin-American countries. To bridge the unfavorable attitude of one of our major international banks, which operates widely in Latin America, the President of the news service finally permitted that financial institution to maintain, for an extended period, a censor in its offices over the news it sent to and received from Latin America.

The point is that our news services, which despite competition are still stronger in the field than those of any other country, are also propaganda agencies. They were started as commercial enterprises, as handmaidens of private trade expansion; they are dominated by business and financial considerations; and in crucial situations to the south have almost invariably been represented by marine officers, government officials or the agents of business concerns rather than by bona fide correspondents. They represent an instrument for combating the encroachments of other powers in Latin America—not on the noble field of truth—but on the field of business profits.

2

In our copious good-will literature, in the utterances of our statesmen, bankers, businessmen and others, are statements that the acts of European countries in utilizing propaganda, the same trade competition, the same pressure to obtain concessions as we do, are sinister deep-dyed plots threatening the safety not merely of the United States but also of Latin America. Only through the righteous efforts of our own country can these menaces be thwarted. Toward the rest of this hemisphere, we have much the same psychological attitude as Japan has for China. But just as the Chinese look upon the United States and England as preferable to Japan, so the Latin Americans frequently think they have more safety in catering to Europe or Japan than to "the Colossus of the North."

This has led us to redouble our pounding on the big drums of friendship and charity.

One of the earliest efforts in this country to channelize good-will efforts in proper hands was the creation in 1912 of the Pan-American Society, promoted by Mr. Barrett, then head of the Pan-American Union. He sent out letters to "a number of prominent Americans interested in Latin-

American affairs." It was an officially promoted organization meant to include only the right people: bankers, manufacturers and businessmen. Such entrepreneurs and financiers as Minor C. Keith of the United Fruit Company, J. P. Morgan, Jr., Huntington, Peabody, Strauss, Vanderlip, Warburg, Speyer, appear on the brief list of the first executive committee. Into such company were inducted Nicholas Murray Butler, a few professors, a few safe reactionary magazine men such as Abbott, Shaw, and Munsey, himself a millionaire. The organization set up its offices at 15 Broad Street in the downtown financial district, with the purpose of promoting "acquaintance between the representative men of the United States and those of the Latin-American republics"; to show the proper people hospitality, and "to take such other steps, involving no political policy, which the society may deem wise, to develop and conserve good understanding, wise friendship and mutual knowledge of each other among the American republics and peoples."

Since then the membership has been kept largely among big corporation figures: steamship men, steel men, railroaders, mining promoters, public utility directors, tobacco and sugar growers, bankers, munitions makers, high-powered lawyers—all with axes to grind, jobs to hold, or with profits to be made, all seeking personal and corporate gain in Latin America.

A few Protestant missionaries and preachers have been taken into the fold, such as Silas McBee (editor of *The Churchman*), the Reverend Frederick Lynch of Bible house (editor of *Christian Work and Evangelist*), and Dr. Samuel Guy Inman, head of Protestant missionary work in Latin America. The name of James Scott Brown, head of the Carnegie Endowment for International Peace, appears directly under that of the steel and munitions maker, Charles M. Schwab of the Bethlehem Steel Corporation.

The society soon came to be presided over by John L. Merrill, head of All-American Cables, leader in the cable war just described. Mr. Merrill to this day is a frequent letter-writer to the newspapers—without ever revealing his commercial connections—on Latin-American affairs. For instance in April, 1938, to the New York *Times*, he praises our policy of friendship to Brazil, ruled by the present Vargas tyranny. Prominent in the Pan-American Society councils is also Mr. James Carson, of Electric Bond and Share, Vice-President of American and Foreign Power Corporation (which controls the major part of all Latin-American power resources), and a director in thirteen American companies to the south.

The Society's close tie-up with the Pan-American Union, its system of making the Secretary of State and the ranking Latin-American Ambassador honorary presidents, have insured the proper interlocking arrangement which made good-will the joint property of the United States government and the large interests busily exploiting Latin-American wealth. The Pan-American Society is thus a semi-official organization.

Sub-organizations of the Pan-American Society, composed of the best citizens of various local communities, were formed. The head of the San Francisco branch has been Dr. David P. Barrows of the Political Science Department of the University of California.

Another subsidiary is the Pan-American Students League, leading spirits of which are, or have been, Merrill, James S. Carson, C. C. Martins (publicity man), and Palmer C. Pierce, though a liberal façade for the organization is presented by such sponsors as Stephen P. Duggin, Waldo Frank, Samuel Guy Inman and others.

The first Pan-American Club was founded in New York in September, 1930, in the James Monroe High School. In May, 1933, a city-wide convention of the League was held, Joshua Hochstein being the faculty director, and adopted the following program: (1) cultural rapprochement, (2) enlightenment of members on Latin-American civilization, appreciation of its culture and ideals, inculcation of a spirit of friendliness, (3) use of American citizenship to maintain amicable and just relations between the United States and Latin America.

Now, students of our schools in many parts of the country are stimulated to write essays and make discourses on Hispanic America. All this is to the good, and quite a few are bound to find out what all the good-will shouting is about. Intermittently the League has published the *Pan-American Student*.

In January, 1932, an alumni chapter was organized in New York, "more mature in its conception of the Pan-American problem and ideal." It publishes *Panamericana*.

The high mark of the student celebrations is April 12th, decreed as Pan-American day by President Hoover, when student addresses are delivered, and the Bolívar medal is awarded. Among the speakers at the most outstanding of these affairs are invited the heads of the Pan-American Society and foreign ambassadors. This year to Columbia University came Mr. John L. Merrill, the President of the Society, Ambassador Pedro Martínez Fraga, representing the Batista military dictatorship of Cuba, various Latin-American musicians and the United States' 16th Infantry Band.

Merrill, Carson, Pierce, Martins and others were active

in forming another organization of the inner business lights of the Pan-American Society and of other influential financiers and industrialists: The Committee (or Council) on Inter-American Relations. This Committee works closely in harmony with the Foreign Trade Association and the Inter-American Commercial Arbitration Council, organized at the Bankers Club, December 8, 1931, and also headed by Merrill.

In the *Foreign Trade Review* of April, 1933, Carson wrote: "I am a believer in Pan-Americanism and I fully appreciate the value of such intangibles as good-will and mutual understanding. They are the very life-blood of the Pan-American movement, but there are other organizations which today efficiently promote these altruistic necessities. The chairman of this committee [on Inter-American Relations], Mr. John L. Merrill, is President of the greatest of them. I refer to the Pan-American Society, Incorporated."

Other members of the Inter-American Committee are, or have been, Colonel Samuel Reber of the Radio Corporation of America, Wallace Thompson, author of various books emphasizing the menace of Indian communism in Latin America, W. B. V. Van Dyke of the American Manufacturers' Export Association, B. C. Hart of the National City Bank, Henry L. Jones of the National Foreign Trade Council. The Committee has assisted the National Foreign Trade Council to study the industrial problems of Latin-American countries.

In the *Foreign Trade Review* for February, 1933, the accomplishments of the Committee were recounted: investigations of the exchange problems in Chile, Brazil and elsewhere, which were preventing the outflow of American profits and bond payments; exhaustive studies of the balance of payments; the giving of money to the American

Arbitration Association; the establishing, through sub-Committee on Inter-American Commerce, direct relations with some 700 Latin-American Chambers of Commerce and with similar bodies in the United States; the giving of funds for scholarships for Latin Americans to study in the United States; advice to various countries on public relations; adequate press contact; active coöperation with the National Foreign Trade Council, the American Manufacturers' Export Association, the Chamber of Commerce of the United States and relations "with various interests . . . endeavoring to find a formula which may be applied to our portfolio investments in Latin America"; promotion of trade; consultation with many American concerns on the expenditure of "substantial sums in the way of subscriptions to various plans for improving relations between the United States and Latin America"; a number of "original reports"; offering of competent research assistance and scanning of "trends and developments of interest to American business men." It may be fairly stated, concludes the account, "that no organization has the facilities for Latin-American research possessed by the committee."

Numerous trade publications in Spanish, English or in both languages tie up with American companies in the Latin-American field and with men represented in the Inter-American Committee. These have changed from time to time. I mention a few.

Before me I have a copy of *Ibero America*, published by I. T. and T., with an impressive photograph of King Alfonso, and dedicated to the Sevilla and Barcelona expositions in eulogy of the then dictator, Primo de Rivera. It appeared about the time that consumers' telephone strikes were sweeping Spain in protest at the new American monopoly and its rate-increases in connection with the high-binder concession which later caused the State Department so many headaches.

With the *Gulf Stream Magazine* (Spanish and English) were connected Carson and his son, James C. Carson of Pan-American Airways; and C. C. Martin, in charge of the Inter-American Committee's publicity efforts. It contains articles by the two Carsons: "Electricity Transforming Latin America," and one on Pan-American Airways. The magazine has the stilted good-will phraseology always to be found in this and similar efforts at commercial publicity. "We who guide the destinies of the *Gulf Stream Magazine* have pledged ourselves to foster, in so far as the written word is capable, a more intimate and binding friendship and understanding between the countries of the Western Hemisphere."

These are indeed beautiful sentiments. The holders of such lofty ideals could never be interested in maintaining unusually high light and power rates and those in parts of Latin America have been just about the highest in the world. They could never have the slightest interest in the problem of making dividends on watered stock or over-valuated power properties.

The active publicity efforts of the Committee are handled through C. C. Martins who, in addition to promoting good-will articles everywhere which usually contain references to the glories of electricity, has managed the Pan-American Information Service of 93-99 Nassau Street, New York, which sends out releases to American newspapers and also covers the Latin-American field with a clip service in Spanish under the slug SIPA. A typical clip-sheet contains the following items:

Fifty-two Millions of Public Benefit Works in the United
   States.
The Economic Situation of the United States.
The Radiological Institute.
Chile and Its Electrical Companies.
Georgetown University, School of Foreign Service.
The United Fruit Company and Its Electrical Vessels.
Telephone Service in Roumania.
Lindbergh Airplanes; Pan-American Airways.

A general examination of the clip-sheets reveals that
while SIPA poses as a serious impartial news agency, its
underlying interest is promoting propaganda for the Power
Trust, airway, telegraph, radio and fruit companies, and
other big concerns. In a twenty page release sent to Latin-
American consulates and newspapers, some years ago, the
Inter-American Council damns most of the news services
and exalts SIPA as the most important, but makes little
reference to the source of its income or its real purpose.
SIPA then claimed to cover 800 Latin-American newspapers
and found entry into more than 300. The report adds: "It
is known that the sheets are read in practically every office
to which they are sent. Many instances have been noted
where editorials show the direct influence of articles from
these sheets." It is used "much more frequently and by a
larger number of papers than is true for any European or
American publicity service," and (though this was a slight
exaggeration) it is "the only mechanism that exists through
which American interests may explain in detail their views
and opinions to the entire Latin-American press." It also
serves some 250 papers in the United States.
   In this analysis, the major concern of the Committee
and SIPA is revealed to be the Power Trust. Among eight-

een examples of supposedly anti-American propaganda in Latin America the report cites first that "In Cuba, México and several other countries, agitation has been going on for some against the power companies, many of which are American."

Naturally no statement is made of how the properties were acquired; no mention is made of high rates or that taxes are often very low, that intimate beneficent relations were maintained with such odious dictators as Machado, or that justified consumers' strikes had engulfed a number of countries.

Well, not even a bona fide news service would likely do that either.

For three years our Federal Trade Commission investigated the propaganda of the public utilities in the United States, the results of which were admirably summarized by Ernest Gruening in his *The Public Pays* and in Jack Levin's *Power Ethics*. This propaganda, coupled with liberal retaining fees, had corrupted most of our high schools, colleges and universities. A large number of so-called educators and instructors in a spirit of incredible avarice, had descended to petty servility and boot-licking for the Power Trust. The public utility interests had brought about the elimination, revision or emasculation of text-books to cut out information about stock-watering, excessive rates, weakness in regulation, low taxation, favorable information on municipal ownership, political control, limitation of franchises, etc. Propagandists were sent out to lecture before the Optimists, Kiwanis, Rotarians, high-school and college students, engineering societies and women's clubs. The head of the General Federation of Women's Clubs was hired to write articles in collaboration with the public utility interests, which brave information was then placed in our leading magazines as unbiased independent opinion. Press and pulpit were bored into, bought up and utilized.

These activities are known as "public relations" activities which, in Latin America, the Inter-American Committee attends to. There, watered stock, pyramiding, high rates, inadequate taxation and other aspects of their operations are often far more exaggerated than at home.

In the Inter-American Relations report we have been considering, it is intimated that steps should be taken to offset such anti-American things as agitation against power companies, against petroleum companies, and American-subsidized air-lines. The Committee is worried about Communists, demagogues, and labor laws focusing on American enterprise, anti-imperialist propaganda. The use of alcohol as a blend for gasoline is mentioned as being "anti-American." [Cuba at that time was finding new uses for its excess sugar-cane and thereby threatened to cut down on its use of American gasoline.] The report went on to declare that the scandals incident to loans and the general public belief that these loans were made "for the benefit of politicians and were obtained by corrupt methods," should be offset. [Of course, the world now knows that many of the Cuban, Peruvian and other loans were obtained precisely by bribery and corruptions.] The Committee opposed the present tariff on products of American interests abroad, but made no mention of our own high tariffs. [Of course tariffs provide one of the more normal means by which a semi-colonial country may build up a more independent economy.]

It is desirable, continues the report, to promote belief in the importance of the benefits of American capital enterprise, to rectify the mistake of American firms "in stressing the wealth and influence of their particular enterprise. . . .

[Who would have ever suspected it?]

"Let us further aid each other especially in terms of trade and commerce and forget for a moment culture and politics.

"What we need is bigger and better methods of transportation and communications and with these established sound commercial relations, lasting peace and greater prosperity must follow as the night the day."

[And how about bigger and better elephants while we're about it?]

The Pan-American Society, Inc., and the committee, take into tow all prominent South American politicians. In March they gave an "exquisite" banquet to Dr. Eduardo Santos, President-elect of Colombia, on the "luxurious" Starlight Roof of the Waldorf-Astoria. Those at the main table were Merrill, Carson, Mr. John D. McGregor, Vice-President of Pan-American Grace Airways, Mr. John Kelleher, Vice-President of the United Fruit Company, Mr. A. Garni, Vice-President of W. R. Grace and Company, J. W. Flanagan, President of the Andean National Corporation, Captain R. Tieber, President of the Texas Oil Company.

The same groups are now seeking to control and direct the new short-wave broadcasting propaganda being promoted by the government. On April 6th, the committee, headed by James S. Carson, Colonel A. Kenny C. Palmer, Director of the Chile-American Association, and John L. Merrill promoted a luncheon at India House, attended by seventeen consul-generals and 150 "specialists in Pan-Americanism" to sell the idea of Yankee business-controlled propaganda to Hispanic America and themselves.

On April 21st, James S. Carson was the guest of honor at the Pan-American day short-wave broadcast from the Savoy-Plaza Hotel, under the auspices of the Pan-American

Center, a ceremony attended by numerous consular representatives and "Hispano-American high society."

Our ear-to-the-ground tells us that the plan is to spike proposals for a government-owned propaganda station and divert any available funds to a subsidy to private radio corporations, thus keeping propaganda entirely in the hands of those who in Latin America have the big stakes and such ever-bleeding hearts—which is very proper, very patriotic, and bound to allay all unworthy suspicions of our ever lofty purpose.

Another business group constantly interested in Latin America is the Chamber of Commerce, which has affiliated bodies throughout the two continents, has many offices, collects data, distributes business information, and everywhere holds banquets for the most distinguished dignitaries. The goodly share of the most important of the Latin-American Chambers of Commerce are also headed by Merrill or Carson or both. They circulate harsh criticisms of Roosevelt and the New Deal.

3

One of the great good-willers of another day was the financial expert, Professor Edwin Walter Kemmerer, who ranged through country after country, fixing up their budgets and currencies. He was given honorary doctorates by the Universities of Ecuador, Bolivia and other countries. He went to Colombia several times, the first occasion as President of a Commission of American financial advisers. Said one local paper: "Besides a fat fee, he was given a medal." He came again in 1930 and "again was rewarded generously."

Now Colombia and some of the other countries are pretty sore about it. They think they were soft-soaped.

Kemmerer was a gold-standard die-hard. He wanted currencies in Latin America kept high and stable as the rock of Gibraltar, regardless of the international trade situation, the price level, or anything else. This was, and is, our official desire. It enables Latin-American countries to buy American goods and pay American debts. It helps prevent them develop an independent economy. In short, Mr. Kemmerer's sound financial ideas were tied to the apron strings of New York financial interests. He was the wizard of South American finance. He helped dictators put their abused revenue sources in order, so they could squeeze out more funds to pay more debts, buy more munitions, and pay their police forces to keep the people down and avoid revolution. He was hailed in Wall Street and he was hailed by the dictators of a continent and a half as a wonder-worker.

Now, even the dictators are wiser, especially as the udders of American loans have gone dry. In Colombia, within three years of his last visit, his scheme was torn up by the roots. It was attacked by both Liberals and Conservatives as "Wall Street Pap" and "the wrong medicine." Among other things, charged Conservative Congressman Silvio Villegas, Kemmerer concentrated the nation's credit in the cities when much of it should have been spread wide over the agricultural districts.

Other good-willers, like Mr. Grosvenor M. Jones, of our Department of Commerce, went to Cuba where he worked on the refunding of the enormous and scandalous debt piled up by Dictator Machado. Another aid of Machado was Professor R. A. Seligman of Columbia University, assisted by Dr. Carl Schoup, who for a sizable fee, put out a 470 page volume, with exhaustive statistics and charts.

Seligman's fundamental concern was to increase taxes— mostly at the expense of the general public, of salaries and of public works—and to avoid properly taxing the foreign sugar, banking power and railway interests. Instead of an income tax, he proposed a tax on house rent (which reminds us of medieval assessments on doors and windows). "Urban property," protested a Cuban pamphlet, "is the one wealth still . . . in the hands of Cubans or residents of Cuba." The whole study seems an attempt to dodge tax-increases on foreign capital and investments, to concentrate tax-power in the hands of the dictator, and to insure payment of the foreign debts, accumulated by bribery and graft.

American educators have also descended on Latin America and proposed flossy urban high-cost systems, with marvelous equipment, but as a rule neglected the rural districts and forgot that education, however well-housed and however technically efficient, is largely meaningless in the face of grave social oppression and inequalities, political tyranny and unjust colonialism.

A swarm of such high-paid good-will experts during our prosperity and armed-intervention days buzzed across Latin America to tell it how to run its affairs—usually to American advantage.

Mr. Hull wishes to begin this practice anew, and seeks a special law to permit the Government to delegate officials, paid by American tax-payers, to such tasks.

The Casa de Españas of Columbia University does much to acquaint academic groups with a knowledge of Latin-American culture and to provide a forum for visiting notables. The Committee on Latin-American Studies at Harvard is engaged in similar activities. The Progressive Education Association, the office of Education of the United States Government, the Carnegie Institute, the Academy of Natural Sciences in Philadelphia, all interest themselves in promoting knowledge of Latin America and good relations. Recently the Rockefeller Foundation for the social sciences has set aside funds and created a special department to carry on research and other activities in Latin America.

Another international institution with one foot in Latin America—but now washed up by the depression—was the Institute of Current World Affairs, subsidized by the Crane foundation. Its purpose was not to sell bathtubs, but to build up good relations abroad and disseminate information.

Its representative in México for many years was the very capable Dr. Eyler N. Simpson, now of Princeton University.[2]

The idea was for its representative to know intimately the fifty or so leading men in México and in the United States, so that he might become a permanent factor in solving international relations, and be in a key position.

He was to study intimately the problems of México, and to provide information for a proper fee to those who sought it—presumably Mexican officials, American businessmen, the State Department, etc. The idea was for him to help both México and the United States.

Dr. Simpson made specialized studies of the henequén and cattle industries for Ambassador Morrow. A fine and conscientious student of broad ideas, Simpson did a great deal of important research. He was very close to young American-trained Ramón Beteta, who today is Under-Secretary of Foreign Affairs.

Whatever may be said for the strength or the weakness of the Institute's program, we are greatly indebted to it

[2] As this book was going to press his death was announced.

even now, after it has given up the ghost, because of Simpson's quite remarkable study of the Mexican agrarian question: *The Ejido: México's Way Out*, published in 1937. This is the most valuable and important study of a single Mexican economic problem ever made by anyone to date. It will be a standard work a hundred years from now, alongside those of Humboldt. Mr. Wallace could even afford to read it.

We are not all dollars. Not all our noble good-will utterances are sugared pills for profit, high rates, bad loans, and undercover news-control. Even business is endowed with mystic righteousness. And even were that not so, the purely spiritual values have been taken care of. In addition to the expansion of the Y.M.C.A. and Y.W.C.A. everywhere southward, there is the active work of the Committee on Coöperation in Latin America—a coalition of thirty missionary boards—headed by Dr. Samuel Guy Inman, a former Disciple of Christ, pastor and missionary—which attempts to evangelize the nations south. This committee evolved from the Panamá evangelical congress in 1916, the same year that the United Press set up its first office, and our great trade drive began.

The work prospered. In the 1927 annual report, Reverend Charles S. Detweiler, Superintendent of North Baptist work, remarks that in addition to the influence of commerce and the movies, political influence is increasing—the annexation of Puerto Rico, the Platt Amendment, intervention in Haiti and Nicaragua, a customs collector in Salvador—and "there is an unmistakable call to the Church of Christ in the United States to keep pace with this new life. The spread of popular education and advance in civilization demand increased effort and expenditure to provide trained leaders in those lands." This was linking God and imperialism with a vengeance.

But increasingly the Committee has realized that, due to growing antagonism to American naval and financial penetration, the work of evangelization must be disassociated in the Latin-American mind from any taint of such imperialism. Dr. Alonso, in the 1929 evangelical congress in Havana, declared: "There are mighty forces working to isolate the small Protestant group in Latin America from the strong Protestant forces in the United States. If they succeed, they will then proceed, with our powerful friends eliminated, to crush us. Combinations like those of Mussolini, Primo de Rivera and the Vatican and their propaganda in Latin America for renewed devotion to the *madre patria* bode no good for us. . . . On the other hand we must oppose with all our might the great industrial and material movement from the United States which threatens to commercialize our life, control our governments and crush our aspirations for self-expression."

There is a vague consciousness of dilemma. Says one annual report: "Before there is a real feeling for Christ in Latin America, He must be lifted out of the clash between Anglo-Saxonism and Latinism. . . . There is a widespread feeling that Protestantism is a form of Anglo-Saxon aggressiveness throughout the world, that we are trying to impose Anglo-Saxonism on them through trade, through our Caribbean policy . . . and through our Protestant missions."

Dr. Inman himself puts his best foot forward. Usually he greets the peoples south as a university professor instead of a missionary. He has often spoken valiantly in behalf of freedom and national autonomy, has consistently opposed the use of marine force; and time and again from the platform has not hesitated to denounce unsavory business and diplomatic practices in the most courageous terms. The magazine, *La Nueva Democracia*, published by his committee and of which he is the nominal editor, is a genuinely open-minded publication. It has drawn the wrath of a number of Latin-American dictators, has been banned in Salvador, Perú and elsewhere on various occasions. Dr. Inman's latest book, *Latin America*, is one of the most capable, fair, and well-informed of all books thus far published about the contemporary scene. Latin Americans have in him personally a true and understanding friend.

The organization has become better endowed as time goes on. Its 1929 report announced a $300,000 endowment for Santiago College. $235,000 for buildings for the Instituo Inglés in the same city. A $250,000 building fund was accumulated for the Lima High School; and the Colegio Americano of Buenos Aires, controlled by Methodists and Disciples, had acquired an eighteen acre campus; and the Committee hailed this school as one friendly gesture of the United States during recent diplomatic difficulties: more than any other organization there, it was "creating a spirit of international friendship." All through Latin America similar improvement of physical equipment is constantly reported.[3]

There is fervor in the effort. In one report, we read: "To be living in Mexico City these days is like walking the streets of Caesara in the time of Paul; such is the hunger and thirst after God that 800 Bibles were sold here in four days! We found Christ in the Mexican Senate . . ."

The public relations activities of the organization are

[3] Other schools of religious complexion or close to the work of the committee are the North American Cultural Institute and Ward College of Buenos Aires, MacKenzie College of São Paulo with 1,800 students, Bennet College of Rio, Crandon Institute of Montevideo.

favorably reported. Dr. Inman is a member not only of the Pan-American Society but of the Instituo de las Españas and the Committee on Cultural Relations with Latin America; he was a delegate to the Pan-American Union Conference of Havana in 1930, was adviser to Mr. Hull at the Buenos Aires Conference. As a Columbia University professor, more recently of the faculty of the University of Pennsylvania, he gained admittance to institutions of learning he could not so easily approach as merely head of Protestant missionary work: the Universities of Chile, Santo Domingo, Lima, the National Institute of Panamá, the Madrid Ateneo, the International Students' Association at Geneva.

School work is important. Dr. John MacKay, the Committee has reported, had continued his work among the South American students with "even greater power than before." Dr. J. H. McLean "has made some happy ventures among the high-school youths." In 1929 the Committee assisted the Institute of International Education and piloted twenty-five Argentine educators during their six weeks' visit to the United States. It was invited by the Mexican government to distribute in other Latin-American countries the Mexican edition of *The Four Essentials of Education* by Tomas Jesse Jones. It hailed favorably the Guggenheim Scholarship fund for Latin America and the allotment of money by the Carnegie Endowment for International Peace to the Pan-American Union to invited Argentine and Brazilian scholars to this country.

The Committee has also given help to the University of México, the World Peace Foundation, the American Mission to Lepers, the Union Seminary of México, the *Christian Union Quarterly*, the Committee on International Justice of the Federal Council of Churches, the Golden Rule Foundation, the University of Denver, Duke University, the Hartford Foundation (missionary training school), the Fellowship of Reconciliation, International House, and the International Clubs' movement in connection with Latin-American matters. For the Fellowship of Reconciliation, Charles Thomson—now of the Foreign Policy Association —went to Central America, where he made "important contacts for Christian fellowship." Other organizations with which the Committee has worked are the Women's Temperance Association and the League of Mental Hygiene. In Brazil its secretary served as chairman of the commission on Rotarian Education and wrote "the first booklet on Ethical Codes (quite a claim!) ever published in Portuguese."

Catholic activities to the south have largely centered on anti-Mexican propaganda, carried on by the high dignitaries of the American church and by the Knights of Columbus. This and other Catholic organizations at one time raised millions of dollars to spread propaganda and take other punitive measures against the Mexican government. Some Catholic elements secured arms and ammunition, violating our neutrality laws, and helped promote armed uprisings. It cannot be said that American Catholics have been instrumental in helping good-will policies, although the National Catholic Welfare Conference has concerned itself with loftier problems.

4

The liberal forces are led forth by, among others, the ex-Reverend Dr. Hubert Clinton Herring, since 1924 until a few months ago, in charge of the social relations work of the Congregational churches of America. He heads the Committee on Cultural Relations with Latin America.

Star names on his executive committee are Dr. John Dewey, Professor A. E. Ross of Wisconsin, Judge Florence Allen of the Ohio Supreme Court, Stuart Chase. To foment better understanding among Americans, every year he leads a seminar in México, where his groups hear lectures and make trips to schools, agrarian colonies and other civic enterprises.

This work began at a very necessary moment when our relations with México were at a veritable cat-and-dog level, and intervention was threatened due to the propaganda and pressure of the petroleum companies. Undoubtedly Herring's seminar, since it attracted community leaders, editors, writers and influential folk, had quite some influence those days in counteracting growing ill-feeling.

He has also led the liberal clans in seminars to the Caribbean, and by and large has done a great deal to acquaint Americans with the real Latin America rather than propagandizing Latin America. The two books, among other publications of the Committee, edited by Dr. Herring, *Renascent México* and the *Genius of México*, which are records of the addresses and findings at the annual seminars, are illuminating contributions, and though I have sometimes been in minor disagreement, his journalistic articles on southern problems have been among the most capable in this country.

Of a liberal complexion are the activities of the Foreign Policy Association, headed by Dr. Raymond Leslie Buell, a patient researcher. While the purpose of this organization is largely to acquaint the American public with affairs abroad, at times its studies have had the dual purpose of also assisting foreign countries.

With this end it sent, with foundation aid, a large commission of experts to Cuba during President Carlos Mendieta's administration—right after Roosevelt had put the Grau government down the chute—to make a general survey and establish a basis for an enlightened program of recovery.

By and large, though in places showing haste, the report of this commission is an excellent and comprehensive study. Its chief merit is its study of Cuban resources, its proposals for diversification of production, its measures for reducing and making more scientific the sugar industry. The report, however, was received with sour faces by Ambassador Caffery and our commercial attaché, both working on schemes to subordinate Cuban economy to the United States and rivet the one-crop system tighter than ever.

Especially good were Leland Jenks' study of the sugar industry, the analyses of the public school system, the race question, the examination into Cuban living standards. But these merits threw into high relief certain defects of the report: the evasion of the problem of domination by American absentee capital, of the militarism of Batista, of the puppet, powerless nature of the unrepresentative government supposed to make use of the findings, a government set up largely through American diplomatic pressure and Batista's guns.

Soldiers had their guns stacked against the bronze statue of the Alma Mater at the University; the buildings had been turned into barracks; high schools and schools were closed. What chance did a wise report on education have to be put into effect? In fact some years later, Dictator Batista solved the educational problem by putting ignorant army sergeants and corporals in as teachers of the elementary and agricultural schools, where they still remain. The university problem was solved by kicking out qualified pro-

were never so bloodily beaten down as in those days. The alliance with the Mexican CROM was subsequently weakened because of that organization's support of the Mexican government's battle with the Catholics. Since then the CROM has largely disintegrated. The PACL was attacked by most Latin-American labor groups as reactionary and an instrument of American imperialism.

Today the more radical Confederation of Mexican Labor (CTM) led by Lombardo Toledano, which has become the all-powerful labor organization in the country next door, is preparing a continent-wide labor confederation. A convention is to be held some time this year. Close contacts have been held with John L. Lewis of the C.I.O., and he has promised to attend. Out of that may likely come a new continental confederation in which Lewis and the C.I.O. have a very large influence. Lewis has already offered the CTM to combat propaganda in the United States against the Mexican oil expropriation, and the CTM has called strikes against branches of American companies in México, with which Lewis was attempting to force collective-bargaining contracts.[4]

The Communist salvation crew was for a long time false-fronted by the Anti-Imperialist League headquarters in Chicago. It was introduced into many Latin-American countries. It stood for complete Latin-American autonomy, but had more lungs than numbers or resources. In a number of countries it was soon officially outlawed.

More recently American Communists have served the Comintern as secret agents in Cuba, Brazil, México and elsewhere. Recently when Hernan Laborde pulled a boner

---

[4] Lewis is reported to have offered support provided México would not sell its oil to Japan. Why he should expect México not to sell where his own United States sells is not quite clear.

in connection with the labor movement, he rushed up to Earl Browder, head of the American Communist Movement, to get things straightened out. The American superiority complex plus rigid Communist dogmatism leads such publications as the *Daily Worker* and the *New Masses* —though occasionally very fine articles appear—into some of the most laughable, distorted and false interpretations of Latin-American affairs to be found in the whole range of American journalism.

6

The World Peace Foundation of Boston has published a number of well-informed but not especially significant volumes on Latin America, the best being Cox's over-cautious study of Nicaragua and our marine intervention.

The Carnegie Endowment for World Peace has backed a number of worthy enterprises. For a time it edited the *Inter-America* magazine. It foments the International Relations Clubs in the American and Latin-American schools, which at intervals study the Latin-American situation, as in 1928-29. As guides, the Endowment sent out Cox's book on Nicaragua; Harvard Professor Clarence H. Haring's *South America Looks at the United States;* Interventionist Judge Hughes' *Our Relations to the Nations of the Western Hemisphere;* Interventionist Diplomat Dana Munro's *The Five Republics of Central America,* and several other volumes of lesser import. It has established a fund, administered through the Pan-American Union, for visiting professors; and it has sent out several representative Americans to tour Latin America.

In 1928 Dr. David P. Barrows of the University of California visited twelve countries. It did not escape the notice of some of the Latin-American newspapermen that Dr. Barrows had been in the American Siberian expedition backing the Kolchak white army and that he had consistently favored marine intervention in Latin America, and was generally known as an "imperialist."

Nor did it escape their attention that the subsequent visitor Mr. Charles Norton, a journalist, had been a consistent and ardent apologist for our interventions and all the aggressive features of our past Latin-American policy.

Nor did it escape their comment that the third Carnegie visitor, Dr. Dana Munro, had written *The Five Republics of Central America*, which whitewashes the American bankers, and had been Legation counselor during our marine occupation in Nicaragua and Minister to Haiti during our marine occupation there and was an advocate of our armed intervention policies.

The present good-will representative, now on tour, is Professor Samuel Flagg Bemis, a rather official-minded authority on American diplomacy.

Early this year, a "caravan" of five ladies, members of the People's Mandate for Peace, started from Washington in a six-week airplane tour of Latin America to urge the governments to ratify the peace and arbitration treaties brought before the Buenos Aires Conference of December, 1936.

Few countries have signed more peace treaties in the past than have the Hispano-American countries, and in few places have they meant less. At the present moment, the southern countries, egged on by the United States, Germany, Italy, England, Japan and Czechoslovakia, are arming themselves as never before. No one has pointed out the fluffy-sleeved mockery of this winged tour of the good ladies better than has Genaro Arbaiza in the January, 1938, *Current History*.

"To the ladies of the Flying Caravan:

"You have just returned from a 17,000 mile tour of Latin America where you went to urge . . . an early ratification of the peace pacts. . . . You have stopped at practically every Latin-American capital and have been greeted by . . . prominent public officials . . . applauded at luncheons and banquets, honored at universities . . . fêted at teas and cocktail parties. I imagine . . . it has been your conviction that Latin America has taken you seriously.

"Well, as far as official Latin America is concerned, . . . you have only provided a good laugh for the gentlemen . . . now in power from the Caribbean Sea to Patagonia. . . . Do you perchance, think that . . . ratification will be an inducement to permanent peace? Just about the time you started on your crusade, Trujillo, the Dominican dictator, was slaughtering Haitian squatters by the thousands, and Trujillo's government is one of the only three governments that have ratified the Buenos Aires peace pacts.

"The treaties you are so anxious to see in force left the basic causes of internal and international strife in Latin America untouched and have gone into the paper baskets of Pan-American diplomacy, already overflowing with forgotten peace pacts. . . .

"Who wants to banish the fear of war down there? War has always been a very profitable business. . . . Many of the gentlemen you met on your tour are playing the game . . . with great personal gain.

"South America is an important territory in the world's armament trade . . . the largest dumping market in that trade. . . . If you had not been so eager about the ratification of those peace pacts you might have seen this technique in operation. And that would have brought you far nearer to the process of international trouble-making than the discussion of peace pacts."

Arbaiza—one of our ablest commentators—goes on to reveal the fevered pace at which Latin America is today arming for war, the intrigues of the great powers in fostering this traffic. He reveals how the Roosevelt administration, which in 1936 advocated peace and opposed the arming of Latin America, has today joined in the scramble and is using every energy to promote the private sales of munitions, war-craft and bombing planes.

It is extremely curious that Latin America has no vital and extensive urge to bring good-will to the United States. The Latin Americans participate in our international congresses; her statesmen are always careful, whatever they are doing, to flatter us; but the driving initiative and control comes from the United States. A good deal of our bid for friendship, I fear, smacks of the sophisticated city gentleman falling desperately in love with a simple apple-cheeked country girl for no good purpose—good-will is inevitably a part of our general trade and investment needs.

Occasionally, Latin-American émigrés, fleeing from local tyranny to this country, attempt to influence various sectors of American opinion in favor of their causes. Occasionally some shaky Latin-American dictator buys up a Sunday section in one or another of our leading papers, as recently in the New York *Herald Tribune*; or a trade commission comes to push coffee or sugar sales; but in general the Latin Americans do not try to convert us to Catholicism; they send no eager bands of school teachers and liberals to look over the American scene. Most of the students and professors who come here for special study do so on funds provided by American institutions.

Strangely enough it is not the weak nations who are

courting the United States, but the powerful United States which is obliged to utilize all of the blandishments. Could the terrible thought be true that after all we need Latin America more than she needs us?

We have been upset by European propaganda in Latin America. And yet no other nation on earth, perhaps not all the other nations combined, have ever carried on or are carrying on as much propaganda as the United States has in the past or is at the present moment.

No other country, certainly, has so many private volunteer bodies trying to influence the Indo-American countries. We send more news, we buy more advertising, we command more publicity space in their papers, we have more eager good-will associations, most of them, of course, directly, indirectly or subtly controlled by big business concerns with veiled interests to safeguard; we have more religious uplift bodies at work there; and these, too, in most instances, depend on large business heads for donations; we have more missions and missionaries; we have more liberals concerned with the fate of our neighbors; and we even export more paid Communist propagandists to Latin America than any other nation.

We are far from being beaten in the struggle to control the southern countries.

And with our new government putsch southward, we are expending more efforts than any single European power.

Have our efforts been wise? What do they mean? Where are they taking us? What do we want? What are the dangers?

CHAPTER

VIII

Our New Role: Salesman or Revivalist?

W<small>E</small> have long had a Jehovah complex about Latin America. Mostly, however, we have emphasized kosher dietary laws rather than the spiritual attributes of our divinity. We have been less concerned with literature, art, social justice, liberty—whatever those vague terms may mean— than with Singer sewing machines and how many bolts of calico can be loaded on a llama's back. If we have accompanied our needles, light bulbs and automobile tires with any philosophical dogma at all, it has been that of "democracy," which it so happens in this instance to be more utilitarian than spiritual, a means to an end which we, with no overwhelming race problems, no feudal problems and with heretofore unlimited economic opportunities, have found useful in promoting orderly government.

Our pro-consuls and marine officers, who have at times descended on Latin America for purely righteous causes, such as collecting debts, forcing ratification of concessions and payment of claims and to dispense quinine, have all been ardent defenders of democracy. Some of our most hard-bitten representatives, once they get abroad, have become almost as fanatically obsessed with the holy mission of honest elections as a Bronx Communist over the virtues of Soviets. How often in one breath our worthy pro-consuls thus engaged in armed intervention used to tell me how

they were saving the country by teaching the local uneducated hordes to vote honestly; then in the next breath, how
the only solution for those countries is the strong man on
horseback.

But the great justification for these and sundry activities
on our part in Latin America in those days was that of
sanitation, long the eighteenth amendment of the Monroe
Doctrine. No matter how many marines and Nicaraguans
or Haitians or Cubans might be killed, no matter what
might be done, we had, at any rate, cut down the percentage of mortality for the rest of the population. Jehovah
Uncle Sam was conceived of eternally in those palmy days
of fabulous loans and marine invasions as a sort of glorified
sewer-digger for the tropics.

Now, however, we have solemnly announced to the world
that our policies have changed; self-determination of nations, even in the Western Hemisphere—even though the
Managua water supply no longer gets its dose of chlorine—
is the recent amendment to the famous Wilsonian doctrine.

Certainly it did look a little ridiculous to be protesting
at what Japan was doing in Manchuria when our marines
were stalking the streets of Haiti. Of course Japan in Manchuria and later Mussolini in Ethiopia, were purely hypocritical imperialists when they committed aggressions in the
name of civilizing backward peoples. We, in contrast, were
wholly sincere in disinterestedly promoting civilization.

But now we—or at least President Roosevelt and Mr.
Cordell Hull—have been declaring for six years that those
past civilizing processes were mistaken, that from now on
an impartial good-neighbor policy shall be enforced to the
hilt—not by the sword but by righteous deeds and smiles.
Ten years ago, if you defended such a policy, if you defended this newer doctrine of the sovereignty of the Latin-

American nations, you were shouted down as a low traitor. Today you are a patriot. You can even sell magazine articles at fancy prices in which you advocate what ten years ago and less was considered high treason. The point is—always be on the band-wagon. But realism is just as necessary now as then.

In all Roosevelt's pronouncements of the good-neighbor policy there really does lurk a repudiation of thirty years of aggressive American relations with Latin America, a sudden spiritual altruism that ignores to a degree our more than $6,000,000,000 of investments in those regions—or has this been merely the rationalization of an inevitable international situation? Is it something which guarantees a new permanent course of action, or has it merely been putting a good face on the present necessity? To what extent has it been carried into effect? Has it failed or succeeded?

2

The economic forces at play certainly have had an effect on the Roosevelt policy.

The forces of expansion in a great industrial nation are inevitable. Our psychological attitude, the Jehovah complex, the long-standing faith that the American way is the best of all ways, the Nordic superiority urge, the faith in sanitation, in democracy—these applied to Latin America, whether justified or not, are in reality merely rationalizations of an inevitable operation of the gigantesque forces of machine production. Those basic economic forces cannot be willed away by Pacifists, cries of imperialism, or propaganda. That they may be understood and partially controlled is a possibility. Unfortunately economic forces have a habit of working their immutable will before anyone is aware of them, what they mean, or where they are leading. We usually understand our sins, if at all, in retrospect.

Those forces of expansion, intrinsic in the modern form of capitalist production, spring in part from the juxtaposition of an industrialized nation to agrarian feudal countries, which tend to become colonial annexes—however much the actual relationship is disguised—of the more advanced economy. Dr. Parker Moon of Columbia University in his notable study of world imperialism has analyzed these forces with sufficient accuracy. Dr. Harry Elmer Barnes in his introduction to Dr. Baylie Diffie's *Porto Rico* has given their meaning with reference to the United States with succinct brilliancy.

Mass machine production, with its corresponding rapid growth of population and large output, requires, first of all, a vast uninterrupted supply of raw products—wolfram, tin, sugar, coffee, hides. These are purchased, whatever the actual form of payment, largely with finished products.

But as the purchasing power of the public in modern industrialized nations, despite higher standards of living, is so greatly inferior to producing power, surpluses of manufactured goods accumulate, also a great surplus of capital. A favorable balance of foreign trade must then be maintained, or the productive system breaks down, whereupon we also have a great surplus of labor supply.

Part of our surplus capital is used in buying up the sources of production abroad, power plants, factories, mines, railroads, packing plants; part is used for outright loans to permit the backward countries to continue purchasing manufactured goods.

This whole process is further accelerated by the relatively low wage in raw-product countries, so that the natives there are in an even worse position to buy back the equivalent of their labor than workers in industrialized countries. The low standard of living in colonial countries leads to a quicker saturation of the markets with finished goods, and this discrepancy between the standards of living in so-called backward and advanced countries also accelerates the accumulation of unsellable finished products in more favored nations.

If for a time the exchange of goods in a form apparently favorable to the industrialized nation may be sustained by loans—i.e., liens on the future, merely another sort of time-payment device—ultimately it is doomed to break down. We have an industrial crisis. The more air (capital) that is pumped in, the sooner the prosperity balloon bursts.

Furthermore there is the competition of other highly industrialized nations, all needing to sell more than they buy—a patent absurdity. Furthermore the investment of our capital abroad leads to the building of manufacturing plants which compete with our own industrial mechanism and also increasingly limit the kind and amounts of surplus goods which can be disposed of in those markets.

As an American writer recently stated: "It has cost America $20,000,000,000,000 to learn the simple economic lessons that a 'favorable balance of trade' is neither favorable nor balanced. All it means is that a 'favored' country exports more goods than it buys back, and writes up the differences as capital claims against the world. If this favorable predicament lasts long enough, these capital claims mount from assets into uncollectable absurdities, and the nation's foreign trade collapses. The favorable balance becomes a boomerang."

As a result, the six billions we have sunk in Latin America will never be collected *in toto*; if we get fifteen percent of it back, we shall call ourselves fortunate; and even if that fortunate, we shall be all the more unfortunate, because that will more quickly restore our tragic favorable balance of trade. The loss of these sums is not the fault of Latin America; it is the fault of immutable economic forces which we did not understand how to control in time and do not yet know how to control. The "simple economic lesson" is far from being learned.

3

This period of loan prosperity had a great effect, as might be expected, on the course of American policy toward Latin America; and many sanctimonious reactionaries in our State Department have not been able, despite the new Roosevelt fiat of good-neighbor sovereignty, to this day to divest themselves entirely of the Jehovah-sewing-machine-sewer-digging complex. This has been one of his most serious stumbling blocks to the making of his policy a success. He has been stymied by the Welleses, the Cafferys and such blue-stocking ilk.

Our economic expansion, those previous good prosperity days, had its contradictions; these led to contradictions in our previous policy. Despite all we read about concentration of wealth and interlocking directorates, the leaders of American finance and industry were never quite a unit with regard to how to get what they have wanted out of Latin America. The ramrod of a debt-collecting institution and the promoter for a vast trading company frequently faced insoluble contradictions. In other words, the policies connected with the promotion of trade, the investment of capital abroad, or the making and collecting of loans were necessarily different, and we were engaged in all three.

Trade demands good-will. It demands economic and

social progress in backward countries. Collecting debts often required force, aggression, destruction of good-will. These forces came into conflict. Thus the recognition of Obregón in México—bitterly opposed by the oil companies—was forced largely through our traders and our Chambers of Commerce which wished to sell goods.

Capital investment in a foreign country often demanded good-will but also opposition to local economic and social freedom which could bring about increased wage demands or regulatory laws.

The need for army-navy national security introduces still another requirement usually running counter to good-will— the seizure of navy bases and other outposts—though the need of allies to the south for the moment imposes friendliness.

Thus, throughout, there was and is a complicated pull of forces that has added to the complexity and contradictions of our policies.

In general, however, our earlier criterion for Latin America was "stability." That was the great unremitting slogan we set up.

This flattered us, for we believed our own system "stable" for all time—despite the symptomatic increase of gang murders. We felt that the United States had reached the peak of all possible human perfection. The idea that we were so stable and assured gave us a smug feeling of superiority over politically unstable countries. It saved us the trouble of even trying to understand why they were unstable. It eased us in our belief in our moral duty to coerce and intervene. Beside if we could maintain stability to the south, that insured us a more interrupted supply of raw materials, and a softer path for American investors and producers abroad.

In a recent governmental broadcast, Sumner Welles,

sending forth one of his constant not overly illumined messages of paternal advice to Latin America, said that the great need in coffee-producing countries was stability. Brazil, the greatest coffee-producing country, is, of course, stable. It is ruled by official murder and force. It is ruled by puppet military governors, bayonets, a brutalized soldiery. This is stability at any price. Thus, the false criterion of stability in good part still rules our State Department.

No one cherishes order and stability more than myself. Unfortunately social evolution of oppressed peoples cannot always be written in terms of political stability. That is to justify dictatorship, social injustice and immemorial wrongs, particularly in present-day Latin America. Having seen many revolutions close up, having followed their courses, I am the first to decry violence in the solution of social problems. Unfortunately that is precisely the solution now imposed by most of the militarized governments of our two continents. They are governments of violence, not of law.

And whether we like it or not, the impact of the modern industrial system with feudal peoples inevitably has created grave maladjustments—social, racial, economic, political—which have resulted in repeated governmental breakdowns. To set up the ideal of stability for a country ruled by a ferocious dictatorship, such as that of Batista in Cuba or Trujillo in Santo Domingo, or Ubico in Guatemala, has been to condemn populations to living death.

To quote the great Argentine educator, Alfredo L. Palacios: "Among us there are unfortunately many partisans of dictatorships. They are those who want 'order and welfare,' and who forget that order and welfare when there is no freedom are contemptible gifts."

The industrial system, itself, demands constantly increasing living standards among backward peoples in order to create an expanding market for manufactured goods. At the same time the ideal of stability to collect loans or secure concessions often defeated this process and caused us directly or indirectly to give aid to old-style feudal tyrannies incapable of creating that general diffusion of progress essential for industrial expansion. Many of the present dictatorships in Latin America can be traced to our mistaken policies, our interventions, our political coercion, our loans. We are still supporting such improper regimes by money, technicians, and naval missions. But we have only ourselves to blame if such governments now or later go home to roost with the more congenial Fascist powers.

4

The 1929 depression changed the whole picture. In all lines of our endeavors abroad, decline and collapse filled the frame. For six years it has been impossible to make any new loans of importance to buttress up governments or trade. It may be many more decades before confidence is regained. Most of the countries have been and are in default. In addition they have built up complex currency, capital and tariff restrictions. Economic nationalism is the new slogan. If new loans are not being made, neither are many new investments, although various concerns, notably the United Fruit, have found the depression favorable for greatly expanding their previous holdings. As for trade—it was knocked into a nine-count flop.

By 1933 we had lost the commercial advantage we had gained during the World War. In volume, value, and percentage we were selling less than in 1914.

With the collapse of the goods-, loan- and investment-markets abroad and with vast accumulations of surplus products in the United States, our major concern shifted sharply to an attempt to revive trade. Good-will suddenly became a greater desideratum than it had been for thirty odd years in American relations.

Roosevelt merely bowed gracefully to the economic facts. As a result he has gotten the credit—and blame—for putting into effect things which Hoover started or planned but did not have, in some cases, the courage, in others, the necessary Congressional support, to put into effect. The N.R.A. was already drawn up in Hoover's day, minus Article 7A. Likewise the new policy toward Latin America was already on its way without being heralded as such with bells and with real change of heart.

The last stand of the old policy of overt aggression, tacitly now in disrepute, was the Pan-American Conference of 1928, held in Havana. There, to override any criticisms of our country, due to armed invasions of Haiti and Nicaragua, a bright galaxy of American prosperity statesmen—Coolidge, Hughes, Kellogg and Morrow—descended on the bayonet-ruled realm of Machado and steam-rollered the conference.

But it was the last stand. Even before our financial debacle, Coolidge shifted ground slightly with respect to México. The stubborn resistance of the Mexican revolution to our blandishments, our dollars, our threats, had driven a dark spear-head of warning into the old policy of aggression. Coolidge, in part, began the present good-will trend when he abandoned the extravagant thesis that every American and every American dollar were under the American flag everywhere, and sent Ambassador Dwight Morrow, of the House of Morgan, to México with a great good-will press build-up to repair the damage done by the aggressive blundering of Kellogg and Sheffield.

Morrow arranged a compromise on the petroleum question, induced Calles to abandon and denounce his own agrarian program, brought about a settlement, really a doubtful truce, between the government and the Church. It was good-will meddling rather than pro-consul meddling. It set back the Mexican revolution and gave American capital a short breathing-spell. Today, however, once more the tide of Mexican revolution has swept away the Morrow dykes.

Soon Hoover was to withdraw the last marine from Nicaragua and make preparations for their withdrawal from Haiti. In other words the logic of circumstances forced Hoover to retrench, to pull in the horns of intervention to the same extent that economic expansion was stalled. Hoover did not call this a policy; he probably felt that it was a temporary unpleasant interlude in the march of America's "manifest destiny"; he had to do it because our economic debacle made no other course possible. It was Roosevelt, not burdened with the sewer-digging philosophy, who was to make a noble virtue out of necessity and herald the new policy, already begun in practice, with drums and banners.

5

The country pressing for attention was Cuba. From 1924 on, economic conditions had grown worse, by 1932 were frightful. Uproarious terrorism by both the government and its enemies made life and property unsafe. Payment on the foreign debt, guaranteed by the State Department, could no longer be maintained. This was bad because $1,500,000,-000 (inflation figure) of American capital were at stake—more than in any other foreign country except Canada. The Platt Amendment made us responsible for a government able to protect "life, property and individual liberty." No such government existed. We were tacitly responsible for the island's financial set-up. And a revolution was brewing which might prove bloody, costly and dangerous to American investments.

Roosevelt, with the aid of Sumner Welles, forestalled revolution by unceremoniously tilting Machado out of office. This was not exactly living up to the announced hands-off policy, but Machado was in such disrepute that the change was greeted with joy here and in Cuba.

Unfortunately Mr. Welles, after having ousted Machado, at once moved heaven and earth to maintain the Machado economic system. The De Céspedes puppet government was set up, largely as a result of Welles' backstage intrigue with various groups, mostly of old-line politicians, to forestall any truly popular movement or popular government.

Welles then proceeded high-handedly to re-write the Cuban constitution for the Cubans and to submit it to the leaders of the various parties in conference.

But the De Céspedes hand-picked government lasted only two weeks. The Cuban revolution seemed on its way in spite of anything. The Cuban people seemed determined to have a real say in their own government.

Thirty American battleships were rushed south—not exactly in keeping with the new Roosevelt policy.[1] It was

[1] In his "Own Story" Roosevelt shrinks the naval display to "several small warships and Coast Guard vessels to certain harbors near which American citizens were living."

At the time, however, the State Department was busy apologizing for the fantastically large naval display on the grounds that Cuba has 700 miles of coast-line—as though to protect American residents the whole of it needed patrolling.

I received a personal letter from President Grau, long after any excuse for the vessels existed, in which he complained bitterly to me about the efforts to intimidate him and to cast doubts upon his government by such naval forces in Cuban waters, and about the undercover intrigues of Sumner Welles with the enemies of the administration.

intervention by threat and force, though no marines actually patrolled O'Reilly Street or raped Cuban girls or danced in Jiggs Café. Every pressure was now put upon the new liberal nationalist government of Grau San Martín to destroy it. We did not recognize Grau, but our Ambassador, Mr. Welles, remained on the scene—to make trouble and plenty of it. Roosevelt declared Grau's government to be responsible only to the army, students, and "a small group of agitators."

In troubled moments in history many strange folk are cast up to importance by the torment, and some of them decidedly unpleasant. This was true of Cuba, but some of those whom Mr. Roosevelt thus labeled as "agitators" were the finest men of the new Cuba that was struggling to be born but which Mr. Roosevelt helped strangle. Some, thanks to our mistaken policy, have since been murdered.

Welles in Cuba was in constant contact with the enemies of the Grau government, especially with the ABC terrorists. The Embassy became a center of conspiracy. One of his last acts before he left was to undo a mediation agreement of the various factions, arranged by the Uruguayan Minister, by which they agreed to support Grau until elections could be called. Welles' personal pride had been hurt by the manner in which the Grau government had done away with his pet De Céspedes government, which he had so carefully helped pick and which had lasted but two weeks. He could not forgive Grau's blocking of his plans and his pet solutions for Cuban affairs. And so Welles made himself thoroughly obnoxious except to a few conspiratorial groups.[2]

[2] One of his more violent critics, the Cuban leader and editor, Sergio Carbo, wrote in an article widely disseminated in Latin America:
"Like Edgar Allan Poe's raven, the sinister diplomat has his claws stub-

Mr. Salomón de la Selva, an educator and editor of the *Latin-American Digest*, wrote of Mr. Welles' efforts at that time, that however successful in ousting Grau, he had "failed miserably . . . First, he insisted in keeping Machado—whom the Cuban people could not tolerate further—in the Presidency until 1935." This failed; then, after Machado was ousted, the Ambassador "rather grossly tended to make the United States Embassy the seat of a new dictatorship, with the Ambassador as dictator and the Cuban President (De Céspedes) as rubber-stamp. Welles' insistence in drafting the Cuban constitution is, for insolence, almost unparalleled in the annals of United States diplomacy in Latin America. And now a condition exists in Cuba for which Welles is largely responsible, although the blame goes higher and falls squarely on President Roosevelt." This condition, said De la Selva, is among other things, "one that signifies the sacrifice of the Cuban people for the sake of safeguarding the Cuban interests of Mr. Vincent Astor . . . the happy-go-lucky scion of Merchants in the Temple, with whom President Roosevelt hobnobs in yachting circles."

bornly stuck upon our blood-soaked country. . . . While Sumner Welles breathes the air of Cuba there will never be peace here, nevermore.

"Since Sumner Welles has been in Cuba, the ranks of the sepoys have filed hat in hand past the North American Embassy. . . . There the insipid mediated government of De Céspedes was incubated and wet-nursed. There was plotted the continuation of Machado's regime, on the basis of the legality of the dishonored Cuban Congress, that was shamefully . . . imposed on us by a meddling in our affairs unprecedented in our history. . . .

"The people point to him in dread, superstitiously crossing themselves. Mr. Welles may be very fine, but it is a sorry coincidence that after each of his campaigns of mysterious visits, dynamite explodes, machine-guns rattle away furiously and the cemetery fills with dead. . . . His head is surrounded by a terrible halo of tragedy. . . . We have had enough of you, Mr. Welles. . . . Your intervention must cease now. Leave us in peace. . . . We are real friends of the American people, BUT WE REJECT SUMNERWELLESISM."

Welles was finally replaced by Jefferson Caffery, a close friend and also a career man, whose status in Cuba was scarcely clear, for Grau still had not been recognized. Roosevelt continued to exercise every pressure against it. Such pressure, plus undercover intrigue, finally did their work.

Fulgencio Batista, head of the army, was flattered by resident American officials; he was wined and dined by the heads of the public utilities interests and other businessmen. The next step was easy. He controlled the armed forces, and he betrayed Grau, who was slowly but bravely winning the country back to order and improved conditions, and despite Roosevelt's hostility was daily gaining popular strength. Grau was ousted by a disguised coup. Surrounded by soldiers who threatened to arrest him, he signed his resignation to save the country bloodshed.

The Batista-Mendieta government, more amenable to American wishes, was thus set up. The wishes of the Cubans were flouted—save for a group of old-line politicians and the ABC terrorists, whom Roosevelt conceived of as representing the Cuban people. A Machado-like regime was re-established under a new name and a new leader, with an even greater military set-up than ever before. It was recognized within a few days of its creation.

Roosevelt states in his own story of the New Deal:

"During this period our Government was unwilling to accord recognition to the Grau San Martín administration because of its lack of general support of public opinion and also because it seemed unable to maintain order."

He and Welles had done everything possible to undermine order during Grau's administration. He had no means of truly gauging Cuban public opinion. He prevented Grau from calling elections.

He recognized the Batista-Mendieta coup—and the old

gang was soon back at the feed-bag. He recognized Mendieta within five days without waiting to see if he could maintain order. In fact he was not able to do so, ever. A bomb even went off under the President's own chair. When taken to task by an American company for failure to give proper protection, Mendieta retorted, "How can I protect you when I can't even prevent bombs from getting under my own seat?"

And why, if the criterion was representative opinion, did Roosevelt shortly after recognize Martínez in Salvador, who had come into power by blood and slaughter and has remained in power the same way, with never a hint of popular support?

Of these events, the *Latin-American Digest* editorialized, (March 12, 1934): "The true-ringing Roosevelt voice sounded cracked, sounded like Coolidge's and Hoover's when it said last December that the Government of Grau San Martín would not be recognized by the United States because it did not have the solid backing of the Cuban nation, and that no Cuban Government would be recognized that did not have that backing and could not control the country and maintain order throughout the island.

"It is a safe bet that President Roosevelt doesn't to this day know that he was ever made to say that, . . . the Good-Neighbor Policy being then just so much bunk.

"Be that as it may, he cannot evade the blame for the indecency of the United States' treatment of Cuba. Whether he hears us or not, yet this we have to say to him: Look at Cuba now, Mr. President!

"You are responsible for the unsuccess of the Grau San Martín effort. You destroyed the first and only truly Cuban Government the beloved island of Martí and Varona has ever had. And you are responsible likewise for the Machado-like terror that Colonel Mendieta is fostering in Cuba."

Another Cuban leader, Francisco Alfonso Hernandez, wrote:

"The heroic attempt to save Cuba from the claws of Yankee diplomacy served only to make this latter a still heavier destructive force that shattered the only thing in which a few trusted—the purity, dignity and faithfulness of the men of the revolution.

"Never since the days of the deeds performed for freedom and independence, never had there been a greater or more worthy effort to gain absolute sovereignty for Cuba than was made by Grau San Martín. . . .

"The 'good-neighbor' policy has become nothing but one of ever so many farces played on peoples every day in order to deceive the unwary. . . . Roosevelt's determination to force Welles on a people against this people's will that clamored to have him withdrawn from Cuba brought about the bloodshed that everyone knows about . . . [He then] sent us Caffery to crown the work of destruction begun by the other. . . .

" 'Good neighbor' has made clear its meaning: one more farce . . .

"Grau's sincere behavior placed him at a disadvantage as regards recognition. His measures against Yankee concerns, in favor of the workers, made him ill-liked by Roosevelt, the good neighbor, who it appears did not find his good-neighborliness returned by such measures. Dr. Grau's last decree intervening in the 'Cuban' Electric Company, placing its administration under the workers, made Mr. Caffery jump and his hair stand on end."

Once a government to Roosevelt's liking had been established, one which he called democratic but in reality was based merely on Batista's bayonets and Batista's treachery, on a few reactionary elements and the ABC terrorists, he then rushed to repeal the Platt Amendment, long a thorn in the flesh of Cubans and Latin Americans. Though he had previously tumbled over two Cuban governments, Roosevelt—sensing the storm of protest rolling up against him in Latin America for his betrayal of the Cuban people and the Grau government—now by his repeal of the Amendment reversed much ill-feeling. The repeal was nice, it was appreciated, it was wise.

But desirable though this was, the fact should not be entirely forgotten that this statesmanlike step was taken with the partly ulterior motive of assisting the new Mendieta tyranny that was the puppet of Sergeant Batista, who still rules the island with bayonets, and who was to murder many and many a Cuban to maintain his improper power.

We took other supposedly beneficial steps for Cuba, which we had declined to do when Grau was in office. Those steps also strengthened military rather than democratic rule.

The Jones-Costigan Act helped out the bad sugar situation by assigning Cuba a quota in the American market. We assigned her a tobacco quota. And of lesser importance, a reciprocity treaty was celebrated.

These measures would equally have saved the Grau San Martín government, and Cuba would today more likely be on the road to a constitutional and orderly solution of its problems instead of living under the constant threat of new revolution against a universally hated regime sustained by bayonets. In other words, both our political and economic measures have been taken to support a regime of our choosing, a regime of tyranny rather than one set up by Cubans.

These steps provided an immediate hurried solution for some economic evils. But they were not destined to promote the truest interests of Cuba. Hull's reciprocity treaty, a temporary subsidy to the Batista tyranny by increasing revenues, in the long run has retarded the process of Cuban crop diversification, thus hog-tying Cuban industry. Though beneficial to export of Cuba's fruit and vegetables in off seasons, it has increased American shipments of those same products and cereals to Cuba—last year by 71.7 percent. Thus on the whole it has been a serious obstacle to crop diversification and sound economy. One big Cuban import under the new treaty is lard. This struck a body blow at the native hog industry. By raising hogs Cuba had a quick means of supplementing its one-crop activities and curtailing large importations of meat and lard. The reciprocity treaty partly halted this and put out of business the two synthetic lard factories near Havana. Another favored item is rice. (Ambassador Caffery is from Louisiana, a great rice-growing state.) This in turn struck a blow at an expanding Cuban industry. Thus, in spite of the temporary impetus, in the long run the treaty has helped perpetuate long-standing economic hardships, by preventing the development of a number of more varied activities. It has hindered Cuba from growing her own foodstuffs.

Cuba's immediate economic recovery was far more effectively promoted by the Jones-Costigan Act which established tariff reductions and a definite quota for sugar, and by the tobacco quota. A flush of life, though insecure, was thus given to the prostrate economy of the island by the sudden dumping of stored sugar stocks on the American market.

The benefits of this act, however, were offset by its promotion of the one-crop system at the expense of other industries. Cuba was thus tied still more closely in an unhealthy fashion to the United States. The proper solution of its economic problems has been postponed; the majority of its people condemned to a pitifully low standard of living.

The crying need of Cuba right along has been, not artificial strengthening of its dominant one-crop system, but new industries, crop diversification, a bit of intensive economic nationalism to free it from economic slavery to American banks and sugar interests. With only four million population, Cuba, one of the richest little lands in the world, is able to produce almost every food supply needed in abundance. Nevertheless the majority of its people live on a level close to the Chinese coolie level. Hull's treaty and the Jones-Costigan Act in their present forms promote in Cuba a system that tends to recurrent disaster. New economic collapse is even now impending.

The only conclusion must be that, despite the repeal of the Platt Amendment and the enunciation of the new Roosevelt policy, the old yard-stick of stability by force and intervention was utilized. Today, the administration is helping to sustain the iniquitous and unpopular Batista regime in power, just as Hoover and Guggenheim tried to keep Machado in office.

6

The new freedom for the Philippines is usually cited as a confirmation of Roosevelt's policy. Actually this was brought about by the powerful beet-sugar lobby, alarmed at the growing production of duty-free sugar in the archipelago. Now that barriers have been set up against Philippine sugar, imperialists are again urging us to break our promises and keep the islands for military and naval purposes, which sooner or later can result only in needless war with Japan.

In the so-called banana republics, one of the weapons

long used by the State Department, aside from marine intervention, was that of withholding recognition to a new government. When such a government enjoyed our displeasure, this was a sure signal for a successful revolt. But just as the successful revolutionist would be on the verge of seizing the coveted plum, a conference of the local Congress or of a picked bunch of servile political leaders would be held, usually on some American battleship, and a provisional president amenable to all our wishes chosen.

As a matter of fact this did anything but promote the stability it was supposed to.

This general practice was given some international legal formulation in the Central American treaties of 1907 and even more in their revised 1923 version. Among other provisions, no Central American government would be recognized which came into power by force instead of elections. As honest elections were unknown in Central America, this inevitably put a seal of approval on exciting tyranny or else imposed on us the obligation to hold marine elections, which though technically honest, could scarcely be considered democratic. The only alternative was to allow, under our protection, existing tyrannical regimes perpetual lease of life.

Under Roosevelt, the 1923 treaty, denounced by various Latin-American governments, has been allowed to go into the discard. Non-recognition, it was intimated, would no longer be used as a club to dictate the internal affairs of the various countries and beat new governments into submission, though this had been precisely one of the weapons used against Grau of Cuba.

The only Central American case that had then arisen was that of the military coup of General Maximiliano Hernández Martínez, who seized power in Salvador in 1932. Stray

Latin-American papers, however, have hinted that this coup was in reality engineered by American influence because of friction with the existing government and the need of a strong military hand to put down growing liberal sentiment in the country. Hernández Martínez immediately cemented his power by wholesale massacres, a butchery not often equalled even in the history of Latin America. Not recognized by Hoover, he provided the one example of a Central American government in recent years able to survive despite such a handicap.

Roosevelt was apparently too busy taking care of Cuba, by withholding recognition in contradiction to his announced policy, to tend to Salvador. It would have seemed a bit ludicrous to deny the popular government of Grau recognition (on the grounds that it was non-popular) and to extend it to Martínez so obviously a bloody tyrant.

Recognition of Martínez' government also had to wait, not until it became "democratic and representative" as was falsely pretended in the case of Cuba, but until Salvador had finally come to a debt agreement—the first Latin-American defaulter to meet her obligations—and had shown her ability to pay up. Most of the outstanding bonds had been sold to the United Fruit Company at 88 and a high rate of interest and protected by a customs collector named by the United States government. Of the actual loan money, Salvador had received not one red penny for any constructive purpose; she merely exchanged a series of smaller debts for one debt still larger than the total at a higher rate of interest.

Now, under Roosevelt, Fred Davis, President of the Latin-American Bondholders' Association said that "it had been found possible to enlist most effectively the good offices of the State Department at Washington in default negotiation." Thus the one example of a changed policy in Central America, though the international treaty bases have been voided, turned out to be in practice, as in the case of Cuba, identical with the traditional policy of thirty-odd years' standing. Recognition depended upon dollar diplomacy as of old.

7

Puerto Rico is not considered part of Latin America except in Latin America itself. For Latin America, Puerto Rico is *terra irredenta*. What we do in Puerto Rico is ever sharply scrutinized by other countries.

Actually the little island is ruled over by an appointed governor, safely protected, none ever quite so generally hated as the present Governor Winship. It is ruled over by American sugar companies, monopolizing the land in violation of the constitutional proviso limiting holdings to 500 acres. It is ruled over by a Congress made up mostly of lawyers and others representing the large American interests. It is ruled over by a brutalized constabulary.

The New Deal has poured a lot of funds into Puerto Rico and has had some grandiose projects which simmered away to nothing very important. The funds were used in part to play politics. Federal paternalism, however well-intentioned, could not take the place of a free economic life. Nor could it serve as an excuse for the brutality with which the Roosevelt administration has treated the Nationalist Party down there. Branded as "agitators" even by Secretary Ickes, harassed, jailed and murdered by the police, the Nationalists have retaliated, and violence has grown into violence, and bitterness into hatred. In this matter we have displayed the same dull colonial stodginess of any other imperialist power.

The head of the Nationalist Party, Pedro Albizú Campos (with whose partially medieval views I do not sympathize), has been railroaded to Leavenworth by a packed American jury.

Albizú Campos wishes Puerto Rico and Latin America to find their own paths to glory. In an open letter published in May, he points to the brutalities of the Fascist nations—the treatment of Jews, Abyssinians and Chinese. He points to the dictatorship of the proletariat, with its blood purges, as a revival of the tyranny of Ivan the Terrible. But he adds that semi-colonial countries need expect nothing better from the so-called democracies. He cites the horrible police massacre of men, women and children in Ponce, Puerto Rico (March 21, 1937), in the name of American democracy; the public massacres in Puerto Lyalty, Morocco, by the French soldiery and the cruisers of Marseilles; the murder of nationalist Arabs in Palestine in the Holy Land by the British army singing "God Save the King."

The most notable application of Roosevelt's new policy promised to be toward Panamá, where a series of serious grievances have grown up, and where the 1903 Canal treaty has become obnoxious to the Panamanians and is in great need of fundamental modification.

For the first time in the history of the Republic, a new President—Harmodio Arias—took power by a coup d'état in which marines were not immediately rushed across the border as had been done previously on every sign of an insignificant dog fight. On the other hand, he owed his success in large part to the fact that our Canal Zone authorities did not permit the existing government to transport troops, per the 1903 treaty, over the canal and the railroad. A sort of inverse interference. Fortunately in Arias, Panamá got the finest, most liberal, efficient and independent executive in its entire history.

The Canal Zone authorities were now to prove more amenable to ironing out Panamá's complaints than any other administration since the Canal was started.

In petty matters the Panamanians were largely placated. There is no doubt that a better spirit, for a time, came to prevail between the United States and the people of Panamá as well as its government than has ever been known. This is very important, for Panamá, being on the crossroads, is watched more closely than most countries by Latin America as the index of the sincerity of all our policies.

Shortly Harmodio Arias visited Washington to get Roosevelt to right injustices to his country. The *Panama American* said, October 2, 1933: "The picture is not of a little man from a little country going to beard an ogre in a big country. Harmodio Arias, in this errand, is the great representative of Latin America decently bent on making to President Roosevelt, whatever the words he chooses, this query: 'What do you mean New Deal and what do you mean Good-Neighbor Policy'—this in behalf not of Panamá alone but of all Latin America.

"Latin America will be on her feet to hear the reply."

El Tiempo of Bogotá (also in 1933), expressing doubts of our efforts to force a reduction of tariffs and thus make Colombia more economically subservient to us, declared that its government should delay until it was seen what we intended to do about Panamá: "A very salutary effect would be had in destroying the very evident fears that we Colombians entertain, if a square deal were given to Panamá at this juncture. Panamá's troubles, which we Colombians feel keenly, result from her having entered blindfolded into a treaty with the United States, depending entirely on the generosity and absolute honesty of the United States in the application of that treaty.

"If now it turns out that the United States assumes a generous attitude to inveigle ignorant nations into signing a treaty and later viciously sticks to the letter of the treaty and to every conceivable advantage that the treaty may give it however detrimental to the weaker nation, no one of these countries will be willing to obligate itself in any way to a document of which the United States is a party.

"The New Deal for Latin America may be a siren's song. . . . Much depends on what tangible results President Harmodio Arias obtains in Washington."

Roosevelt was generous. Immediately he righted a series of petty injustices and later embodied the changes in signed agreements. In addition he promised to Arias a thoroughgoing modification of the unfair terms of the 1903 treaty. Shortly after negotiations were begun. Preliminary news items indicated that the United States was making a generous concession, a real effort to iron out past injustices.

But if some petty agreements have been signed, the proposed treaty, though adopted by the Panamanian Senate, has since been quietly buried by us. Marine officers, the War Department, private interests, Mr. Hearst, stuck their knives into it, and Roosevelt has never fought it through, has never kept his promise to Panamá.

8

The most recent test of good-neighbor policy has been that of oil expropriation in México. There is no doubt that under any previous administration at this very moment diplomatic relations would be hanging in the balance, troops would be at the gates of El Paso and Laredo; we would be on the brink of war to protect properties, many of which had been acquired by fraud, violence and murder.

Had Roosevelt made any such moves, he would, of course, in twenty-four hours have tumbled down the whole edifice of good relations that he has labored for six years to build up in a continent and a half. He would have augmented the chances of the Fascist powers in this continent. This forbearance and recognition of México's sovereignty shows more restraint and decency than could be expected of any other great power on earth today. It is a particularly noble example in this hour of international aggression and brutality.[3]

In many ways the oil expropriation in México and our policy toward this act marks one of the most epochal events of our times and a turning-point not only in political relationships, but in economic policies. It definitely opens the gates not merely for a recognition of political sovereignty of the Indo-American countries, but eventually for their complete economic independence, and this without customary international disturbance, and interactive coercion and rebellion.

Early in the nineteenth century the Latin-American countries obtained political independence. They were reconquered almost at once, first by British economic imperialism, then by American economic penetration, both of which tended to make political sovereignty in many quarters merely a hollow pretense, just as it still does in Cuba. The

[3] Secretary Morgenthau rather pettishly marred the picture by seizing upon this moment to cease purchasing Mexican silver and in addition forcing the price down on the general market. If the State Department accepted expropriation on the basis of Mexican law, subject to proper indemnification, then it seemed rather stupidly inconsistent to simultaneously make it harder for México to pay—unless the State Department is insincere.

proper goal of Latin America must be to achieve economic independence. The Mexican oil expropriation is one of the first important guns in that battle, which will be a signal feature of the next few decades in all the southern countries.

Thus Cuba becomes the darkest blot on the new Roosevelt policy, and México its brightest expression. In Cuba and Central America the old pattern of dollar diplomacy has been partially followed, making the Roosevelt policy in certain instances more verbal than real. And yet Cuba has sloughed off the Platt Amendment, a definite gain. Panamá, after a few petty concessions, has been forgotten. But neither nations nor individuals correct all their past mistakes in a day.

Particularly to be commended are the signed promises of the United States never to intervene by force in any Latin-American country. This and the other worthy achievements I have mentioned—in the confused application of the Roosevelt policies and their repeated undercover betrayal by old-line career members of the State Department—are permanent and notable gains on the road to better continental relations.

If one chalks up the fine works of the Roosevelt administration in Latin-American matters, not against its own shortcomings, but against those of half a century or more of relations, then Roosevelt stands out as the most original and constructive Executive in that respect that has ever sat in the White House. No one can take away the merited praise for these worthier achievements.

However, it is necessary to check the results, not merely with the past, but with present and future needs. To correct a past mistake is not necessarily a guarantee for the future nor against the commission of things which may prove costly despite the remedies achieved.

It is certainly well to remember that when the economic factors that brought about the Roosevelt policy change again, our policy is likely to change correspondingly, and old-style aggression may be resumed. Permanent legal gains and valuable precedents will have been established, but we need to know now as never before whether or not we are headed in the right direction in Latin-American relations.

In fact there is every evidence that behind the scenes, the Roosevelt policy toward Latin America, though retaining an ever more exalted phraseology, has already changed for the bad. Once more the old-style naval and military missions are being used to help buttress up reactionary governments and make sales. Once more displays of military might, such as our frequent bombing flights over Central America and our armed planes sent to Argentina are being made. The utilization of naval missions and of our commercial attachés to promote the interests of our armament venders is again going on. These and other things indicate that once more our good-will protestations are becoming hollower, daily less sincere.

For a moment Uncle Sam crawled out of his clothes as a sewer-digger and took a job as a sandwich-board man advertising a revival meeting, with a tract in hand. Occasionally he took a furtive drink at the old stand. I am not entirely convinced by either disguise.

Perhaps there is something in the way the *Latin-American Digest* editorialized September 11, 1933: "Relations between the United States have come to such a pass that when the United States does not do a criminal act, it is pointed to with pride. It is as if I passed a neighbor in the street and expected him to give me praise because I did not stick a knife into him."

Facetiousness aside, the acts and policies of both Hoover

and Roosevelt obeyed changed economic conditions at home and abroad. The Roosevelt policy, in practice a hybrid thing dictated by varying circumstances in different countries, is a product of the depression and the growth of economic nationalism to the south of us. Even so it is far preferable to our previous Jehovah paternalism, armed intervention and constant meddling.

To the extent that Roosevelt's doctrines are actually applied—and there is plenty of back-sliding—they hold far more possibility of our working toward a real community of nations in the Western Hemisphere, with benefits to our neighbors and to ourselves than with the old-style Big-Stick methods. But under the cloak of these policies, a number of things, dangerous to the peace and safety of our country, are now occurring. Under the cloak of those liberal policies, Roosevelt is in fact now pushing us toward possible war in Latin America.

CHAPTER

IX

Don Quixote Rides the Pampas

No more dangerous words for the immediate peace of Latin America were ever spoken than those uttered by President Roosevelt in Buenos Aires in December, 1936. Taken literally, his advocacy of democratic and constitutional government in the Western Hemisphere was a call for mass revolutions in most of the twenty countries to the south of us. To put it bluntly, he spoke his glowing words to one of the worst assemblages of diplomatic cut-throats ever gathered in one salon anywhere in the world, an assemblage for most of whom his words could have no echo of reality. His plea could be and was accepted by those governments merely as polite diplomatic nonsense. But for the peoples of Latin America, his words, had it not been so well known they were merely stage decoration, would have represented a clarion call for revolt.

In his message to Congress, January, 1936, as several times previously, President Roosevelt declared that never in the four and a half centuries of modern civilization had there ever existed a greater "devotion to the ideals of self-government than exists in the twenty-one American republics."

The moon, too, my children, is made of green cheese. We are just Little Red Riding Hoods, supposed to believe that a wolf is a grandmother. The contention that the American republics to the south are nice free democracies is silly poppycock. To say so is to abet and promote tyranny.

At no time since independence have those long misgoverned nations to the south had governments which have more callously flouted the will of the people. Few are even constitutional governments. Except for México, to some extent Costa Rica, Panamá and Colombia, those governments represent military tyrannies run by narrow military cliques or one-man despots. Two such, Chile and Uruguay, have become fairly liberal in permitting free press, political expression and civil liberties, though an occasional emergency decree briefly takes these away; and from interval to interval the heavy official hand terrorizes too careless journalists and others. Argentina, within a very limited range, has also permitted some democratic rights. But the basis of all these regimes is military force, governments by coup. This is traditional in Latin America, the product of many conflicting economic and race factors, but merely because traditional, such governments are not thereby rendered democratic or just or desirable.

One need not blur the issue by calling a despotism, even if enlightened, democratic. A number of countries certainly have as odious and frightful regimes as have ever plagued the earth and mankind. In short, most of the governments of the New World are based precisely upon those dark principles of defilement of the individual, of oppression, of lack of democracy, of hatred and disregard for the rights of neighbors, which our President has repeatedly predicated as a cause of war and aggression.

We have already mentioned the secret conference that was the aftermath of the Buenos Aires assembly—a special meeting of the powers of the continent, exclusive of México which continues her political and economic reforms for the people, various Caribbean countries, and the United States, for the purpose of arranging a mutual undercover agreement to assist each other to suppress all popular movements and to insure a continuance of despotic governments now in power. This has given rise to what is known now as the secret Black League of South America of which Argentina is the moving spirit.

This accounts, in part, for recent scurrying back and forth of diplomatic representatives between Argentina and Brazil, and Argentina and Chile. It has resulted recently in the setting up of a common police bureau in Buenos Aires to be maintained by that country, Perú, Bolivia, Chile, Uruguay, Brazil and Paraguay, for suppressing all political opponents of the military tyrannies which rule those countries and handing them back across the borders to be jailed and killed. In all but name, there is a sort of Fascist League of South America, and its chief purpose is to oppress the people.

No worse tyranny exists anywhere than in Brazil, where Hull and Roosevelt talked so bravely about democracy. Thousands there have been murdered; thousands of political prisoners crowd the jails. Bayonets alone sustain "my friend" Vargas.

In Argentina, Roosevelt also called President-Dictator Justo "my friend," though Justo sat where he was through Uriburú's overthrow of constitutional and popular government, and Justo's successor, Roberto M. Ortiz, occupies his post by bayonets and fraud.

Uruguay, where Roosevelt also stopped, was long the democratic Switzerland of Latin America, famed for its free government, its progress and enlightenment, but even before the Pan-American Conference five years ago, that traditional system had been overthrown by Dictator Terra.

Only through widespread revolt throughout most of

South America—revolt which I do not necessarily advocate —can Roosevelt's postulates for peace and democratic government in the Western Hemisphere be promptly established, and probably not even then.

However, the various dictators, much as they dislike the word "democracy," were not overly alarmed by Roosevelt's tilting at windmills. They know that Roosevelt honored them by choosing this broad platform of the Latin-American nations from which to announce America's intentions to the world. Of course, from that angle, he demonstrated merely the old paternalism behind the new beard of goodwill, an assumption that the United States has the right to be the spokesman for both continents. All too soon we shall find out differently.

The dictators know of the administration's partially bad record in Cuba; they know that in Puerto Rico we have been stamping out the Nationalist independence movement with violence.

They are, however, quite willing to be called great democratic governments, even though some have openly declared themselves corporate states. These Sancho Panzas of the President's Latin-American family are indeed willing to follow him to the extent that it is to their interest to do so and just as long as his policies do not endanger their own crass dictatorships, just as long as his slogans of democracy are not taken seriously.

Their faith in his peace plans was vividly revealed by the fact that immediately after his visit, the various nations hastened to place some of the biggest orders for armaments in the history of the continent. Chile alone ordered 100,-000,000 pesos of air-bombers.

2

Despite these sour notes of realism appended here to a beatific but scatter-brained moment in our foreign policy, I was heartily in favor of Roosevelt's peregrination, glad of the non-intervention accord arrived at, though not at all in favor of the neutrality and war-embargo plans he proposed —a sure road to war. Nor do I like the gross attempts to pull the wool over people's eyes as to the real situation.

The emphasis upon trade in the President's speech in Buenos Aires, his linking it up with peace and democracy, perhaps gives the clue to the most practical phase of his excursion. It is nice to have commerce linked up with noble sentiments. It is nice that Mr. Hull believes in lower tariffs and the promoting of trade. We may not believe that the free market he postulates in international trade—if it ever existed—will return in our day if ever. Though the efforts of Mr. Hull are not necessarily based on sound economic principles—merely a wish fulfillment of something desirable but not existent—they are carried on sincerely for hoped-for profit, prosperity and unhampered freedom. He valiantly seeks to permit American merchants to freely sell where no individual freedom to sell exists. Within that range Mr. Hull's works are highly commendable. No one can for a minute doubt his patriotic devotion.

It will do no harm, however, to inject the proper realism into all that idealism, nor will it do any harm to remind ourselves that of all the nations of the world, we did and still do, despite great reductions, squat behind enormous tariff walls of the sort for which President Roosevelt and Mr. Hull so denounce the reactionary powers of Europe and which they declare are "suicidal" and war-producing.

We, as much as those powers, have been to blame for the steady increase of trade barriers throughout the world, for economic nationalism, with its attendant controls over currency, capital export, and trade rationing. We are quite too belatedly trying to rectify policies which have maimed ourselves and the world.

The game of world trade, however, has changed faster than our comprehension of it.

The Latin-American countries—once the load of our bayonets and our dollars was lifted from them—like good mice, at once played while the cat was away.

They, too, erected high tariffs and instituted all the mechanism of economic nationalism and exclusion. In their case, however, being semi-colonial countries, they were following a wise and necessary system of self-preservation and national development, however embarrassing that system may be for a nation like ours with surplus goods to sell. Such steps are necessary for them to achieve economic independence, to offset advantages gained by large industrial and capitalist nations over centuries of development—advantages of political power, great navies, great wealth, technical efficiency. Only in such ways can Latin-American countries—as we did at an earlier stage in our own national life—build up their own industries, promote the use of their own domestic resources for the benefit of their own people, and achieve real nationhood.

Hull and Sumner Welles are now thundering over the radio against this.

The nations of the world, Mr. Welles tells us, should abandon their programs of self-sufficiency, permit a free flow of goods, letting each country produce what it can most cheaply and sell where it wills.

That indeed would be an ideal world. Nations could well

afford to do that if all were not armed to the teeth, including the United States; if many of them, including the United States, did not maintain monopolies or semi-monopolies on key products; if many of the nations, including the United States, did not have heavy financial investments in other countries; and if many countries were not in a deplorable debtor class with respect to the more powerful nations.

Dr. Puig Casauranc, head of the Mexican delegation to the Montevideo conference, declared in this connection:

"It is . . . necessary that other voices representing the opinion of countries in less advanced economic stages . . . that have not yet reached a high industrialization, a super-production of manufactured articles, . . . should speak out, should come forward and tell this Assembly why it has been necessary to raise in almost all our countries those serious restrictions to international trade; why 'high tariffs' and the 'control of exchange' and 'import quotas' and all kinds of restrictions to international commerce have been inevitable. . . ." Rather than "the mere enunciation of high and generous purposes . . . it may be necessary to dig down into deeper causes . . ." It is not merely a question of trade, nor is it merely a problem of paying for imports with exports. Also there is "the law of comparative cost, which determines the quantity and kind of merchandise and services that can be exchanged." As "agricultural countries and producers of raw products . . . these countries are almost all of them lands whose economy is of the colonial type . . . exporting raw materials . . . importing manufactured products. . . .

"A country that is little industrialized cannot and never will be able to pay with its exports for all merchandise imported unrestrictedly and will find itself, in consequence, compelled to pay the balance in cash. These cash payments bear very definitely on the rate of exchange which is unfavorable to the debtor country and paralyzes its commerce. If that situation is prolonged . . . credit is . . . resorted to because of the impossibility of making payments in cash . . .

"By an instinct of national defense, a country in that situation bars the importation of merchandise and resorts to high tariffs, to the control of exchange, to import restriction . . ."

It was necessary also, Dr. Puig insisted, to examine into the question of wages and not merely of credit. For all credit inflation is "illusory" so long as "there is no proper proportion maintained as to what the worker receives, thus making it impossible for him to acquire what he himself produces . . ." This gap is even greater in the southern countries. "While there exists this enormous lack of proportion between wages received and dividends declared, how will it be possible for the great productive masses . . . to be able to purchase the world's production in this era so exceedingly productive? Where will you get your customers?" The masses are not even able to buy shoes.

But because of this unjust system, a powerful nation like the United States should not "expect or demand . . . that their exports should be larger than their imports of raw materials." The weaker countries must protect themselves, he concluded, against these evils by tariffs and other economic devices to control commerce.

These are sound views. When the United States was a semi-colonial country, it built up its industries by means of protective tariffs, by putting terrific handicaps on foreign goods. Throughout our history we have practiced economic nationalism in order to become wealthy and strong. Now that we are powerful we seek to deter other less developed nations from doing the same. Now that we are in a superior economic position, apparently it is to our advantage to see that other nations, still in a semi-colonial status, do not themselves use the same instruments that we earlier used. We cannot stop them, however, and in the long run it will be to our own disadvantage to do so, merely to promote the reputations of diplomats for having temporarily stimulated more trade.

We ourselves scarcely live up to the Hull-Wellesian ideal. We ourselves have still one of the highest tariff barriers in the world. I congratulate Mr. Hull on trying to lower it and save as much of our foreign trade as possible, though his proposals are inadequate for the present world situation. But we are not likely to live up to even our own limited preachments.

Japan today can produce certain textiles more efficiently and at lower cost (even were wages there to be equalized with ours) than any country. But not only do we maintain a high tariff against them, but have also subjected them to a quota, limiting the amount of the imports. This, Mr. Welles, is not practicing what you preach to Latin America.

Cuba can produce sugar more cheaply than any country in the world, with the possible exception of far-off Java. But we protect our artificial beet-sugar industry at Cuba's expense. We have given Cuba certain petty advantages in our market only to the extent that it does not interfere with that highly anti-economical industry of ours. This, Mr. Hull, is hardly practicing what you preach.

For this reason Cuba should junk the present reciprocity treaty, rationalize its sugar industry, put its people on the land from which they are excluded by the monopoly of large American companies, put more emphasis precisely on self-sufficiency, and attempt to bring back some of the general welfare that existed even under Spanish rule during much of the eighteenth and nineteenth centuries.

No, what Hull and Welles are really demanding of the Latin-American countries—which are the ones that above all others should resort to proper tariffs, and protective currency and quota and exchange devices—is that for the sake of American merchants they do not try to achieve economic freedom, do not try to build up new industries, but remain dutiful little colonies under Uncle Sam's tutelage.

The southern countries will be foolish indeed if they heed the two northern good-will apostles. In the long run we ourselves will be far more benefited by balanced systems of national economy to the south which, if successful, will raise the general standards of living and make the masses consumers of world goods.

Merely for immediate benefits and an elderly statesman's hobby, we should not attempt to halt that process. In order to retain merely a small preferred market, we should not constantly, as we do, try to block the creation of a vast new market, that in a decade or so, will prove of great profit to American merchants.

The American specialists, who for so many years had ranged over Latin America (fixing up supposedly sound gold-standard currencies) so that the various countries would be chained to dollar exchange and would maintain high standard money to make possible their buying high-priced American goods, have seen their work melt away in every country on the continent. In a jiffy nearly every country, beginning with México, has learned the tricks of managed currency, exchange control and quota limitations on trade.

They went further and adopted the motto "buy from

them who buy from us." By controlling all international banking operations, they can regulate all purchases of foreign exchange and in this manner and by setting up quotas and by other expedients, largely determine just where outside goods were to be purchased and in what quantities. The barter system came into being.

We were the last of the great nations (we so believed in rugged individualism) to wake up to this pernicious state of affairs—and only after a body blow had been struck at our commerce with Latin America. Germany, Italy, Japan, to mention only the black sheep among the nations, were busy long before us in promoting the sort of treaties with Latin America which Mr. Hull now claims will help save the world from war. When we got around to reciprocal favored-nation agreements, the Fascist powers had gone on to barter arrangement, subsidy and currency juggling. Our good officials apparently could not realize to what extent the world had gotten down to a barter basis or to government-controlled trade and planned economies. It is a bit ridiculous for us to enunciate lofty and noble principles for carrying out a policy we should have followed long ago and which we did only when we were forced into it by our carelessness and short-sightedness, a policy which even now is antiquated.

To what extent Latin America can be influenced, merely by favored-nation trade and good-will, to alter their commercial relations with the rest of the world on our behalf, remains to be seen.

It is nice for us to believe still in laissez faire and free competition, which is the basis of the Hull trade policy. But laissez faire does not exist in international relations or trade wars or in modern national controls. The free market is today a myth, and the nation which depends on it can be left in a very precarious position. Trade in any given quarter can be wiped out overnight. Mr. Hull is building on sand— quicksand.

3

We now have reciprocal trade treaties with nine of the Latin-American countries.[1] What effect have those treaties had on our commerce? According to State Department releases, those treaties have salvaged American trade to the south and are responsible for considerable recovery. What are the real facts?

After our trade slumped so low in 1932 and 1933, it began slowly to rise. The general recovery in business in the United States assisted this, plus even more rapid recovery in Latin America. This recovery began to occur before any reciprocal trade treaties were in existence. Long-delayed buying of raw materials, due to depleted stocks in the United States, caused large and sudden demands for Latin-American products. The United States won back trade in all countries, along with Germany, Japan and Italy. England, though her trade registered ups and downs, definitely began to lose out.

1937 was our banner post-depression year in the Latin-American markets, though our sales were far from equalling those of our prosperity years in either value or amounts. Nor have we gotten back such a large share of the market, even though we are in a better position in most countries than any other nation.

The world rearmament boom—and today trade is a war-propelled mechanism—lasted in Latin America and United States up until the end of 1937. In some of the countries,

[1] In March we denounced the treaty with Nicaragua.

this false trade inflation kept on well into 1938; several countries are even still going strong.

But our own trade and that of most of them are slumping again. We are no longer making the huge purchases we were making in the early part of 1937.

From seventeen of the twenty countries, we bought less in February, 1938, than February, 1937 (from —3 percent from Ecuador to —71 percent from Argentina, and —76 percent from Bolivia). Comparing the first four months of the two years, the decline for Argentina is now nearly 80 percent. This means that our exports will go down badly. Exchange controls in the various countries automatically attend to that. Argentina is again reverting to a quota system to stop excessive American sales.

Purchasing power below the Rio Grande is already hard hit. The various countries will largely have to move heaven and earth to get rid of their products. In such moments barter bargaining reënters stronger than ever. Reënter Germany and Japan. The American slump may even provoke to the south a new series of serious political upheavals, revolutions and wars.

There is another interesting aspect of our now historic 1937 trade revival. In 1920 we sold more than we bought in twelve out of the twenty countries, viz.: Argentina, Costa Rica, the Dominican Republic, Ecuador, Haiti, Honduras, México, Nicaragua, Panamá, Paraguay, Perú and Venezuela. In Uruguay our exports more or less equalled our imports. But in 1936, we sold more than we bought in only five countries, viz.: the Dominican Republic, Haiti, México, Panamá and Perú. Trade with Bolivia was about give and take. Today, according to February trade reports, we are selling more than we buy in fourteen countries, and our purchases seem likely to fall off even more. This sharp falling off of our exports with the controls existent in Latin-American countries, will mean an even worse, more abrupt slump for our trade than if such things, as of old, were left merely to chance.

The free international market was much more in existence in 1920 than in 1933 or 1938. There is today no free market anywhere in Latin America. Iron-clad controls on trade have been set up almost everywhere.

Had we the means to make barter arrangements in the style of Italy, Germany and Japan, in 1936 for instance, we would have sold approximately 30 percent more goods than we did. Now, we could prevent any slump at all, for we still have the goods to barter, an excess of goods. But cash and carry and our love of the free market that doesn't exist prevent any such process. Our rugged merchants would rather sit among their piled-up goods and twiddle their thumbs than participate in an organized system of foreign trade.

As a matter of fact, our good merchants have cried again and again for government help in foreign commerce ever since this republic began—and usually have gotten it, are getting it now. That help, however, is based at present on childish reverence for trade principles that no longer operate. That help is chaotic, devious, rarely efficient. It is usually more costly than it needs to be for benefits derived, and all because a false pretense of a false laissez faire theory must be kept bravely alike. Our government and our merchants positively insist on being romantic.

Mr. Hull loses no chance to denounce improper German methods, especially subsidies to promote foreign trade. Yet our very high tariffs, which Mr. Hull reasonably tries to lower, have long been a subsidy to our foreign trade. American business firms are thus enabled to charge American citizens higher prices and sell far more cheaply abroad. In Nicaragua, I bought an American typewriter—despite heavy freight charges and duties—more cheaply than I could have bought it inside the United States itself.

As a matter of fact, when our trade was booming in 1920, we were resorting to the most extravagant trade subsidies ever known in history. We were pouring out our golden dollars in the form of uncollectable loans. These gave us a favorable balance of trade. It was a hit-and-miss sort of subsidy considerably less efficient than the present channelized efforts of the Germans. The Latin-American countries got more direct benefit from the subsidies than we did, and the cost was probably at bottom more than the extra trade was worth, and to this day our trade is blocked by the piled-up obligations which must be paid off and which prevent proper purchase of American products or normal trade relations.

Now, in any case, we cannot subsidize our trade in that fashion. But our government's purchase of gold and silver is little else than a subsidy to our export trade, a subsidy amounting to billions, and probably all told a far greater subsidy, though less efficient, than any supplied by the German government to its merchants. Direct subsidies, as a matter of fact, would cost us less and be more intelligent.

The one amazing thing is that without directly subsidizing our trade last year, except in certain countries, or utilizing all the weapons available to the Fascist nations, we have held as much of the market as we have. Partly this was due to the proximity of various countries, to good shipping facilities, to the specialized nature of certain American products, superior quality, etc.

But very little of the trade we held and very little of the recent temporary gain can be ascribed to the Hull reciprocity treaties. Much of the gain was due merely to a normal increase everywhere, our own productive revival and the better economic condition of the Latin-American countries. In some instances also various abnormal factors operated favorably.

Politically the most important country with which we have a Hull-style treaty is Brazil. There American trade has failed to keep up with German trade, though we buy more and have heavier investments. We have been in second place for several years now, and Germany continues to increase her exports there. The reciprocal trade treaty is obviously no barrier to barter, currency manipulation and subsidized exports. Our treaty contains clauses to safeguard our trade against such practices. Actually there can be no such safeguard. The Aski marks and barter work the better the more a truly free market is set up by others. Only to the extent that Brazil abandons the principles that Hull seeks to promote in all countries can she restrain German trade. She does not have to favor us to sell her coffee, which in the American market is not subject to the governmental controls she herself imposes on foreign trade. Here she enters the market in free competition. But she does have to extend favors to nations that have a controlled market and drive barter bargains.

Although the trade picture elsewhere on the continent again darkens, even so we can look to quite some increase in our exports to Brazil, for if our steel mills, down to below 30 percent of production, no longer can order as much vanadium and tungsten and manganese, our use of coffee actually increases with depression. Our purchases from Brazil—if due for a temporary slump as a result of the failure of our one important steamship company doing business there—are likely to hold up fairly well. The gain there will not be especially due to the reciprocity treaty but to other special factors: purchases in excess of sales, constant diplomatic pressure, lifting of present exchange restrictions on dollars.

Also, we have given Brazil a $60,000,000 gold credit. This again helps our trade by indirect subsidy rather than by the principles advanced by Secretary Hull. Though we denounce Germany so hotly for her subsidies to her foreign trade and her barter system, hypocritically we pretend that $60,000,000 gold credit to Brazil to help her reorganize her banking and monetary structure is not a trade subsidy. Certainly it is less effective than the German method, which has the merit of benefiting German merchants directly rather than throwing German wealth out the window to be partially dissipated by foreign governments.

Economically, the most important country with which we have a reciprocal trade treaty is Cuba. There the considerable gain has been due chiefly to the large shipments of sugar under the Jones-Costigan Act. This act sets a definite quota for Cuban sugar and protects it against tariff-free colonial sugar, sufficient to give it a slight advantage over European and other outside sugars. There is also a definite quota for Cuban tobacco.

The Jones-Costigan Act is therefore diametrically opposite to the free-market principle of the Hull reciprocity treaty. It rests on a concealed system of barter. In Cuba the Hull treaty thus implements barter rather than the free market. Fortunately, in this case, the barter is for American goods and not German goods as in Brazil. We buy much more from Cuba than she buys from us. We are also helped by Cuba's preferential tariffs, based on the buy from those who buy from us principle. This, too, is an artificial compulsion entirely at variance with the Hull theory.

The fact is that Hull's reciprocity treaty, as we have already seen, definitely injures certain phases of Cuban economy and helps to block the permanent improvement of Cuba's low standard of living, hence in the long run implies defeat for American trade through lack of proper Cuban purchasing power.

Colombia is the third most important country having a reciprocal trade treaty with us. In 1936 our sales there showed a 30 percent gain over the previous year, and in 1937 another gain of 41.4 percent. But our purchases continued to be nearly three times as large as our sales. Perhaps the Hull treaty permitted Colombia to sell more in the American market, though other factors were far more important. And a three to one adverse balance for us does not sound like good business. Recently Colombia's sale of oil to us has increased, due in part to the temporary stoppage of Mexican oil exports—again an artificial factor.

Actually, despite Mr. Hull's treaty, Colombia has strict control of foreign exchange, so that it does not at all permit a free market. It can throw trade where it pleases. Furthermore this exchange control does not apply to Aski marks, thus giving Germany an immediate advantage. In other words we are presenting Colombia with a trade-ideal on a silver platter, which we can abide by and she does not.

In addition, our purchases of Colombian products serve to implement not merely our sales, but also payments on loans previously made to Colombia. Our sales to Colombia are therefore dependent on how much we collect on our debts. The more we collect, the less we sell. In other words, in 1920 we subsidized a big trade with loans. Today we are subsidizing the loans with trade. We now get money rather than selling goods. We are now paying for our false generosity of the twenties.

Isn't it a good bargain, some may ask, if we get, in exchange for small sales, both goods and money? The answer is that the bankers get the money; American factories fail to find a market; American workers fail to find jobs. We have to buy more. Thus the reciprocal trade treaty in the case of Colombia—to the extent that it has had any effect at all—has been also to pump more funds into the hands of the bankers.

In Guatemala, another reciprocal trade country, our purchases have increased far faster than our exports, which have remained nearly stationary. Now, our imports are also dropping off. In February, 1937, we imported $1,174,000 of goods, sold $607,000; in February, 1938, we imported $772,-000, sold $554,000.

In Honduras and Nicaragua, in 1936, both our exports and imports declined. In 1937 our exports to Honduras increased and showed gain on into 1938, but our purchases have now fallen off badly, and the country is putting up many barriers. In Nicaragua, decline continued through 1937, and in February, 1938, sales dropped about 40 percent as compared to February, 1937. The trade treaty has now been abandoned by us (March 10, 1938), because of alleged violations on Nicaragua's side.[2]

German and Italian trade is picking up in Nicaragua.

In Haiti, another reciprocal trade treaty country, there was a small gain in American sales in 1936, but this was lost in 1937 and 1938. In Costa Rica, despite a Hull treaty, exports have remained about stationary.

---

[2] Nicaragua depreciated her currency and to a corresponding amount increased her duties, though in terms of gold córdobas there was no change. Actually this meant a double increase in the cost of American goods in Nicaragua, though in terms of the American dollar, the duties remained stationary. Quite apart from the arguments pro and con, a striking example of the futility of the trade treaties, when currency and exchange controls exist, was provided.

Only in Salvador have there been considerable increases, but our purchases there, comparing February, 1937, and February, 1938, have dropped 37 percent, and sales are beginning to turn downward again.

In some of the Central American countries our exports were saved from large decline or held up well because of the recent expansion along the Pacific coast by the United Fruit Company, and other concerns, which have been shipping in new equipment, e.g., to quite abnormal trade factors.

In 1937 there were gains in American trade nearly everywhere to the south. In general, they were far larger and more rapid in those countries with which we have no reciprocal trade treaties than in those with which we have. This probably does not mean the trade treaties are to blame, but rather that they are fairly negligible, and that other factors account for expansion or decline.

Our appreciable gains, the ones that give Latin-American trade figures for 1937 such a bright complexion, were otherwise made in Argentina, México, Ecuador, Perú and Venezuela, countries with which we have no special treaties. These increases are due to special, impermanent factors. In México the 1937 gain of 43.9 percent over 1936 was due to a big public works program, to the government's nationalization of the sugar industry, to its active promotion of agrarian *ejidos* and consequent large purchases of farm machinery, etc. It was due to our Treasury's silver purchase program, which was a definite subsidy both to the American silver industry in the United States and in México and also to trade with México. Thus, increased Mexican trade was a product of so-called governmental paternalism on both sides of the border. Far more than to anything else, it was directly due to the trade-subsidy principle, similar to that of

Hitler, which we busily denounce except when we practice it. That increase of trade was due to principles diametrically opposed to those envisioned by our good Secretary of State. In the same way—also in good part by government action—our trade with México recently has been badly smashed.

In Argentina the big 1937 increase of 66.5 percent over 1936 figures was largely due to purchases of munitions and American bombing planes. Argentina's believed need for such war materials, plus American diplomatic pressure and munitions-company salesmanship, caused her temporarily to set aside her trade restrictions on imports from the United States to permit us to sell more than we bought. In any case, the result was due to governmental regulation and governmental purchases, not to any principle of the free market. These munitions sales, in fact, were at the expense of more permanent and normal trade relations.

To Perú we have granted an increased sugar quota. American capital expansion always increases to the south under dictatorships, and new American factories have been going up there which have caused unusual importation of machinery. This, naturally, is not a normal trade expansion. The factories set up will compete with American goods in the near future.

At present, with the United States' rapid decline in business prosperity and the excess stocks of raw materials now on hand, purchases of Latin-American products are again falling off in a dizzy fashion reminiscent of 1931-32. Reciprocal trade treaties or no, our sales there are bound to decline correspondingly. In fact, decline in our sales is already to be noted in four of the reciprocal trade treaty countries. Four still show slight gains, but in the case of Brazil only are these likely to continue. Of the eleven nonreciprocal trade countries, only three have as yet showed loss in this period, the rest still showed slight gains.

It requires minute examination of the complex factors involved, and this with respect to each individual country and its products, to arrive at any conclusions regarding the effect of the Hull treaties. The evidence would be far too involved and technical to present here. But the conclusion can only be that the treaties, though in several instances not beneficial to the other country, have not particularly done any harm to us beyond causing us to pin our faith to inadequate measures. They have mostly had but negligible effect. Trade today is determined by far more important varied factors. The Hull treaties, like so much of the hazy New Deal processes, represent an attempt to deal with merely superficial effects rather than causes. In short, if not as a rule damaging, even if in some cases of slight benefit, relatively the treaties are unimportant and unrealistic.

How can trade flow unhampered, even with such treaties, with the existing load of debt in Latin America? Here is a factor ten times as important as any reciprocal agreement. Puig Casauranc, head of the Mexican delegates at the Montevideo Pan-American conference, pointed this out forcibly and brilliantly time and again. But his proposals merely to consider the matter were entirely smothered under Hull's leadership—and mostly in committee.

Before the Committee of Initiatives, December 4, 1933, Puig stated:

"Gentlemen: Could it be regarded inopportune, barren or foolish that at a meeting where twenty debtor countries are represented this theme of so great importance should be looked into when an investigating committee of the United States Senate has seen fit to do so? . . ."

In acquiring these debts, "The peoples of our America

were not alone guilty of dolorous failures. It was clearly shown that a greater guilt lay upon their 'tempter' and that likewise this tempter was the party that even with regard to the riskiest investments hid the facts from the people, the tempter's own people, no less than from the peoples to whom the tempter sold capital."

When bankers place loans, "no care is given then to the need soon to rise of forcing all kinds of restrictions on international commerce in order that the debt obligations be fulfilled, and no importance is attached to the condition devolving upon our peoples who are forced to live a miserable life, bearing with a tremendous depression made acute when not altogether caused by the outflow of our insignificant metallic reserves in the service of these debts. And when we fail to observe our debt obligations religiously, the reasons that we have for so acting are not looked into. We are merely blamed for not living up to our sacred commitments!"

Puig insisted that any promotion of sound trade demanded an examination of the problems of currency and of credits. He asked for light on these problems which the gentlemen representing the United States could give. He did not propose any attack, for he well knew, he stated, that those who had wrought so much evil in America had also been "victims" of their own "absurd monetary and credit system."

Following the Montevideo conference, *La Prensa* of Salvador stated that it was not disappointed in the outcome for it had fully expected failure, even though México's proposals had raised a brief hope.

"The capital matter of intergovernmental debts and of debts contracted with North American bankers in years past, was skilfully dealt with by Mr. Hull's sagacity, who founded his evasiveness in arguments which, had someone wished to contest them, could have done so on the basis of the historical reality of most of the contracts. And let us speak naught of the problem in which the Cuban republic painfully struggles. That was the Achilles' heel of the delegation presided over by the North American Secretary of State, and it was necessary to avoid the blow that could have proved mortal."

To cite another factor: How can Mr. Hull seriously believe in a free market when American steamship services to each of various regions are monopolized by a single company which can immediately suck the juice out of any reciprocal trade treaty arrangement, and even stall commerce as they are now doing. I quote the Minister of Costa Rica to Washington, who on May 8th spoke, curiously enough, over a State Department short-wave propaganda hook-up to Latin America:

"The merchandise of the United States has to support a greater cost of production and the highest freight rates. The agricultural products of Central and South America suffer a double evil: less value in the market and greater cost of transportation.

"The freight rates from New York to the Plata River have suffered considerable increase from 1934 to date. I will give the data on three or four articles exported to the United States.

"On automobiles and accessories there has been a freight rate increase of 18 percent; on agricultural machinery, 6 percent; on hardware, from 8 to 10 percent. . . .

"The rate on tinned meats has increased 40 percent; that on hides, cured or raw, 20 to 25 percent; on wool, 35 percent; quebracho extract [tanning fluid], 100 percent.

"For many countries coffee is the principal wealth. Its price in the American market has diminished more than 30 percent, and as if that were not enough, freight rates were upped in 1936 to date from 10 to 20 percent."

Aside from the numerous controls that destroy any free trade ideal in our own country, those controls are even stronger to the south.

The political institutions of Latin America were born of free trade, as a result of the effort to break through Spanish imperial monopoly. The result was independence and open markets for British, later American, goods.

But gradually Latin America began to emerge from its colonial status. New laboring and industrial and middle classes are emerging. They demand, now, as Earl K. James puts it, "a positive State, to control and create new wealth, not merely to act as a policeman."

Latin America had to begin a new struggle, not for political independence, but for economic independence. Economic nationalism was born, just as it was much earlier in the United States. Mr. Hull may not know it, but the free market in Latin America began actually to disappear in 1900—over a third of a century ago. It has been disappearing almost entirely since the World War. It has now disappeared.

And yet Mr. Hull wishes us now to follow the pattern of ideas he gathered sometime before the Spanish-American War. He is imposing them on us now. He is thereby merely moving in a shadowy world of unreality—except that strange shapes therein have hard corners on which our country needlessly barks its shins.

4

I am glad Roosevelt went to Buenos Aires. I am glad that he spoke for democracy and peace on a continent that sadly needs both. I hope that it will increase our trade. I hope that it will save us backyard trouble if we do get into another war. I hope that all this will happen even though his neutrality proposals were knocked into a cocked hat. I am merely a bit sorry that he had to be nice to all those little gilt-braid Hitlers and spoofing Mussolinis that at present infest those regions of the world.

More recently Roosevelt again has set himself up as spokesman for all the twenty-one nations of the two continents (Canada out in the cold). On Pan-American day, April 14, 1938, he once more averred that the ideal of the American Republics is "democratic liberty." [If he refers to governments, this is simply not true.] "Our instrument," he continued, "is honor and friendship; our method is increased understanding; our basis is confidence. [Words, words, words, meaning exactly—nothing.]

"The twenty-one American Republics," he continued, "present proudly to the rest of the world a demonstration that the rule of justice and law can be substituted for the rule of force, that resort to war as an instrument of policy is unnecessary, that international differences of all kinds can be solved through peaceful negotiations.

"We, [the three hundred millions of citizens in the American Republics]" he declared, "know how to maintain peace. It shall not be endangered by controversies within our family; and we will not permit it to be endangered from aggression coming from outside of our hemisphere . . . an international understanding unique in the world. [Were it only true!]

". . . Particularly I am glad that in December of this present year, representatives of all our governments will once more assemble—this time in the great capital of Perú." He spoke of "my friend, the President of Argentina." He praised the Foreign Minister of Brazil.

We know only too well the sort of government, the undemocratic and brutal tyrannies that are Brazil and Perú. We know how remote Argentina is from being a democracy. We have followed the complicated threads of Latin-American politics. In a succeeding chapter, I shall analyze the aggressive Power politics and imperialism of Argentina, and her present efforts to form a Black League of her own. To anyone who has grasped the significance of the international forces at play in Latin America, President Roosevelt's words can sound only rhetorical and wholly unrealistic.

One can be just as fond of peace and honor and justice among nations as is Roosevelt, but such things do not come to pass through hazy poetry of idealism, which disregards the actualities of the situation. Roosevelt's words are off in the clouds. They are the words of Don Quixote, holding his heart, on the eve of tilting at windmills.

First of all, Roosevelt has no authority to speak for the whole of the Western Hemisphere. This is colossal and unjustifiable paternalism.

He has no right to fool people regarding the true nature of the governments to the south.

Certainly he does not fool Europe. He does not fool the Fascist governments. He does not fool England. The Chancelleries of those countries know exactly what they are doing in South America, what is going on. They do not need to resort to old-style aggressions to get what they want.

Certainly Roosevelt's words do not fool the dictatorial regimes of South America. They do not fool imperialistic Argentina. They do not fool Dictator Ubico of Guatemala, building up armed forces, in the hopes of carrying on a holy war to unify Central America by force of arms. They do not fool the blood-torn nations of the Chaco War. They do not fool Dictator Trujillo of the Dominican Republic, who is flirting with Germany, who has recently slaughtered twelve thousand peaceable Haitian citizens.

Roosevelt's words certainly sound hollow to the oppressed peoples of South America. They know that their governments are not founded upon justice, liberty or democracy. They know their governments little desire peace and honor as indicated by Mr. Roosevelt's words. The folk to the south feel that Roosevelt's administration, in actively supporting tyrannies such as those of Vargas in Brazil, Batista in Cuba, and Benavides in Perú, is betraying the people of the continent.

Mr. Roosevelt's words are not fooling the American munitions merchants who are doing a bigger land-office business in Latin America than ever. The munitions merchants are not fooled, because they know that the State Department, the War Department, the Navy Department, the Department of Commerce are assisting them in every way possible to sell armaments to the so-called continent of peace. They are not fooled because they are allowed to work hand-in-glove, share patents, profits and business contracts with the munitions concerns of England, Germany, Italy and Czechoslovakia.

Mr. Roosevelt surely does not fool himself.

Does he wish to lull the American people into a false sense of security? For the only ones he may have fooled are precisely the American people.

CHAPTER

X

We Fight Fascism

In 1922, Juan Terry Trippe was the head of the little Long Island Airways System. In 1931, Trippe was President and General Manager of the vast Pan-American Airways company.

This simple biographical item drapes a dramatic story. It is the story, not merely of the evolution of Mr. Trippe, but of the rapidly evolving relations of the United States to the Latin-American world. It tells of a real revolution in world affairs and international communications.

Before the World War, Great Britain, except for the Caribbean area, was largely dominant in Latin-American affairs. Before the World War, we had no news services to speak of in Hispanic America. Outside of the Caribbean, our industrialists had no American-owned cable service. They had no extended banking system. They had a relatively small capital investment. We scarcely had any airplanes that would fly safely, let alone carry our influence over two continents.

In pre-war days, it took three weeks to a month to get to Argentina. Today we can fly there from Miami by regular plane service in less than five days, or if we are in a hurry—as our recent army pilots—in twenty-eight hours' flying-time. The far tip of the southern continent is thus brought as close to us as New York is to San Francisco by train. Panamá is closer by air to Miami than New York is to Chicago by rail. Three days' plane trip from New York brings you to Lima, Perú; three days' rail trip westward will not take one across the Rocky Mountains. Many places in Latin America are closer by air to Berlin than they are to the United States.

In twenty years our whole international life has been altered. Our relations to South America have become intricate, complex. The guide posts are gone. We have had to create new ones. With breathless swiftness, as history records such things, we have had to make decisions, with no precedents to help us, that may eventually spell peace or war, prosperity or disaster. We are beginning to realize, though still not very vividly, that the coming struggle for power in Latin America is at our door. What are we going to do about it?

The Monroe Doctrine won't settle it. Nice platitudes about democracy and friendship and international justice won't solve it. The battle is being fought on other ground entirely.

We have already observed part of America's expansion south. Whatever policies we follow, that expansion, in one form or another continues.

The drama of Mr. Trippe is the drama of American expansion southwards—territorial, commercial, financial, military, and cultural. There we collide with the Latin-American feelings of national sovereignty, there we collide with native imperialisms, with bloody dictatorships, with reactionary regimes and very advanced regimes. There we collide with the growing tide of revolutionary sentiment which demands democracy and freedom. And there we clash sharply with the rival ambitions of other powers.

Airways play a big role in the complicated criss-cross of

conflicting ambitions. Without the pioneer work of Pan-American Airways, the company weather reports, landing fields and radio service, the recent mass flight of our army bombers to Argentina would have been impossible.

By 1930 the Pan-American Airways, only a few years old, was already operating over one hundred planes, had eighty-nine airports in thirty-one countries, and flew routes of 22,000 miles for flights totalling 3,000,000 miles, carried 30,000 passengers, and over 1,000,000 pounds of baggage and cargo. It had become overnight the largest air transport company in the world—and the safest. By 1938, Panagra (the South American Panamá-Buenos Aires route) carried 20,953 passengers, flew 11,095,386 passenger miles, carried 2,500,000 letters. How was this imperial concern built up in little more than a decade?

The German *Scadta*, operating in Colombia, even earlier saw the opportunities of expansion and in 1920, and again in 1926, its head, Dr. von Bauer came to Washington, to try to obtain mail contracts and permission to cross the Canal Zone in order to initiate flights to Miami.

A young army officer, Captain J. F. Montgomery, getting wind of this, sensed the great possibilities and interested Mr. Richard Bevier and his father-in-law, Lewis Eugene Pierson, of the Irving Trust Company and one of the high-ups of the American Smelting and Refining Company (a Guggenheim interest) and of the Electric Bond and Share Company. Both concerns are strong in Latin America. The Electric Bond and Share Company was then hand-in-glove with Dictator Machado, and our Ambassador there was a Guggenheim and especially interested in aviation, so that when Montgomery began commuting between Washington and Havana, he had easy entrée and quick promises, which eventually brought him a Key West-Havana flying contract.

This, he had foreseen, was the key to eventual control of the whole continental system. Without this bottle-neck, no rival promoter could get anywhere. The Pan-American Airways, Inc., was organized, and an alert reporter of business etymology might have seen that the little segment would inevitably grow into a continental tapeworm.

Reed Chambers, head of the Florida Airways (then on its last legs), backed by Charles A. Stone of Stone and Webster, Percy Rockefeller and Richard Hoyt, the latter close to the National City Bank, also got the Pan-American aviation bug. Trippe, who had left his Long Island company, backed by Cornelius Vanderbilt Whitney, also had the same fever of international expansion. These three groups finally got together and formed the Aviation Corporation of the Americas as a holding company for the operating Pan-American. Trippe was put in charge.

The next step was to absorb everything already in the road. A small Puerto Rico-Santo Domingo line and the Compañía Mexicana de Aviación were brought in by stock-payments. Pressure was next brought on airplane manufacturers to take up stock at $15 a share, with option rights on additional shares. This accomplished, official doors could be pried open.

Washington authorities were brought into line, and a special commission detailed to help get the Latin-American contracts, thus making the promotion semi-official. Lindbergh was hired as technical adviser, and he combined goodwill flights with business. By 1929, the company and Pan-Americanism was an established institution in the Caribbean with regular flights and equipped airports.

The next deal was with the Grace Line, owners of steamships, banks, plantations—a great economic power on the west coast of South America, able to hinder or promote any new enterprise. The Grace people became half-owners of that section of the service known as Panagra, and 14,000 miles could then be put under operation, with appropriate airports, a vast radio service, and weather observation stations. All this displayed great initiative in a pioneer field.

But before Trippe could get in on the ground floor on the east coast of South America, the NYRBA company, backed by Rand of Remington Rand, secured mail subsidies from South American governments to fly from Argentina to Miami.

Rand's weak point was that Washington had not yet been tapped. Pan-American Airways, it soon turned out, was strong enough to block all efforts of the NYRBA to get American subsidies, and so in August, 1930, the latter sold out for 75,000 shares of Pan-American stock. Thus Pan-American Airways, thanks to astute organization ability, big political and financial backing, enormous governmental subsidies, fine service and much pioneer work, achieved a near monopoly of international air service in Latin America. In Perú, the Faucett Aviation Company, partly controlled by Panagra, now also operates most of the domestic lines.

The Germans (first in the field), the French and Italians are now pushing in strong with trans-Atlantic passenger services to replace long-standing mail services from Africa to Brazil. England hopes soon to take a hand; the Dutch have plans. The commercial war of the air in South America will soon begin in earnest. On international flights, Pan-American is on the ground floor. Last year it established a new diagonal route through southern Brazil, via Paraguay and northern Argentina, to Buenos Aires.

But it is well to remember that there are nine planes daily

out of Buenos Aires, flying for Rio, Montevideo, Santiago and other points, run by German, French, Italian, Uruguayan, Argentinean and American companies. The Germans, of course, already have by far the biggest air network of South America.

2

During this same period, other great American financial and business interests were spreading many networks over the southern countries. The International Telephone and Telegraph Company, had already found Dictator Machado a pliable agent for the awarding of a juicy contract. Soon its lines were to extend over the continent.

It bought up the All-American Cable Company, with its 27,624 miles of cable. This company, organized back in 1881, had been a pioneer in the field, an offspring of the old Central and South American Telegraph Company. This purchase was a culminating step in a vast scheme of continental amalgamation. In 1920-21, the I. T. and T. took over the various Puerto Rican and Cuban telegraph and telephone systems, making arrangements with the Bell system through fifty-fifty ownership of certain properties. By 1924, the I. T. and T. made its stranglehold contract with Dictator Primo de Rivera of Spain, which gave it unabridged control there and made possible the further rounding out of a vast system over what was once the great Spanish and Portuguese empires. The following year I. T. and T. set up a dual service for México to fight Erickson, but since has bought into the Swedish International, and in México now shares ownership. By 1927 I. T. and T. had forged into control of the domestic services in Uruguay, Chile, Argentina and Brazil.

By 1929 it drove out the United States and Hayti Tele-

graph and Cable Company, getting the lines of the whole
Antillean system, thus connecting Cuba, Haiti, Santo Domingo, Puerto Rico, St. Thomas, Curaçao and Venezuela.
In 1930 it secured the controlling interest in the Peruvian
system. The I. T. and T. also went in for radio communications, as early as 1922 getting hold of the Radio Corporation of America, and in 1928 set up radio services in Argentina, Brazil and Chile.

All of this drive for monopoly control in all the countries of the continent was achieved by stock barter, inflated
sales prices, the piling of values on values, the creation of a
super-complicated holding structure of pyramided service
charges and monopoly control of supply companies, which
helped conceal the watered stock, the drain of profits, and
excused high rates. It was a more intricate bureaucracy than
those of many of the governments where it operated.

The Electric Bond and Share Company, through the
American and Foreign Power Company, of which Machado
had been an agent, also started with Cuba as a springboard.
Under the wing of Morrow's benevolence in México, it
secured control of all the light and power resources of the
country not already held too tightly by the big Canadian
corporation. They moved on south and swept every country
into the net except Perú. There the Italian company held
out for a fabulous price, which but for the 1929 depression
would have been paid.

Many of these operations required little outlay. Payments
in stock to existing companies, the issuance of new stocks to
the public, and other high-finance deals easily turned the
trick. Hence high purchase prices were no obstacle. With
international monopoly control once established, high rates
could then take care of any inflated values paid. Monopoly
power was the goal sought.

It would take too long—and it is easily enough available —to give an extended account of the United States financial empire in Latin America: the great sugar companies in Cuba; the United Fruit Company, which practically made and unmade Central American governments; the Standard Oil; the Guggenheim mining and nitrate interests; meat-packing in Argentina; the great Ford rubber plantation in Brazil; the holdings of Bethlehem Steel Company, in Cuba, México, Brazil, Chile; Grace and Company on the west coast of South America; the big steamship companies— Munson Line (now bankrupt), Panamá Mail (now eliminated), Standard Fruit, Grace Line, the Red "D" Line, the Delta Line, the Norton Line and others.

These vast enterprises are now supported by a complete chain of banks, of which the National City Bank takes the lead, with twenty-six branches in Cuba, numerous branches in Santo Domingo and Haiti, Argentina and Brazil. It operates in México, Chile, Colombia, Panamá, Perú, Uruguay, Venezuela. Seven branches are maintained in Puerto Rico. The Chase National Bank operates in Havana, where it is very powerful and in Panamá and Puerto Rico. The First National Bank of Boston is strong in Cuba and Argentina.

It cannot be said, however, that American banking to the south as yet has the standing or provides the extensive services of the British or German banks, but it has been greatly aided in the past by dollar diplomacy and in the future will likely be aided by means to be called good neigh-borliness. Crowder's intervention in Cuba finally smashed Spanish banking control there. Knox's dollar diplomacy smashed French and British banking supremacy in Haiti, Santo Domingo and parts of Central America.

The Maritime Commission, under Kennedy, was also busy trying to improve American steamship services south.

When the Commission arranged to transfer three Panamá-Pacific liners from the coast-to-coast service to the eastern ports of South America, it was declared: "Aside from the desire to cultivate South America as an outlet for American exports and to oppose a united front to the encroachments of foreign powers, the Administration also is reported desirous of assuring a supply of minerals needed in war time of which there is some scarcity in the United States."

With the final collapse of the big Munson Line this year, leaving the United States without any adequate passenger, mail or swift freight service with Brazil, Uruguay or Argentina, the commission has hurried to call for sixty-day bids to recondition the Panamá-Pacific liners for prompt service. To the east coast of South America, even with these additions, the French, British, Italian and German steamship services will surpass ours.

In February the commission promoted the consolidation of the Grace Line and Colombia Steamship Company, and a division of the field, with the secession of a number of vessels to the Atlantic, Gulf and West Indies Steamship Company (AGWI). "The effect of the new arrangement," the press was informed, "will give us the finest trade fleet in this area (the Caribbean south to Venezuela) and by strengthening and stabilizing remaining services, tend to make them increasingly self-supporting." As with foreign countries, our steamship lines south are all well government-subsidized.

3

The United States has also tried to keep up with the armament-sales game of the European powers in Latin America, is doing so more energetically than ever today.

Following the World War, there was a race to dump

excess equipment in the countries to the south. Boundary disputes were at once magnified to grave proportions. Guatemala and Honduras—prodded on by rivalries of the United and Cuyamel fruit companies—almost went to war. The Leticia trouble saw the wholesale arming of Perú, Colombia and Ecuador. The Tacna-Arica imbroglio was revived and almost led to war between Perú and Chile. An old boundary dispute between Chile and Argentina was pricked into life, and the famous statue of peace, the Christ of the Andes, threatened to crumble under artillery barrages. Jealousy was fomented between Brazil and Argentina.

United States munitions companies sold airplanes, cruisers, submarines, guns, ammunition. It was a great day of profits and graft. Loans, with State Department approval, were poured out to further encourage these purchases. Bolivia was mortgaged up to 90 percent of her national income, and American military and naval missions blossomed over the continent—the same sort of thing that we are now so angry about Germany and Italy doing.

This munitions traffic of the twenties, backed by all the weight of the State Department, the War, Navy and Commerce Departments, has all been exposed by the Nye Senate Investigation. It is one of the filthiest stories ever spread on white paper. It revealed the propaganda methods, the graft, the collusion of Latin-American officials and munitions salesmen, the tie-ups with European munitions concerns. Our American army and navy missions were but sublimated salesmen for American munitions firms. Generals and admirals were on the pay rolls of those companies. While our War, Navy and State Departments coöperated in this arming of a continent, the State Department simultaneously was busy talking peace, holding arbitration conferences, trying to settle international disputes and going through all the mumbo jumbo of being interested in the welfare of our neighbors, while actually undermining order and stability.

Those same munitions companies were selling both to recognized governments and revolutionists. Those naval and army missions, as has been disclosed, were teaching the police forces of the Latin-American dictators how to put down insurrections and break strikes with tear gas bombs. "More than 150,000 Latin Americans," says Genaro Arbaiza, "were killed with the marketed wares."

That same sort of thing is going on today. The broken threads have been picked up again. Once more Latin-American armies are being expanded and there are nearly 350,000 men under arms. The munitions game again goes merrily on, and our part therein flourishes. Nothing effective has been done to put any check on the earlier evil practices Presumably the same filthy deals are being practiced. Fifteen or thirty years from now—perhaps after a bloody war brought about by such activities—we will have another investigation and uncover it.

We now have naval missions in Brazil and Perú and are thereby giving improper aid to two of the worst Fascist-like regimes on the continent—illegal governments, ruling by force and blood-purges, and utilizing the knowledge of our naval officers to maintain themselves in power against the wishes of the people. Our State Department feels we need to offset strong German and Italian influence and so our navy officials are down there to promote American sales.

Brazil has ordered war vessels from us. The Brazilian battleship *São Paulo* was reconditioned in the United States Brooklyn Navy Yard. In January, 1934, our Navy Department helped the New York Shipbuilding Company prepare its bids for Brazilian cruisers, and in January, 1937, it helped the Brazilian government draw up specifications for destroyers. Three of the nine destroyers planned are being built with plans drawn up by United States government engineers. The Du Ponts some time ago put up a powder plant in Brazil, and they, and allied concerns, the New York Shipbuilding and Bethlehem Steel, have a ramified sales organization throughout the south.

September 5, 1934, Senator Clark stated at the Nye hearings (quoted by Arbaiza in *Current History*): "It is a fact that the Secretary of Navy stated at the time Congress passed the act to authorize the naval mission to various South American countries that one of the purposes of it was to sell armaments. . . ."

On May 7th, Mr. Hull stated: "We have long been exerting ourselves in every way possible consistent with our situation . . . in . . . aiding and coöperating in bringing about disarmament and conditions of peace. . . .

"We have been among the last to continue to talk about disarmament and peace while some other countries were going forward with armaments right and left. . . .

"We think peace and disarmament, we dream peace and disarmament, we proclaim peace and disarmament. We strive for it day in and day out."

Oh, Lord, their right hand knoweth not what their left doeth! Mr. Hull talks, dreams, proclaims and strives for peace and disarmament and is helping to arm the southern nations, supposed to be so pacific, with every possible instrument of death.

He never pulled a bigger boner in our diplomatic history than when he offered to lend Dictator Getulio Vargas of Brazil battleships from the American navy. Perhaps this was what he meant when he said at the Montevideo Congress: "Our churches have direct contacts with all groups;

may they remember that the peacemakers are of the children of God."

Quite apart from the bitter animosities that his proposal provoked in other quarters in South America and the naval race that we at once intensified, why, in God's name, should we lend battleships to a dictator who has snuffed out as many lives as Hitler has, who has destroyed the liberties of his country, who has driven its decent citizens, thinkers, teachers, poets and writers, not murdered, into forced exile?

Equally unjustifiable was our treaty-loan of $60,000,000 to the same tyranny. Mr. Morgenthau is evidently Jewish enough to recognize tyranny in Germany but not in Brazil, though shortly after this loan was granted, it took special undercover pressure by American diplomacy to prevent wholesale persecution of the Jews down there.

As in the twenties, we are sending military missions, selling munitions and talking peace and international justice and spouting about the great idealism and democracy of all the nations of the Western Hemisphere. Plain Hull-abaloo! Grandiloquent Blah blah. Soft soap. Eye-wash.

Never have we gotten the Latin-American countries to sign so many peace pacts. And never have we sold so many war materials.

Our government also helps sell war-planes to South America. The Pan-American Air Congress at Lima last year was for that purpose. The Italians showed up with a whole carierful of planes and "stole the show" and sold their planes and became the air-advisors of the Peruvian government.

Our mass flight of six Boeing "floating fortresses" to celebrate the inauguration of the new President-Dictator, Roberto Ortiz, of Argentina, was also a muddled combination of good-willism, airplane salesmanship, and threat—all the complex factors that go into present day international relations. The *Herald Tribune* of February 27, 1938, specifically commented that the "practical benefits of such a demonstration to this country's aircraft industry, which is striving to protect its South American market against European inroads, are incalculable."

Many flights are not even publicized. In February of this year, 62 American planes see-sawed back and forth over Central America, ostensibly on a good-will mission, but also to remind those countries of the might of the United States. Nicaragua was buying more Italian munitions. In April, another gang of American bombers menaced and smiled in South American skies.

We aren't saying good-will and peace with flowers—except over the radio—we say it with battleships and guns.

4

In this and previous chapters, I have already considered the building up of our cable communications, the expansion of American news services, the vast network of publicity and public-relations carried on by private companies. Our news agencies, though still dominating the field, have been hard-hit by the new cheap services of Europe, all government-subsidized.

Our government has at least imitated England, Germany, Italy, and Japan in sending out officially sponsored propaganda broadcasts to Latin America.

Efforts to reach Latin America by propaganda on the air were studied in December, 1937, at official suggestion, by the National Conference for Educational Broadcasting, the Pan-American Union, and World Wide Broadcasting Foundation. Later, through coöperation of the Interior Department, the Pan-American Union, the National Broadcasting

Company and other agencies actual broadcasting was started.

February 26, 1938, Roosevelt appointed an interdepartmental committee specifically to consider methods of utilizing radio channels to combat other foreign propaganda and strengthen United States cultural ties with Latin America. Frank R. McNich, head of the Federal Communications Commission, was put in charge, and the committee included representatives of the State Department, the Post Office Department, the Interior Department, the Commissioner of Federal Education, the Agricultural Department, Dr. Alexander V. Due, director to the Bureau of Foreign and Domestic Commerce, and Lee Pierson, President of the Export-Import Bank, and close to those controlling the great American business and munitions expansion in Latin America.

The Federal Communications Commission promptly allocated four new short-wave lengths to General Electric, World Wide and other concerns, for broadcasting to the south. On March 4th, regular broadcasting service was inaugurated by a G. E. short-wave broadcast by Sumner Welles, Fernando Lobo, the Chargé of the Brazilian Embassy in Washington, and Dr. L. S. Rowe, the old faithful of the Pan-American Union.

This was followed fifteen minutes later by talks in Portuguese by Berent Friele, President of the American-Brazilian Chamber of Commerce, of which our old friend Merrill is the leading light, and Dr. Luis de Paro, Brazilian Consul-General, and included a musical program featuring Moemi C. Bittencourt, Brazilian pianist, and Elsie Houstin, Brazilian soprano, and an orchestra.

Daily broadcasts are now maintained from 7:30 to 11

P.M. in Portuguese over a 9.44 megacycle, six times signal strength, and in Spanish on a 9.35 megacycle.

The National Broadcasting Company is also sending out international programs, and distributes five hundred schedules to newspapers and others as far south as Argentina. Toscanini is now being broadcast over short-wave, with all comments in Spanish.

Columbia operates Station W2CE, programs of special interest for women and for "fostering better relations," in charge of Elizabeth Ann Tucker. It was inaugurated on May 10, 1938, with an illuminating program, "To Feminize Latin America." Roosevelt has asked for reciprocal programs from Latin America. Perhaps it will kindly favor us with speeches "To Masculinize the United States."

However, most of this is wasted effort, for none of the stations have powerful enough short-wave transmission to reach very far into Latin America, even were they not blotted out by German and Italian interference. They are not heard well, if at all, south of Cuba.

In May a bill was proposed to erect a $3,000,000 government short-wave transmitting station in San Diego, with which our government could propagandize Latin America, and the people there have the great privilege of listening to the pearls of wisdom that fall from the lips of Hull and Welles. According to one of the drafters of the bill, Senator William G. McAdoo, the purpose was to promote those two Siamese twins, our commerce and our ideals.

Senator Dennis Chavez of New Mexico, co-author of the bill, suggested that the station should be located in the southwest in order to use the background of culture of a region settled by Spaniards and Portuguese. Just how this would seep over the radio, he didn't explain. It would also remind South America that we were broadcasting from a region stolen from México by force of arms. It apparently made no difference that San Diego is a remote point from most of Latin America, and four thousand miles west of Rio, or that transmission of programs from Washington to California would run up a fantastic bill. Other Congressional measures were introduced. Representative Maury Maverick of Texas naturally wanted the station to be in San Antonio. Representative Green of Florida wanted it in Jacksonville, Representative Cellar of New York wanted it in New York.

The nation, it was argued, needed to be saved—but save it, boys, by rolling the good old pork barrel, said the patriotic solons of our glorious Republic. As Raymond Clapper pointed out in the World-Telegram (May 16, 1938):

"You would think that the location of a radio station would be a matter for engineers to decide. But no, the politicians will decide it, not on engineering principles, but for political reasons."

The Office of Education also wanted control of the station, for the head would thus "become a most important Poo-Bah as editor in chief." The State Department of course wants it so as to reinforce its good-will-munitions program of save the dictatorships in the name of democracy. Somebody certainly will have to decide how much time shall be given to crooners and how much to discussing Latin-American tariffs and to sales talks on democracy and light bulbs.

And, lastly, the control of the broadcasts is also sought by men connected with the special business interests in Latin America. Such companies already have a close tie-up in the ownership of the radio corporations and with the international programs already put out by such private agencies. Among other things, the radio companies feared that if the government set up a station, they would lose control of small local stations which might ask for a hook-up with the federal programs.

Mark Ethridge, President of the National Radio Association, warned the Senate committee considering the matter, that the proposal for a government station was "entirely in disaccord with democratic principles." Maybe he is right, but his motives may not be entirely without self-interest. In any case, the Senate committee listened to a lobby of the radio corporations on the matter and dropped the idea of a government station like a hot potato.

More important than saving us from the dreadful Fascist in Latin America, more important than our endangered national security is the question of private business initiative and profits. More important than either is political log-rolling.

It is perhaps fortunate that conflicting selfishness has stalled the matter, for all this is a wrong-headed departure from traditional American policy. Though all Americans have a sort of fine Christian Endeavor attitude toward the world at large, we have never yet permitted our government to go in for official propagandizing of the heathen. Mr. Welles, they say, has his heart set on a government station. But we should remember that Mr. Welles is somewhat suspect by the Latin-American people. And if our good statesmen talk democracy long and hard enough to the Latin-American people, the latter may actually decide to get rid of their present dictatorships—and the State Department, which has enough griefs and doesn't want any dictatorships upset, would again be charged with meddling in the internal affairs of its neighbors.

In fact, a number of Latin-American diplomats are said to have suggested to the State Department that the Presi-

dent's good-neighbor policy is pretty new, its disinterested-
ness not entirely proven, the certainty of its continuation
under a new administration not at all assured. The Germans and Italians are a whole ocean away and their efforts
are not so alarming, but the United States is next door, and
intensive official propaganda would immediately arouse old
fears of aggression and prick into new life old epithets of
"imperialism."

We have at times been irate over German, Italian and
British propaganda activities in our own country. Foreign
powers are all in the same boat in Latin America. There we
Americans are merely foreigners along with Germans, Japanese and Italians. The southern folk are pretty well fed
up on foreign propaganda, and our coming in on the tail
end of the procession with a blare of drums would be the
last straw. At present they are getting Japanese, Italian,
German, Russian, English, French and Spanish short-wave
broadcasts, and are pretty sick of the jumble.

Of course our dispatches, we claim, are not to be propaganda. Propaganda is only what the other fellow sends out.
Thus recently at India House, 1 Hanover Square, Mr. Frank
D. Mason, Vice-President of the National Broadcasting
Company, which has been handling much of the official or
semi-official United States publicity drive on Latin America,
has stated that broadcasting should never be used as "a
weapon of propaganda." He continued, "In carrying out
this service of broadcasting, none of us, in our international
activities, have any commitment to any ideology, any race,
or any religious creeds. We wish only to serve in holding up
the events of the world through an unblemished mirror,
without distortion."

Our government has stated it will not use propaganda—
the broadcasts will be purely educational. As one Latin-

American critic promptly retorted: "The Colossus of the North has tried every means to rule us. Now it wishes to insure our servility by boring us to death."

As a matter of fact our government broadcasts are larded thick with propaganda. They are a steady drone for the Hull reciprocity policies. Mr. Welles, in a recent propaganda broadcast for our government, told Latin America how evil a thing is economic nationalism, that it creates false prosperity, and endangers peace. This is the rankest sort of propaganda—grossly against the true interests of the Latin-American countries seeking economic independence.

Do we imagine that in the long run Latin America will be less angry at our government, at our propaganda, than we become at loud foreign propaganda dinned in our ears?

To hold up events of the world to the mirror of truth for the benefit of Latin America, I suppose, is a worthy ideal. But no one can help carving the mirror a bit. If we don't want to influence Latin America to accept our way of thinking, if we don't want to get something out of the effort, why all the Hull-abaloo?

Our broadcasts, even if truly educational, inevitably become propaganda for a way of life, the American way of life. They seek a purpose, to create friendship, to sell goods, to bar other foreign competition. They stress democracy. But for Latin America, democracy is still a revolutionary concept, capable of tumbling down governments. To advocate it is propaganda. It is propaganda far more revolutionary there, far more an alien doctrine than either totalitarianism or communism.

5

One instrument of propaganda, on which we have well-nigh a monopoly, and which returns to American coffers as much profit as perhaps any other industry in the field today, is the movies. Here again, it is argued, no element of propaganda enters. Any addict of the movies, with an I.Q. above fourteen years, knows that they reek with propaganda. Even movies, seemingly quite innocuous when carried abroad, immediately assume propaganda importance. Such movies dovetail so well with our mode of life, our opinions, our outlook on all things, that to us they seem truthful in a universal sense. These are usually the least truthful movies. The foreign audience finds itself looking at something entirely alien to its culture, its sentiments and thoughts. To a Latin American, Hollywood movies overflow with propaganda. Frequently just as in murderous and corrupt Chicago or holy blue-nosed Boston, they are suppressed. *The Road Back* and *They Gave Him a Gun*, for instance, were barred in Brazil and Chile.

Since Latin America, the biggest outside cinema market we have, accounts for a very large slice of earnings, much effort is now made to cater to the wishes, opinions and prejudices of the countries to the south. It is no longer possible to have a Mexican villain lest the cinema company lose rich royalties. Other countries feel equally touchy about their citizens. We are now witnessing the amusing fact that all the villains are invariably Americans, but all foreigners are invariably good folk. We will end up by propagandizing ourselves.

6

As do the European powers, we also give out scholarships and professorships. Fully eight years ago, the John Simon Guggenheim Memorial Foundation extended its scholarships to Hispanic America. The Carnegie Foundation allocated funds to the Pan-American Union to bring in professors. A comprehensive program is under way for the exchange of professors and students with all the countries. Hull is pushing it.

We have sent far more official good-will emissaries to Latin America than any other country. A few have blazoned in the headlines such as Hoover, Lindbergh, Morrow, Roosevelt, but many others less heralded and some not heralded at all have played their roles.

The United Fruit Company, the Pan-American Airways, the steamship companies, and other American business organizations have directly or indirectly subsidized many authors to write articles and books on South America. Free fares have caused the number of shallow fly-by-night travelogues of tourist fliers on Pan-American Airways to multiply like a rash on the publishers' lists. I could name at least two books by prominent authors in part the product of free passes on United Fruit steamers. This is a fine thing when it does not impel a writer to distort his conclusions. In the latter case, the efforts should be frankly labeled "Paid advertising;" the arrangement would then be entirely bona fide.

All in all, between private and government agencies—even before we recently began to take special steps—we have a more elaborate system of propaganda built up in Latin America than has any other nation on earth.

Many such activities are not publicized at all, any more than the German government publicizes all its efforts. All the departments of our government are coöperating in the policy of promoting American influence to the south. Even our intelligence departments are hopping about; our own secret agents and spies are busy in many lands.

Recently Secretary Ickes protested to a Congressional Committee against cutting off his budgets for foreign educational travel funds on the ground that this would hamper the important work of the Department in promoting Pan-Americanism. This he said, if also done to other departments, would seriously curtail activities. Our government is carrying on all sorts of secret promotion work to the south.

Secretary Wallace is pushing propaganda in many ways. He considers the Pan-American policy as "the basis of all our foreign policy," and has asked the Senate budgetary committee for funds to establish in Puerto Rico or the Canal Zone a tropical agriculture college, to "permit" southern countries "to become better producers of classes of tropical agricultural products that do not compete with our domestic products."

Even with this kindly assistance, we would hardly recommend that Brazil quit growing cotton or that Argentina, Chile and Perú cease growing wheat and fruit, or that other countries abandon crops necessary for them or providing a profit on the international market. It is the old story of expecting Latin America to forget her own interests in order to be a satellite helpful to the United States.

April 6, Secretary Hull requested Congress to lift the ban on the constitutional provision which prohibits American government employees or officials from accepting "any office or profit or trust" of any sort "from any king, prince or sovereign state," in order that our government might detail experts to South America to aid in engineering work, roads, sanitation, finances, irrigation, fisheries, etc. He based his argument on the beneficial results already resulting from military and naval missions.

The last argument can be discounted. The black, even corrupt record, of such American missions in the past has been exposed by the Nye Senate investigation. To aid in constructive civilizing efforts should not be based upon such improper reasoning. Also such experts would increase the sales of American goods, more important, they tell us, than any other consideration.

But inevitably such missions and such officials have a political significance. Ambassador Guggenheim, during the bloody Machado despotism in Cuba, used his experts to assist that government, which was oppressing and murdering the Cuban people. The same is true whenever we send experts to unpopular and tyrannical South American governments. We are today thus helping to oppress various Latin-American peoples by our aid and sympathy to such regimes. We have become an active—if often unwilling—party in half a dozen countries to gigantic political injustices.

Already the corresponding committee has reported favorably on the Hull proposal. But Congress should pointblank refuse his blanket request. What is more we should pull our naval, military and aviation missions out of Latin America. Permission to American officials to aid foreign governments should be granted only in specific instances and only after the most careful scrutiny. To carry out Hull's wishes would strengthen still further improper alliances we already have with certain South American governments.

More recently the State Department has asked Congress for funds with which to set up two new divisions for improvement of our cultural relations. Actually this money is to be spent not to propagandize Latin America but to propagandize the United States in behalf of State Department policies, and provide canned material for dutiful writers, newspapermen and radio broadcasts.

7

The Roosevelt administration has made some notable gestures toward Latin America. Highly to be applauded as statesmanlike acts were the repeal of the Platt Amendment, which previously made Cuba merely a protectorate, our acceptance of the non-intervention treaties proposed by Latin America, and finally our refusal to be stampeded into bad relations and possible intervention in México because of the taking over of American-owned oil properties.

But after this has been said, there have been grievous mistakes. Increasingly the State Department, at the cost of more important principles, is drifting into a policy that, in the name of good-neighbor treatment, is increasingly unsound, even hypocritical; deeds ever more divergent from utterances.

Our good-neighbor policy rests in great part upon certain falsehoods, misconceptions, and non-existent conditions. Some of these are:

1. *The belief that the Western Hemisphere is a unity, that all countries in it have identical interests, merely because they are in the same part of the world.*

Does France have the same policy as Germany? They have different policies, in part, precisely because they are neighbors.

a. Brazil needs the market of Germany and Japan for her more than 2,000,000 bales of cotton, her manganese, her tea, her iron, her vegetable oils, her excess coffee, just as she needs the United States for a market for her coffee. Her international policies must obey these necessities.

b. Over 35 percent of Argentina's production normally goes to England, which has $2,000,000,000 invested in the country. To England, Germany, Japan, Italy and other countries, Argentina must sell her wheat, cattle, meat, hides, corn, her major products for which there is no market in our country. Her international policy *must* show friendship to England and Italy.

c. Uruguay must sell meat and wheat to England and Germany, and her international policy is oriented accordingly.

d. Chile must sell her iron, copper, nitrates, fruit to Europe as well as the United States.

e. Many Latin-American cultural bonds naturally are strong, and should remain so, with the Latin cultures of Europe. Paris and Madrid and Lisbon are normally the cultural capitals—so far as the outside intellectual influences are concerned—for the various South American countries.

f. The Latin-American countries are more divergent, racially, than many countries in Europe.

g. The economic, social and political interests of México and Argentina are probably more different than those between Finland and Italy.

2. *The belief that the Western Hemisphere is a brotherhood of democracies in contrast to the evil dictatorships of Europe.*

Governments to the south have rarely represented the people less than at present. Some are worse tyrannies than any in Europe, their danger limited merely by their relative weakness in the world scene. In Perú, under Benavides, who set aside an election and seized power in violation of the constitution, and rules without a Congress, the jails are full and hundreds are in exile.

Vargas, to maintain his evil power, has killed wholesale and destroyed all self-government and all civil liberties. Sumner Welles has taken American journalists to task for endangering our friendship with him. Birds of a feather, they say, flock together.

This February, in Rio de Janeiro, Ambassador Caffery presented a vellum-bound book containing a Portuguese translation of Roosevelt's speeches at the Buenos Aires 1936 Peace Conference. The Christmas-like gift carried a dedication "to my friend." I suppose heads of governments and politicians have to make such gestures, but let them not be made—to use a little official eloquence ourselves—by sullying the fair name of Democracy.

President Martínez of Salvador, Ubico of Guatemala, Trujillo of Santo Domingo, and Dictator Batista of Cuba, have waded through blood to get where they are and stay there in defiance of the wishes of the people.

The complexion of the various governments differs widely. But it is pure cocaine-dope to argue that democracy exists in the Western Hemisphere or even the larger part of it. Few of its governments have the slightest basis in democracy.

Josephus Daniels, our Ambassador to México, for whose efforts there I have the highest admiration, stated in lyrical tones on May 6th at Chapel Hill to an academic group interested in foreign relations:

"There is not in the Western Hemisphere any government upholding doctrines of the totalitarian state, no avid eyes on the territories or possessions of their neighbors, no control in any republic by Communists or Fascists or Nazis, no persecution of races."

If only Paradise were that close!

3. *The belief that the Western nations are peace-loving as opposed to the war-thirsty nations of Europe.*

Recent wars and recent international injustices have shaken the southern continent time and again. In the last few years we have seen any number of near-wars in Central America and to the south; Tacna-Arica, Leticia, the Cuyamel-United Fruit-Guatemala-Honduras imbroglio in Central America, and others less publicized. Even while Roosevelt was uttering these wrong platitudes, Dictator Trujillo, in the Dominican Republic, was butchering 12,000 peaceable Haitians—men, women, children and babes. Nicaragua and Honduras almost went to war over a postage stamp. Other troubles were brewing and are still brewing along with new ones. Never before have the southern countries put out so much on armaments.

The Chaco War in South America, only just ended, was one of the bloodiest on record.

Argentine power politics prolonged it, and keeps the peace terms still unsettled in order to bring both countries under her influence as definitely as we control Cuba, or France controls Morocco. At this moment certain official elements in Argentina are charged with secretly plotting the future seizure of Brazilian iron deposits. Ubico of Guatemala is building up war forces and dreaming of conquest—the unification of Central America by force.

Balance of Power intrigues threaten to tear the southern continent assunder.

4. *We are showing friendship to the governments, not to the people of Latin America.*

We are helping to support tyrannies of the same brutal sort as those we cry out against in Europe. Roosevelt in his Chicago speech suddenly decided to quarantine aggressor nations. Retorted a Peruvian writer: "How about quarantining equally irresponsible and menacing nations in South America?"

Haya de la Torre, one of the outstanding leaders of South America, has said, in *La Nueva Democracia:*

"If, in the United States, there is a government that seriously looks after the welfare of the people, i.e., democracy, its outlook should not be one for the United States and different for Indo-America. It is not proper to defend democracy in the forty-eight American states and ignore it in the twenty Indo-American states, in the name of non-intervention.

"As a matter of fact intervention has never ceased . . . even without sending marines. They [the United States] intervene morally and sometimes merely negatively, keeping silent when a tyrant of those regions tramples on the principles and rights that are above all national frontiers, because they are human and universal. Who remains silent, indorses.

"It is necessary that the United States condemn such governments in Latin America in the same manner that it has just condemned the Fascist nations of Europe.

"Among our people the good-neighbor policy is looked on dubiously."

It is perhaps no business of the United States, though we have often made it our business, what kind of governments South America may have. But certainly we do not need to scrape and bow to governments which are the shame of the continents, to send them money, offer to lend them battleships, sell them armaments, send them naval missions to help them keep down the people. We are playing the game with petty brutal minorities temporarily in power rather than with the people of Latin America.

Futuro, a semi-official labor organ of México, after discussing Sumner Welles' "imperialist" policy in Cuba and elsewhere, has this to say of his support of Vargas of Brazil: "It is interesting to note how Sumner Welles places more value, much more, on the horizontal solidarity which welds all the rich exploiters of the earth that give substance and force to the great 'Fascist International' than to the Monroe Doctrine itself, a vertical concept which seeks to circumscribe the imperialist sphere of hegemony."

Sumner Welles, the magazine continues, has acted the same as Eden and Chamberlain, "mouthpieces for British Capitalism." When Fascist activities needed to violate English "freedom of the seas" to fight Spanish democracy, "they merely had to let the English imperialists choose between the freedom of the seas and their tender sympathy for Hitler and Mussolini."

Lombardo Toledano, head of the Mexican labor movement, thus derided Roosevelt's Pan-American conference. "When the Chaco War was under way, no danger was considered imminent for those countries, but now that it is over Mr. Roosevelt sees a danger to peace in this hemisphere?" What is the nature of the danger? "Everybody knows it may be a war between imperialistic elements seeking their economic rehabilitation or to maintain and develop their privileges in the world markets.

"The United States intervened in the last European war to convert its debts into credits." The Latin-American countries which entered in "obedience" to the United States, "were ignored at the peace conference. . . .

"Now as a new war appears imminent," he continued, "the United States urges us to be prepared to strengthen her position and consolidate her influence in this rich and virgin portion of the planet. The theme of her industrial leaders, and bankers—America for the United States—may be finally a reality."

The only basic aim, he insisted, is "complete economic and political submission of the Latin-American nations to Yankee imperialism."

If the oppressed people of Latin America could speak at this moment—their newspapers, their political rights, their means of expression are everywhere suppressed—they would cry out a mighty protest at the falseness of our good-will protestations; a mighty curse against us would rise up from many parts of the two continents.

5. *Our belief Latin America loves us because we are now friendly instead of aggressive, that whenever we wish it, Latin America should be glad to love us.*

Latin America's interests are today varied and international. Only by force or political and economic pressure does she bow specifically to our will. The southern folk consider us, as we do them in our more sober moments, as foreigners to whom they owe nothing except for value received.

Even the reactionary governments there that apparently so favor us, do not see the salvation of the Western Hemisphere or their own salvation as residing in putting themselves under our direction and tutelage. They are willing and glad to be friends with us, but not to lose their European and Oriental friends by doing so.

Latin Americans feel that since their countries gained independence, they have been more endangered by the United States than any other power.

The United States has meddled more in their internal affairs, has committed more aggressions, has seized more territory by force. The southern folk have no illusions that the European powers would be more generous, but they feel that their best safety lies in a system of checks and balances between the various investing and trading powers, to play one against the other. This they are doing, however nicely they respond to Roosevelt's hazy revivalist phraseology.

The Latin-American countries are under no obligation to be "democratic," to trade exclusively with us, to follow our political pattern, to follow our foreign policy rather than their own. They are not obliged to think of any interests except their own. It is for them to decide whether they want Japanese or German goods instead of ours. In fact the competition of the various powers greatly benefits them.

Alexander Hamilton ("Publius"), the father of our constitution, said in the XI Federalist paper:

"By prohibitory regulations extending, at the same time throughout our States, we may oblige foreign countries to bid against each other for the privileges of our market . . . Suppose, for instance, we had a government in America, capable of excluding Great Britain . . . from all our ports . . . Would it not enable us to negotiate, with the fairest prospect of success, for commercial privileges . . . ?"

Why should we Americans expect Latin America, now in a somewhat analogous position to the Thirteen Colonies, not to use its bargaining power to improve its position with us by dealing with Europe and Japan and vice versa? The statesmen of the south are doing just that. They would be simple-minded fools if they didn't.

"The expansion of commercial relations," said Puig Casauranc at the Pan-American conference in Montevideo, "should not and cannot be sought on a basis of emotion; . . . only on the basis of real and mutual advantages."

6. *The belief that, as Admiral Leahy stated, we have to have a navy to protect the whole continent and uphold the Monroe Doctrine.*

First of all, Admiral Leahy should keep his nose out of foreign political policies and tend to his assigned job of creating an efficient navy and providing information how to bring that about.

His remarks called forth a declaration from the national convention of the Hispanic Fi Iota Alfa in Troy, New York: "Until Hispanic America is united, the Monroe Doctrine will be an imposition by force which we cannot with dignity accept, and Pan-Americanism will continue to be considered by the people of Hispanic America one more instrument of penetration. . . ."

The Monroe Doctrine has never been accepted in principle by Latin-American nations. For us it is a totem pole to dance around. In Hispanic America it is considered a collar of servitude.

If we wish to protect the investments of our bankers and secure needed resources in Latin America that is one thing. But the Latin-American countries have no illusions that the Monroe Doctrine is primarily to protect her. In the past the Monroe Doctrine has cost them land, territory, wealth and independence.

The nations to the south, on the way to standing on their own feet, resent our paternalism, resent our acting as spokesman for two continents.

The Monroe Doctrine is in a definite twilight stage, still dimly significant, already half gone. If we persist in parading it, quite likely we will ere long find some of those we are supposedly protecting have allied themselves with our enemies, have joined with European powers against us.

Welles, who on May 5, 1938, declared that "our fellow citizens will insist that their government be prepared to coöperate with the other American Republics, should it become necessary at any time to repel acts of aggression through which any non-American power or powers may attempt to acquire domination over any portion of the Western Hemisphere."

But the problem in Latin America is no longer to protect the various countries there against armed invasion from Europe—not likely to happen—but to prevent a repetition of the technique used in Spain of sub rosa intervention under the guise of neutrality. Such intervention could easily pay complete outward respect for the Monroe Doctrine. We have agreed ourselves not to intervene by armed force in a Latin-American country. But we have no assurance that other countries will not clandestinely do so. To be consistent with our policy in Spain, we would have to assume a fake neutrality position.

And if a Latin-American government of Fascist or military complexion, faced with revolt, asks for aid from Germany and Italy, and the latter sell her munitions and send "volunteers" and experts—they are doing it right now—there is nothing in international law or the Monroe Doctrine to stop them. We ourselves have properly declared that the Latin-American governments are sovereign, quite free to carry on their own foreign relations. The Monroe Doctrine does not cover such contingencies at all.

Far more likely than our being called upon to defend Latin America we shall be required to stay neutral or to back one set of Latin-American governments against another set, and both sets allied with one or another European nation.

7. *The idea that the New World should form an economic and political alliance independent from and against the rest of the world.*

This is the goal sought by Roosevelt in proposing his neutrality and embargo ideas at Buenos Aires. It is the goal he proposes to seek at the forthcoming Pan-American conference in Lima. It would seek to put the resources and economic and political power of Latin America at the disposal of the United States.

However much temporary advantage we might gain from such a sprawling, impractical and anti-progressive step, in the long run the dangers to peace and a sound world system would be greatly increased. Under our leadership the Latin-American countries would be much more likely to be dragged toward war. It would expose them to attacks from European nations to which they are not now exposed. It would lead to endless conflicts with the rest of the world. Indeed it would become an absolute necessity for European empires to smash through such a closed-door economic set-up, by force of arms if no other alternative presented itself. It is an attempt at a new kind of imperialism. If isolation is impossible for the United States, it is equally impossible for the Western Hemisphere as a whole, and would prove an even greater war-provoking policy.

This program, too, also runs counter to the hypothesis of the Hull trade drive. But this policy mayhap explains, despite that fact, our eager effort to make reciprocity treaties, particularly with Hispanic America.

In connection with such a proposed treaty with Colombia, *El Tiempo* of Bogotá wrote as early as September, 1933:

"In questions of international commerce, the predominant motive is not always one of good-will.

"These considerations move us to infer that perhaps what is being attempted [by the United States] is to initiate an American get-together movement for the purpose of isolating these nations [of Latin America] commercially and forming with them a league of interests that will virtually separate them from Europe in the field of the international exchange of products. Colombia has been chosen to begin with, in order to establish an easy precedent . . . But as the consequences of such a step must needs have serious international repercussions, we believe that it is necessary to devote to the negotiations started in Washington for the celebration of a commercial treaty, an attention at once keen, unsleeping and constant."

8

1. *Our government should at once get out of the propaganda business in foreign lands.*

The Latin-American countries, to the extent that they restrict foreign government propaganda, should also restrict ours.

The heavily weighted official nature of our propaganda is increasing Latin America's suspicions of our good intentions. Of all the men in the State Department, Welles is best known to Latin America for his record in Haiti, Cuba, Colombia and elsewhere, and he does not command their confidence. Even Goebbels of Germany or the Italian official radio stations are not so clumsily blundering with their propaganda. They get in plenty of Fascist and Nazi doctrine, but do not clutter up the air with such obvious official mouthpiece speeches. The too frequent addresses by certain State Department officials who have acquired an unsavory name to the south, are harmful.

2. *Our government should quit helping out in the dirty armament business.*

The arms thus sold are likely, one of these fair days, to kill our own citizens. We have no assurances that the battleships we have sold to Brazil, the planes we have sold to Argentina, the munitions we have sold to Perú, will not eventually be turned against us. Our merchants constantly declare they do not want government aid, that they want merely to paddle their own canoes. Then why should we especially devote the energies of so many departments to promoting munitions sales, of all things?

One of the topics set to be discussed at the Pan-American conference this year in Lima is "moral disarmament." Morals, in Latin-American political and international relationships, despite fine words and false-front treaties, have been pretty well disarmed. How about physical disarmament? We know why that is not being discussed and can't be discussed.

"Moral disarmament." Just sweet Hull-abaloo! Some day the world's politicians are going to sink and suffocate in the mire of their own perfume.

3. *We should at once recall our naval and army missions home from Brazil and Perú and Guatemala, our air mission home from Argentina.*

They have no proper business there. They are helping unpopular governments, which means they stand against the people. They are helping our munitions venders. They are helping oppress the peoples of those countries.

4. *We should get rid of our official language of patronizing condescension and superiority.*

Mr. Hull recently said that we could not expect the South American countries immediately to restrict their trade and relationships with European countries. Suppose an Argentine politician were suddenly to come forth with a statement: "We do not expect the United States to break off her trade and other relations with England and Japan immediately, that will have to be a gradual process of adjustment." We'd think he was plain nuts.

Mr. Roosevelt recently spoke in the name of all the

twenty-one countries of the Western Hemisphere. By what right? By what authorization? However lofty his sentiments, he should know that Latin-American countries secretly or openly resent such paternalism.

That indefatigable heresy-hunter, Congressman Samuel Dickstein, spoke heatedly in Congress on April 19th about Nazi propaganda in Brazil, stating that "it was the duty of the United States to prevent the propagation of this sickness."

Maverick of Texas has made similar declarations.

It would seem this is Brazil's business, not ours. Humorously enough the very day Dickstein spoke, Vargas was putting into effect Nazi-like decrees against the Integralista Nazis and against the Germans in Brazil.

9

The only possibility for sound American influence in Latin America is to stand squarely with the democratic and progressive forces of those countries. We can gain nothing by imitating the political tactics of the Fascist powers, though we might learn something in the field of economics. We can gain nothing of permanence by trying to bid against Germany for influence with a semi-Fascist government in Brazil that temporarily exists in defiance of the will of the people. Why should we go around licking the boots of dictators? Or copying their methods?

In the long run we will gain by the downfall of feudal regimes in Latin America, whatever the temporary loss to American property. We will gain by such economic strengthening of the Latin-American countries. We will gain by progressive measures to raise the standards of the people, the large majority of whom are not now purchasers of world goods but who can be converted into one of the largest mass markets in the world. In that great German-United States democratic-Nazi protectorate known as Brazil, the average *monthly* factory wage, according to official figures, is $11.05. How much American goods can we hope to sell to the Brazilian masses?

Where free peoples exist we shall not have to worry much about the intrigues of foreign reactionary powers to control them. We shall always have headaches when our neighbors are ruled by dictators of the present brand. To make improper deals with them is to write our strength in water.

In those few countries where the people have a right to express their opinions, anti-Nazi and anti-Fascist sentiments have swayed the people and their governments. Boycotts have been staged. Active curbs have been created. And yet in México, most democratic of them all, we are losing out rapidly. We are losing out because our oil companies and a few stiff-necked gentlemen won't talk over the price of their properties. We are losing out because we won't let México sell her oil in the United States. We are losing out because we stopped silver purchases and pushed down the price as a punitive action to injure México. But we sedulously court Brazil, one of the worst dictatorships on the continent. Mr. Welles, you remind us all too unpleasantly of Mr. Chamberlain, whom you so greatly admire.

10

We are in a further dilemma, of course, because the powerful American corporations in Latin America are making close deals with the Fascist powers. For immediate dollar profits, they are promoting Fascist trade. Our armament concerns are dividing up the market with the Fascist countries, letting Germany dominate in some countries, Italy in others. With them our merchants of death are sharing markets. They are sharing orders. They scramble for concessions, but they respect each other's territory and merely take a commission on the business. No patriotism and no frontiers deter our merchants of death.

The I. T. and T., through its subsidiary All-American Cables, on May 9th inaugurated a new direct super-radio circuit between South America and Rome, and on May 16th solemnly dedicated another with Berlin. This directly facilitates Nazi and Fascist penetration and propaganda. It is well to remember that the head of I. T. and T. is also head of the semi-official Pan-American Society and patron of the Pan-American Students' League, that he is busy promoting radio broadcasts to counteract Fascist propaganda while equally busy making money out of that propaganda.

Either Nazi and Fascist penetration is perfectly legitimate and our government should waste no time sending out counter propaganda, or it is not. If American business is not alarmed, why should our State Department work itself up into such a lather to protect American business?

Our whole Latin-American policy is based on the postulate of protecting American trade and business interests. But many of those interests have heavy deals with the very nations and the very business firms of governments against which the American taxpayer is supposed to shell out money to protect American business. American business to the south is getting heavy orders from German munitions firms. Our State Department combats Nazi trade and propaganda and works overtime to preserve the peace menaced by all these undercover American business arrangements. Our State Department to do this must support tyrannical

South American governments at the expense of the people tyrannized over.

It is all a game of button-button-who's-got-the-button. The button seems to be the profits of this year's balance sheet. This gives us no time to wipe the drops off our nose.

It is not so childishly simple as this either. As elsewhere in the world, our interests in Latin America are being increasingly caught between the nut-cracker of the extreme left and right trends. The seriousness of this is that our officials are not at all interested in democracy abroad. We are not taking a brave stand for democracy and peace. Far from it.

In Latin America we are not supporting the forces of democracy and freedom any more than we are in Spain. We are actively supporting Fascist trends, under the noble cloak of brave words about freedom, democracy and international justice. Those sleek words no longer have meaning in connection with our actual policy. We are merely playing a conventional game of power politics on the southern continent. Would we play it better if we weren't such arrant hypocrites?

CHAPTER

XI

Argentina's Imperialism

A SUNDAY afternoon in February, under the blazing mid-summer sun of the great city of Buenos Aires, the new President of Argentina, Roberto M. Ortiz, was escorted to the National Palace by a squadron of San Martín mounted guards. In the breezeless day, the blue and gold pennants on their long lances drooped slightly. Overhead circled the Argentine air force, over 100 American- and Italian-built planes. With them manoeuvred the six American army bombers that had swept down from Miami and over the sky-flung Andes to take part in the inaugural ceremonies.

This flight of American war planes was in imitation of the numerous Italian mass flights across the South Atlantic during the past half dozen years, an attempt to outsmart the Fascisti at their own game. It is a definite bid for Argentine friendship—or at least for orders for airplanes and munitions.

A prominent Argentinean writer scanned the skies. "Those American bombers from so far away—why do they point their guns at us? Do they come as a threat or for friendship?"

"Both, my friend," replied his companion.

"We live in a degenerate world," replied the other.

"Among more enlightened savages, it is customary to leave your guns behind you, when you come in friendship."

The bid for Argentine friendship is part of Roosevelt's policy, as he expressed it to President Ortiz, of "a constructive and fruitful . . . inter-American coöperation." This can hardly mean two nations just smiling at each other in a friendly fashion. Nations aren't sixteen-year-old sweethearts. Roosevelt has not told us, but it was to be presumed that we should eventually learn whether all this grandiose phraseology, all the fuss and feathers meant the promotion of trade, or to save American investments, or a plan for new loans, or a political alliance, or—as the embattled planes might suggest—a defensive war alliance. However, both the United States and Argentina are pledged to no entangling alliances.

As I write this, part of the answer has already been vouchsafed. Apparently in good part it was a build-up for the justification of sending American army officers down to Argentina to train the Argentine air force. We are thus helping to promote a type of Argentine imperialism that scarcely corresponds to the lofty doctrines of our President. We are helping to promote the Black League of Latin America.

Who is Señor Ortiz? What does he propose?

The new Dictator-President is a powerful-set man, slightly corpulent, with large ears, big smudge eye-brows and puffy lids over stern black eyes, a wide, full, but firm mouth in a wide face, and a bulldog jaw. At least one of his ancestors came from the Quiché highlanders and bequeathed him a mighty nose, with enormous nostrils that plunge up high, without any dip between the eyes, into a broad forehead. He comes from a well-to-do land-owning family and dresses like a very sober businessman, which he is, being worth over four million dollars in his own right.

A lawyer, he has risen to his present high post, not as an army officer as is customary, but through politics, his own wealth and Big Business connections. He has been an attorney for some of the largest British corporations in Argentina, and is very close to British and Italian interests.

In 1918, he was elected a member of the Buenos Aires Ayuntamiento, or City Council, on the liberal ticket of the Radical Civic Union, under the leadership of President Hipólito Irigoyen, which for thirty years provided Argentina with its most enlightened, democratic government. Later Ortiz was appointed to the National Chamber of Deputies, where he specialized in financial affairs.

In 1929, depression hit Argentina, a sharp financial crisis. The government of President Irigoyen took severe measures to combat it, measures which promptly angered the large proprietors, feudal, military and ecclesiastical elements, and also British capital. A typical military puppet of these interests, General José F. Uriburú, in 1930 overthrew the constitutional government of Irigoyen by armed force and commenced a reign of terror against the people's party.

Ortiz—today's hero of our tale—thereupon deserted his liberalism, and his party, leaving his political friends quite in the lurch. A good opportunist, he climbed upon the military band wagon.

Uriburú outlawed the candidate of the majority Civic Union Party, broke it with violence, and with the army and newly organized Fascist groups, put Agustín P. Justo into power with a typical machine-gun election. This military reactionary coup and subsequent fake plebiscite shattered a long tradition of peace and democracy. Democratically elected governors were ousted and replaced by appointees, mostly Fascist.

Under the new totalitarian regime, Ortiz became Min-

ister of Public Works. In conjunction with foreign concessionaires, he further developed the harbor facilities of
Buenos Aires and promoted road-building—a trunk road
through Mendoza over into the Andes, another down to
the southern lakes region, the building of large irrigation
dams. These deals made Ortiz a very wealthy man. He fig-
ured more importantly in the councils of the military, Conservative and Fascist clique that had seized power.

More recently Ortiz became Minister of Finance. He
was a wizard. He was instrumental in refunding Argentina's
debt by means of domestic loans at a lower interest rate.
In one year the debt to the United States was reduced
from $258,000,000 to $153,000,000, a phenomenal achievement, and in line with Ortiz' program of nationalistic autonomy.

He was promptly picked by the army ring and a small
group of plantation owners and industrialists, the new
"Concordia" group of Conservatives, Fascists, and Renegade Radical Civil Unionists to become candidate at the
September last elections. He did not have to campaign
much; the army tended to that.

But although the Civic Union Party had been kept down
by military force and sporadic terrorism for seven years, it
still enjoyed the confidence of the people. Though practically outlawed, unable to function at all in the rural
districts, it presented as its candidate, ex-President Marcelo T. de Alvear, a man of very high caliber, who had
been driven into exile by Uriburú and Justo, not even allowed to run at all six years before. Now, in this recent
election, many of the campaigners and candidates of the
Civic Union Party were threatened, maltreated and jailed.
La Critica, one of Buenos Aires' largest dailies, with nearly
a million circulation, which supported Alvear, was tempo-

rarily suppressed, along with other opposition papers. The day before the elections the police concocted a fake tale of a presidential assassination plot and used it as a pretext to discredit and jail political opponents.

In spite of all this coercion, in spite of the fact that the Ortiz group and the army counted the ballots, Alvear *polled a majority of the popular vote.* But partly through fraudulent manipulation of the electoral college, Ortiz was named President—against the majority will of the people. So great was ill-feeling, so obviously was the government outvoted, that congressional, local and provincial elections, supposed to have taken place in January, were illegally and arbitrarily postponed until doubtful State governors could be set aside by military interventors, control perfected, and a steam-roller vote for the ruling Concordia-Conservative army party guaranteed—in short, a semi-Nazi election.

Thus Ortiz heads a totalitarian regime, largely defiant of the will of the people, not in the slightest democratic. However—along with a warning to political leaders as to the kind of doctrines they should not support, a pledge to build up the armed forces, to run a stern government—he expressed a great belief in democracy, still does.

It was on the basis of these inaugural statements that Secretary of State Hull generously praised Ortiz, declaring that his speech was an "inspiration" and eloquently lauded the new dictator for his "faith in the preservation of democratic institutions."

Hull at least made a noble effort to sell the Ortiz administration to the American people as a democratic regime. Undoubtedly this revealed Hull's high-minded determination to promote inter-American justice and peace.

For although Ortiz had been put in by chantage and

army force to head a totalitarian government, and as a civilian front for military elements, he is no mere puppet. The new Dictator-President is remarkably capable. It is he who has been behind most of the program of the last six years of national planning, a species of economic self-sufficiency and nationalism, based on Big Business prerogatives. Ortiz handled the refunding of the national debt and was prominent in the organization sometime previously of the new national-owned Central Bank, the gold reserves of which at present are well over 100 percent, though legally they need be but 25 percent. Fortunately fine crops, with the exception of last year, have given Argentina a long period of economic recovery.

Ortiz has been close to the Argentine Industrial Union—a Big Business group of Buenos Aires—and, with Senator Sánchez Sorondo and others, worked out a far-reaching plan for finances, taxation, trade, agriculture and industry. This plan, providing for a decrease of Argentina's dependency on foreign trade, adopted the made-in-England slogan of buy from them who buy from us, imposed rigid controls on exchange operations, established strict governmental control of trade, and in secret was laying the ground for future imperialistic invasion of Brazil.

Undoubtedly Secretary Hull is anxious to add another reciprocal trade treaty feather to his cap, something that Argentina, despite all sorts of blandishments, has long resisted. But such a treaty would mean the junking of Argentina's whole scheme of recovery. As the latter plan is dear to Ortiz' heart, it is doubtful whether he will change the previous policy. If he yields to Hull's desires, it is doubtful whether such a treaty would be any more faithfully observed than similar ones have been in Brazil and Colombia.

Argentina has other objectives—and they are not those of Mr. Hull, nor of peace, nor of following American leadership.

2

The shift in emphasis in our South American relations from Brazil to Argentina—traditionally hostile to us—is epochal. In large part it has been promoted by Sumner Welles who, when Ambassador to Argentina, became "enamored of the fine manners of the aristocratic Argentine land-holding class"—I quote a member of the State Department. As Brazil has fallen more and more into the clutches of Germany and Italy, to that extent we have sought to move closer to Argentina. But the United States still has a difficult task if arrangements with Argentina are to go beyond mere polite remarks of friendship.

First of all, British influence is overwhelmingly predominant there. No serious international diplomatic move is ever made without consultation with British interests. It is generally recognized that it was the fine hand of Great Britain that caused the failure of Roosevelt's neutrality and embargo plans at the last special inter-American conference held in Buenos Aires. Friendship with the United States, by the very economic facts of the case, will have to be conditioned by Argentina's close ties with Britain. Great Britain's investments there, over $2,000,000,000, are three times as great as ours. England customarily takes nearly 40 percent of Argentina's products; we take but 13 percent and often less, this year probably not more than 7 percent. We cannot hope to play other than second fiddle in Argentina until we can buy more Argentine goods—which we don't need.

Will Rogers once remarked that Argentina exports wheat

and gigolos, that we get the gigolos but we ought to get the wheat. As a matter of fact we don't need either. We love our sacred family, and we have more wheat than we can sell. So it is with most of Argentina's products.

Argentina's subservience to English diplomacy means that many of Argentina's attitudes are similar to those of England, and the new Chamberlain line-up with Italy will have great influence in the southern country. Argentina is really part of the queer English-Italian axis, not of the Washington-all-points-south axis.

Another basic pattern of Argentine policy is friendship to Italy. Over two million Italians have emigrated to Argentina. Many of them are wealthy; they exercise great economic influence. A large part of the population has Italian blood. Ortiz' new Foreign Minister, José Maria Cantilo, has been Argentina's Ambassador to Rome the past five years, and his new cabinet appointment is a direct concession to the new British-Italian combination. When recently he left Rome to take up his new post, he was fêted by all the Fascist big-wigs, with significant words as to the future role of Argentina in world affairs.

A third traditional pattern of Argentine policy is "continental solidarity," which Ortiz mentioned and for which Hull lavished him with praise. But "continental solidarity" used in Argentine diplomatic lingo for a long time, does not conform to Washington's ideas on the matter. It means specifically Argentine hegemony in South America, a definite sphere of influence policy similar to that of the United States in the Caribbean. It does not mean solidarity of the two continents, of the Western Hemisphere; it means direct Argentine domination over Uruguay, Paraguay, and since the Chaco War, economic penetration of Bolivia by Argentine capital. Traditionally it included an alliance with

Perú, and bonds are again being strengthened there. Perú, too, is now in good measure, part of the Italian-British axis.

The new dictator of Argentina stands four-square on these long-standing policies. In addition he has announced a big armament program, in part a military policy to keep the dissatisfied people down, of course in the most democratic fashion. Our new friendship with Argentina quite likely will enable us to sell a few more airplanes and munitions. But that will merely mean that the trade quota Argentina allots us will be so used up that other more legitimate trade products will be barred. By selling more munitions we of course argue that we are furthering our broad policy of peace in South America. We are also helping to maintain a non-popular totalitarian regime. If a truly popular regime should arise in Argentina it might likely be very resentful toward us.

3

Argentina is a great country, a wealthy country, a powerful country. The Pampas, next to the Mississippi Valley, represents the greatest stretch of level prairie anywhere in the Western Hemisphere. Like the Mississippi, it lies mostly in the cool temperate zone, though it is also favored by reaching back into the tropics, so that eventually it can produce more varied products than even the Mississippi, practically all the agricultural products now utilized by man.

Though, in area, only a third the size of the United States, nevertheless Argentina is five times the area of France, twenty times the area of England; it is one of the largest countries in the world. Certain years, it has exported more wheat than the United States and Canada combined.

It exports three-fourths of the world's corn which enters into international trade. It exports more wool than any country except the continent of Australia. It leads the world in shipments of cattle and hides. It produces more linseed than the United States. It is expanding its cotton and sugar industries; is one of the leading tobacco-producing countries of Latin America. It is the sixth wine-producing country in the world. It has twenty-five million acres under alfalfa alone.

This remarkable economic development has been achieved with a population of only 13,000,000 people. Though Buenos Aires is one of the great cities of the world, the third largest on the two western continents, the country is still very sparsely settled. Though the unequal distribution of wealth imposes grave social injustices which weaken the general social fabric, Argentina has the largest per capita trade of any large country in the world.

There are certain anomalies in this situation. In the nature of its products and the character of its development, Argentina in many ways is at the stage of development of the United States prior to the Spanish-American War. Even far more than the United States was then, it is predominantly an agricultural country. Some great textile and small iron factories have arisen, but as yet, in nearly all manufacturing lines, despite a new policy of economic nationalism, the production is inadequate to supply even Argentina's domestic needs, let alone throw her, except for a few specialized items, into the export trade. Argentina definitely lacks certain metals and other raw materials for self-sufficing manufacturing.

Another similarity to the United States, some thirty or so years ago, is that Argentina feeling herself to be wealthy, relatively prosperous and powerful, now has the youthful impulse of military and geographic expansion. In the next few years this imperialistic urge is likely to shatter the peace of South America.

Another anomaly of Argentina's growth is that, while the country is not particularly industrialized, its agricultural development obeys the laws of modern industrialization. More than any great agricultural empire in the past, Argentina has had available a greater body of scientific, technical and mechanized farm methods; and more than any other great agricultural empire in the past, she has had a greater market for her products.

Still another anomaly is that Argentina, though predominantly agricultural, has found herself in a world of jarring imperialisms, of greedy power-politics, and, though not an industrialized nation, is rapidly building up a powerful national military machine, the strongest army, the strongest navy, the strongest air force on the southern continent. Living in a world of power-politics, Argentina, instead of attempting to build up true continental solidarity, is frantically imbued with the cheap envy of trying to surpass vast Brazil, to assume not only the leadership, but the political, military and economic overlordship of the southern continent. With respect to all her near neighbors, she has utilized the same type of Machiavelian power-politics, of greed, of balance of power, of intrigue, which has made of Europe such a hornet's nest. In other words, Argentina, though having an agrarian economy, is decidedly imperialistic.

An anomaly of this situation is that Argentina, despite her power-politics and imperialism, is still semi-colonial. Over $2,000,000,000 of British capital are invested there; about $700,000,000 of American capital; an enormous amount of Italian, French, German money. And while

Argentina can use a great deal of capital, in fact needs still more capital, at various times it has had a temporary surfeit beyond all possible need for the immediate advancement of the cattle-range and wheat farming. At such times this capital has reached out into Paraguay, Uruguay, Bolivia, even into southern Brazil, Perú and Ecuador. Here again is a phenomenon similar to that which already characterized the economics of the United States prior to the Spanish-American War.

4

On the far southern end of the continent, Argentina is in a geographic central position somewhat analogous to that of Germany in Europe. Turn the European map upside down and imagine the Seine, the Danube, the great rivers of Central Europe, all finding their outlet through Germany into the North Sea, and you will then appreciate that the tensions on the Old World Continent not only would be even more terrible than they are, but that Germany's bargaining position would be even stronger.

Thus from a large part of southern Brazil—the rich states of Rio Grande do Sul, Santa Catharina (with its big mineral deposits), much of São Paulo, Paraná and above that the southern half of Matto Grosso region—the rivers all drain into the Plata near Buenos Aires. There flow the Taquary, the Paraná, the Iguasú, the Uruguay, the Paraguay, the Paranahyba, the Pilcomaya rivers—all mighty streams—their vast fan-like net of tributaries cover what is today the wealthiest part of Brazil.

The life of Paraguay is compassed by the three mighty rivers, the Paraná, Paraguay and Pilcomaya, all of which converge upon Buenos Aires. Paraguay also is bottled up by Argentina's control.

While Bolivia's rivers mostly flow into the Amazon, in that direction lie the densest jungles of the continent, a vast undeveloped region, and even if these barriers should be surmounted, the distance to the Atlantic would still be thousands of miles. Bolivia's normal outlet to the Atlantic is through Argentina and Paraguay; and to say Paraguay, is also to say Argentina.

Here then are the makings of a first-class struggle for empire and power, and with such cock-eyed political boundaries as exist in that portion of South America, this struggle is as inevitable as the fall of a dead leaf in an autumn wind. All the peace talk of Washington, all the peace talk of Argentina and Brazil, are meaningless in the face of the economic and geographic realities of the situation.

Some witty Frenchman said the Chaco War reminded him of two bald men fighting for a comb. But the Chaco is today the frontier of the continent, the new zone of settlement and expansion, the clashing goal of four nations.

When our settlers pushed from the Old Northwest, from Illinois and Ohio, on into Minnesota and the Dakotas, the phenomenon was utterly remote from Europe, of little significance. Now Europe well knows that the struggle for the Mississippi Valley was the most important fact in the world affairs of that day, one of the momentous events of all man's history.

Today, we feel equally remote from the Chaco, but perhaps half a century hence, the settlement and control of that area will prove far more important in the new balance of world affairs than all the present fretful struggles of a dying Europe. Hitler, looked at from the perspective of centuries, is a drop in the bucket compared to the fateful tide of Chaco events.

With modifications, we have other parallels in all this southern jealousy in our own earlier westward movement. Thus Buenos Aires becomes the New Orleans of the southern half of the southern continent, the outlet for a vast wealthy agricultural region, a region which eventually, like Ohio and Pennsylvania and Illinois, will also be the great manufacturing world of the south. Imagine then that the building of the Erie Canal and our trans-Appalachian railroads had been delayed half a century, that instead of a port weakly held by far-off European powers, a strong nation—far stronger than the Thirteen Colonies—had sat on the mouth of the Mississippi, that New Orleans had advanced to the position of the largest and wealthiest city of North America.

The Westward expansion of the United States might have been an entirely different story; war might have been our meed much sooner. More than one statesman, though loving our Union, declared that in the last analysis, provided Spain and later France were not cleared out of the mouth of the Mississippi, all the hardy Middle Western Americans would prefer to be under the Spanish or French flag than under the Stars and Stripes. The economic life of our Western settlers, their very existence, depended upon belonging to the same nation that controlled the mouth of the Mississippi.

Imagine further that the west bank of the Mississippi, up to about St. Louis, was controlled by the same strong nation that held the mouth.

The result would have been war. It would have meant that the strong nation at the mouth of the Mississippi would most likely have reached out and taken the rest of the valley, while the Thirteen Colonies remained a smaller nation on the fringe of the Atlantic.

But in the case of Argentina, Brazil is also powerful. Similar forces are being set in motion to that which opened up the Erie Canal and the railroads, but they come late. Argentina has a far head start.

Here then are the seeds of future war in South America; in my opinion, one not far distant; war which will see meddling by European powers, if necessary, under the guise of non-intervention. Not merely meddling: both countries will inevitably seek European alliances.

Today, the United States, along with the European powers, while talking peace, is busy arming the nations concerned at a greater rate than ever, sowing for that grim day of reaping.

5

Still another factor is influencing Argentina. The country lacks mineral deposits. It has very little coal and iron. Brazil has fine deposits of both. The future of Argentina's mighty agricultural empire is in doubt. In our own country, Wallace has stated—and he is right—that we can never hope to recover our old position in the world market for our farm products. All over the world the movement toward national agrarian self-sufficiency proceeds apace. Almost everywhere there is a surfeit of agricultural products. With the new mighty strides in scientific knowledge and chemical agriculture, the future for any nation depending on agricultural export looms still darker.

For ten years now Argentina has been working on a program of greater economic self-sufficiency. This road seems uncertain unless she can be assured of certain vital mineral resources. Part of the goal of such self-sufficiency is precisely to secure such resources.

Furthermore—though Argentina has long been a spearhead for England in Latin-American affairs, and is still deferential to England, her greatest market, the power having the greatest investment there—Argentina now harbors considerable disillusionment of her friend and protector.

The new Empire tariffs, the rapid promotion of agricultural expansion inside the Empire, is working increasing hardship upon Argentina's long-favored place in the British economy. England, which in the past has taken nearly half, sometimes more than half of Argentina's products, is turning more and more to her own colonies. Argentina is beginning to see that while England wishes to control Argentina economically, to have it as a great storehouse in time of war, that this interest is due to no altruistic or friendly motives. Such motives basically do not exist in foreign relations, however much statesmen like to talk about them. The fact is Argentina has been hard hit by the empire tariffs. Argentina sees that England wishes to keep her in a subservient role to be utilized only when needed.

Argentina has long drifted in fancied security that her wealth and prosperity were inevitable, that her great resources could cope with any emergency, that the Pampas was mobile gold easily plucked, that her place in the world market was forever secure. She is now waking up to the bitter reality that the present is very doubtful, the future still more so. She is waking up to the reality that her proud position as the commanding power in Latin America is being challenged by Brazil, daily becoming more industrialized.

Brazil, for climatic, racial and other reasons, was much slower in developing, but in varied natural resources is the richest nation on the face of the globe. The future, therefore, apparently belongs to Brazil because of her rich iron and coal deposits, her oil, her copper, tin, manganese, silver, gold, platinum, wolfram—all the metals necessary for modern industry and war purposes.

Just east of northern Argentina lie some of Brazil's richest iron deposits, and the belief is strong in Brazil today—and doubtless munitions venders of all nations have strengthened this idea—that Argentina, at the first propitious moment, intends to strike hard and steal this portion of her neighbor's land, especially as it forms such a natural, economic and geographic unity with the La Plata region. Argentina sees Brazil forging ahead as an industrial nation. São Paulo today is a city of over a million inhabitants; a great industrial center. Argentina's jealousies have been aroused.

There is precedent for aggression in Chile's armed seizure last century of the nitrate fields of Bolivia and Perú.

As a result, certain of Argentina's statesmen have been definitely shaping economic and political policies toward the eventual conquest and consolidation of the whole great valley region which they already partially possess and to a great extent control. With this accomplished, Argentina would be one of the most powerful nations on earth. Otherwise, she will gradually assume less relative importance, much like our own South after the Civil War.

On the other hand, Brazil, like the United States in the case of New Orleans, has a strong *Drang nach Sud*. Brazil is really two countries. It actually split apart during part of a long period of the colonial era and was ruled as two different colonies. The great Amazon region to the north is an economic unit, and its population is a mixture of Indian-Negro-Dutch and Portuguese. The southern part of Brazil, a healthy plateau country lying in the temperate zone, is far more European in race and culture. Railroads—counter-

part of the Erie Canal and our own trans-Appalachian lines
—have tied this region to Rio de Janeiro, but it is a trun-
cated region so long as Buenos Aires, or Montevideo, remain in alien hands. Artificial bonds, plus language and
culture, make it look north to Rio; but natural economic
and geographic forces exert a perpetual pull south toward
Argentina.

6

This is no new conflict. It began back in colonial times.
It was carried on by Portuguese and Spanish frontiersmen.
It continued after independence.

In 1826, soon after Argentina and Brazil separated from
Spain, war for control of the Banda Oriental (now Uruguay) was launched between Brazil and Argentina, a bitter
struggle. Uruguay, in good part through British diplomacy,
eventually was set up as an independent country, a buffer
state.

Since then the story of its domestic politics for the better
part of a century has hinged on intrigues by Brazil and
Argentina in its internal affairs. Brazil needed Montevideo
as an outlet for its great inland river system. Argentina
needed it to round out its agricultural valley-unity.

In 1842-52, for over ten years, war again was carried on,
this time by Rosas, dictator of Argentina, for control of
Uruguay. For eight years Montevideo was under siege. A
combination of Uruguayan and Brazilian forces, backed by
France and England, held Rosas back. For a long time it
was an indecisive struggle, but in the end the combined
odds were too great for Rosas; he had to give up his imperialist pretensions, and Uruguay remained free, but for a
time definitely under Brazilian influence. Later it swung
into the Argentine orbit.

The story book is not closed. Congressman Enrique Dickman has recently revealed in the Argentine Congress maps prepared by the Integralistas (Nazis) showing Uruguay a part of Brazil. The Integralistas would not feel they were Nazis unless they had something outside the fatherland to conquer, and so they have made plans in German-Austrian style to reduce that country to a province of the larger State.

Today the Uruguayan dictatorship of Terra and Baldomir has swung into the Brazilian orbit, and Uruguayan-Brazilian-German capital is unitedly seeking concessions in Paraguay, Bolivia and Uruguay itself.

This conflict between Brazil and Argentina over Uruguay has lain at the root of many armed difficulties for more than a century. Those difficulties are now maturing. The historical moment for their being tested approaches. Brazil's *Drang nach Sud* and Argentina's Valley expansion are coming head on.

7

Another goal of Argentine imperialism became Paraguay. Some of the loudest denouncers of American territorial expansion and imperialism have been Argentine writers, such as Ugarte, Lugones and others; and yet in Paraguay, Argentina for long had a sphere of influence, an economic hegemony almost as definite, as overpowering, as ours in Cuba.

This economic conquest of Paraguay by Argentina was a long and gradual but determined story.

From 1811 to 1840 Paraguay was governed by the famous Dictator Dr. José Gaspar Rodríguez Francia, an austere theocratic absolutist ruler, who believed in complete isolation. Francia was succeeded by Carlos Antonio López, who ruled constitutionally for ten years, then by his son Francisco López, educated in Europe.

Don Francisco returned to Paraguay with a French concubine, European ideas and an overwhelming ambition. He seized power from his father and soon plunged Paraguay into the power-politics of the locale. He himself was plagued by Napoleonic ambition to become the conqueror of the continent. He built up the best-trained army ever seen in South America and thereby precipitated the bloodiest war (1865-70) in its history, a war from which Paraguay emerged with territorial integrity and honor, but with only 25,000 male citizens alive.

This war definitely grew out of the conflicting imperialistic ambitions of Argentina and Brazil, the century-old conflict over supremacy in the Plata River region. Don Pedro II, Emperor of Brazil, intervened in behalf of the pro-Brazilian party in the customary electoral struggle in Uruguay. López II, dictator of Paraguay, decided to support the opposite party and thus give his flourishing army a chance to prove itself.

Argentina, though secretly backing the party opposed to Brazil, was anxious not to have war, nor did she relish a third party meddling in. She had no desire to give the Napoleonic figure of López and his crack army a chance to experiment. López was flatly refused permission to cross Argentine territory to get into Uruguay.

The result was a complicated struggle in which for once Argentina and Brazil were on the same side. Aided by Uruguay, they declared war on Paraguay, a long and bloody struggle seldom equalled, one of the most bizarre and dramatic episodes in the stories of the nations.

Weakened by this five year struggle, Paraguay for years had to submit to outside influences. To rebuild her economy, she had to make concessions to Argentine capitalists. Argentine influence became supreme in Paraguay. The Argentine firm of Carlos Casada has a concession of more than four million hectares extending from Puerto Casada, on which are two hundred kilometers of railway, 80,000 head of cattle, and three thousand people. It is estimated to be worth close to two million dollars. North of this from Puerto Sastre stretches the property of another Argentine cattle company engaged in the quebracho industry, also worth $2,000,000. Steamships, railroads, exporting agencies, make an Argentine network of economic influence in the smaller inland country.

But here, too, Argentina's advance has of late been challenged. Heading a leftist movement of officers and peasants, Colonel Rafel Franco seized power on February 18, 1936. A group of reactionary military elements thereupon formed the "*Frente de Guerra,*" advocating Fascist doctrines. It was closely in contact and partly inspired by the Green Shirt Integralistas of Brazil. It assassinated the student leader Felix Agüero, and in August, 1937, allied with the old Liberal Party, succeeded in overthrowing Franco and bringing into office the present puppet dictator Felix Pavia.

Eusebio Ayala, former Liberal President, had already become convinced that Argentine control over Paraguay should be checked by catering to Brazil. His relative and associate Dr. Bordenave had earlier negotiated for railway connections with Brazil. General Estigarribia, also his aid in the Liberal movement, is also pro-Brazilian, closely linked with the military circles in Brazil and Brazilian-dominated Uruguay. They have been instrumental in a deal which has turned over Paraguayan resources to the German Thyssen interests. In this the Pavia government has assisted.

It has arranged for new rail and highway connections with Brazil.

These developments tie up with Italian, Japanese and German interests in Paraguay. Paraguay has been buying river gun-boats, airplanes and ammunition from Italy, fomenting the acquisition of tannin and cotton properties by the Japanese.

Argentina is pinning its hopes at present on the candidacy of Dr. Gerónimo Zubizarreta, lawyer for the large British interests in Paraguay and intransigent in his stand for the extreme demands of the country for the entire Chaco as a result of the war with Bolivia. He resigned from the Paraguayan Chaco peace conferences rather than be a party to the recent agreement. Upon the outcome of his efforts will probably determine the supremacy of Brazil or Argentina in Paraguay and peace and war in the Chaco.

8

The northward expansion of Argentina across the Pampas is the equivalent of our Western movement; and—just as we clashed with England, Russia, Spain, France and Mexico—Argentina has repeatedly been led into difficulties with her neighbors. Part of the goal of this colonizing expansion has been the Chaco of Paraguay and the Chaco of Bolivia. In 1876 Argentina tried to appropriate another slice of it, but President Hayes awarded it to Paraguay.

To fulfill her goals of imperialism and conquest, as well as her policy to checkmate Brazil at all turns, Argentina has long been determined to gain a foothold in Bolivia, similar to that in Paraguay, to expand there her economic and political control.

This has been more difficult because of the aloof mountain position of the central government of Bolivia, and because Bolivia, such a large country, is far more exposed to multiple influences. Bolivia borders on Perú, Chile, Brazil, and Argentina, and the intrigues of those four powers in this landlocked land, have given Bolivia one of the most bloody domestic histories of any nation on the continent. Bolivia long ago reached perfection in instability and disorder. Probably it has had more constitutions, more governments, more revolutions, more assassinated Presidents than has any other country on the continent.

The early part of Bolivia's history was filled with an effort by Perú to annex the country and make it part of a greater Perú. This, the surrounding countries, especially Chile, which feared the strong power on the Pacific that might result from such territorial amalgamation, sought to prevent.

On her side, Chile, in the War of the Pacific, seized Bolivian territory touching on the Pacific, and hemmed her, like Paraguay, into landlocked isolation in the center of the continent. Inevitably this threw Bolivia toward Argentina and Brazil, and started Bolivia on a restless quest for some feasible outlet toward the sea. The old enmity against Chile has never really been healed.

Of recent years, to dispute Argentina's desired economic and sphere-of-influence expansion into Bolivia, came also American capital—American mining, oil and banking interests.

But by 1903, in combination with the Bolivian government, the North Central Argentine Railway (owned by the government), pushed a connection from La Quiaca on the frontier to the capital at La Paz, and a side line down through the rich Potosí mining region to Sucre. This defi-

Congress, on September 10, 1932, was at the bottom of the fight. Oil was also endangering the peace of Argentina. "Notwithstanding many warnings," he said (not mentioning the Standard Oil Company by name), "this nefarious influence has been allowed to insinuate itself into the life of our northern provinces and make possible grave difficulties for Argentina and for all South America."

Dr. Inman quotes the *New York Times*, of December 24, 1932: Petroleum was becoming ever "more important a factor in Bolivia's distrust of Argentina's impartiality. Bolivia has been cool toward Argentina ever since the latter refused to permit the construction of a pipe line into Argentine territory, thereby causing the closing down of production in the Santa Cruz fields. If Bolivia gets a port on the upper Paraguay River she can land petroleum in Buenos Aires cheaper than Argentina can bring her own petroleum from Comodore and Rivadavia.

Here was an imperialistic struggle—though the causes were multiple—in which control of Bolivia's oil was an important issue.

Argentina, backed by British capital and diplomacy, though also furthering her own interests, had sought control of Bolivian resources and had been denied. It thereupon blocked Bolivia's outlets for the development of the Santa Cruz region by the Standard Oil. Though the Standard Oil Company denied helping Bolivia, the Argentinean government closed down a Standard Oil propaganda radio lest it involve Argentina's supposed neutrality. In any case the United States provided a large share of Bolivia's war materials, including airplanes and American pilots. Argentina and England helped Paraguay, although England, as usual, was not averse to profiting from both sides. Whenever a Paraguayan plane crashed, the Bolivian rushed to it to scratch off the paint to prove it was an Argentine war machine.

There was no doubt that Argentina was one of the instigators of this war, that thereafter she deliberately helped prolong it, that even today, while posing as a peacemaker, she has dragged out any settlement in order to wring concessions from both parties. As Hubert Herring wrote in the *Christian Science Monitor*: "The chief sinner is Argentina . . . deliberately egging Paraguay on in order to weaken Bolivia and to give Argentina the chance to extend her economic thrust further up the upper Paraguay River and beyond."

Behind the negotiations of the failures of the League of Nations and of the Pan-American Union, all the painful diplomatic efforts of the United States, was the constant intrigue of Argentina to prevent a settlement until she could enforce one on her own terms. Saavedra Lamas was given the Nobel Peace Prize for finally bringing about an accord in a conflict he had helped provoke, had prolonged, and had partially settled all for purely selfish reasons. He deserved any decoration except the one he received. The matter still remains undecided.

For a time, after a truce was declared, Argentina tried to force Paraguay and Bolivia to elevate the disputed area into the new Republic of Santa Cruz. This would provide Argentina with a new puppet buffer state and further cut off the possibilities of Brazilian economic penetration into Bolivia. She has not entirely abandoned that idea.

Since Bolivia was so badly defeated, she has—despite her animosity—been forced to turn to Argentina for economic succor, and also to get her to aid in securing the best terms possible from Paraguay. American capital, already having placed wild-cat loans in Bolivia, could not go in deeper. The depression had ended that phase of dollar diplomacy. But Argentina was thriving, well out of her short depression, with an excess of capital.

And so, finally a provisional Bolivia-Argentina pact was signed, January 21, 1936—following a series of negotiations by Horacio Carrillo, Ex-Minister of Foreign Affairs—for a ninety-nine-year lease of the eastern region between Santa Cruz and the Argentine frontier. 100,000,000 pesos are to be expended building railroads, roads, and other improvements. It was proposed to colonize the region and exploit its oil fields, including those which under Argentinean pressure had been expropriated from the Standard Oil.

The Standard Oil wells and refineries at Sanandita and Camiri have been taken over and are now run by Yacimientos Petroliferos Fiscales Bolivianos—really as much an Argentine as a Bolivian government concern. The petroleum agreement signed between Bolivia and Argentina, November 19, 1937, definitely replaced the Standard Oil with Argentine government control.

Argentina has now permitted the building of pipe lines into her territory, thus allowing Bolivia economic outlets, which if it had granted five years previously would have probably prevented the Chaco War.

The new Ostria-Gutierrez treaty between the two countries is far more than a commercial arrangement. It is also a political alliance. Both countries agree to inform the other of activities of their neighbors (Brazil and Chile), though these are not mentioned by name, and to take mutually precautionary steps.

Today Bolivia and Argentina are in close alliance. Special sports events are arranged between the two countries.

The interchange of commercial missions is constant. Visiting officials are given parades in the two capitals.

And so Argentina is on the way to complete its "Caribbean penetration."

9

Brazil has not been unaware of the imperialistic pretensions of Argentina and has sought to block her influence in Bolivia, as she has sought to block it in Uruguay and Paraguay.

Years ago, an effort was made by Brazil to drive a railroad into Bolivia, and the Madeira-Mamore line was built through a terrible jungle region—the most expensive pieces of construction in the world, a job which cost untold lives and vast sums, and which today is almost overgrown again with tropical forests. It is still used to connect up Bolivia with the Madeira and Amazon rivers, and then again by river, via Villa Bella. This, if it gives access to a rich rubber, cacao and sugar region, 1,000 miles—a whole empire— must still be crossed for anyone to get on up to La Paz.

More successful is Brazil's line from São Paulo to Porto Esperança on the Paraguay River. This has opened up to Brazilian settlers the eastern part of Bolivia. Further up the river is the new flourishing center of Puerto Goiba.

Brazil, prior to the Chaco conflict, also generously offered Bolivia Puerto Suárez on the Paraguay River, only 399 miles from rich Santa Cruz. It provides some outlet for coffee and rubber, but it is unsatisfactory as an ocean-head port. Until the river is dredged and straightened, only small vessels can navigate that far up. In any case Paraguay can still bottle up all commerce down the river and impose any duties she sees fit. More successful, as a result of the Brazilian government's close relations with German capital, is the new air route, described in a previous chapter, which so closely connects the ramified German-Brazilian and German-Bolivian systems and gives rapid access to the rich Santa Cruz region.

Today Bolivia is somewhat like Persia before the World War, the north was controlled by Russia, the south by England. Today Argentina is dominant south of Parapeti; Brazil is the predominant influence in the north. She now hopes, through a new rail line via Paraguay, with the aid of German and Uruguayan capital, to tap Bolivian oil fields not controlled by Argentina.

The result of Argentina's continental ambitions has been a factor in the armament races which periodically have disturbed the tranquillity of the Southern Hemisphere. It has led Brazil to reach out for alliances to offset the menace of Argentina. The most feasible has been Chile, which, next to Argentina, is the best armed of the southern nations. Argentina already has a traditional boundary dispute with Chile over islands in the Beagle Channel, and despite the Christ on the Andes, feelings have never been too kindly between the two countries. A tariff war of long standing was almost paralyzing all trans-Andean communications, and for a time trains quit running entirely. Brazil has not found it hard to make overtures.

Thereupon Argentina modified her attitude toward Chile, but in December, 1936, Brazilian Foreign Minister Macedo Soares journeyed to Santiago and secured a close rapprochement, and in March, 1938, General Góes Monteiro, chief of staff of the Brazilian army and former Nazi Integralista sympathizer, journeyed there in turn. The bands played, soldiers paraded, receptions were held, Monteiro was made "the Illustrious Guest of Santiago."

Missions constantly passed between Brazil and Chile;

special treaties bearing the marks of a secret alliance have been made.

This has further moved Argentina to try to split the two countries apart. This was one of the reasons, other than that of colonization and financial penetration, that caused her to seek influence in Bolivia, and more recently led her to extend her influence on into Perú.

Perú has always been the traditional enemy of Chile, ever since the brutal aggression last century of the latter country in wrenching away the nitrate fields. This old dispute has been settled, with considerable concession on Perú's part, and a great deal of hullabaloo about a new friendship pumped up, but the old suspicions die hard. Recently at Argentina's insistence, Perú modified the clauses of her commercial treaty with Chile. Semi-official comments in Chile said that Perú had been bullied into this by Argentina. Perú was obliged to issue an official statement that she had modified the treaty of her own volition and in friendly accord with Argentina.

Right after Roosevelt talked peace at Buenos Aires, the Argentine government sent a fleet of eight warships through the Straits of Magellan and up the long coast line of Chile straight to Perú. The vessels were on their way to cement the new alliance with the bull-necked dictator there, General Oscar Benavides.

Chile hastened to put 100,000,000 pesos into war planes and to expand her navy.

The scars of the old Leticia trouble are far from healed. This year Colombia, above her already large appropriations for armament, added an extraordinary budget. In Perú it is rumored that trouble may be expected again when the present international commission there folds up its tents.

Perú also has a lively boundary dispute going on with Ecuador, whose government is largely under Colombia's thumb. Thus Chile, Colombia and Ecuador all line up on the Brazil axis.

As a result the whole continent is tied into a system of balance of power, with secret military understandings. If a spark falls, it would likely set the whole continent aflame. Thus great Argentina, with its satellite buffer states, plus Perú, on the one hand, and Brazil, with its tie-up with Colombia, Ecuador and Chile, on the other, are two powerful divisions that endanger the peace of the continent and the world.

Venezuela, somewhat apart, tends to the Brazilian axis. Brazil is making strong efforts to promote trade with Venezuela in return for oil, which would be bought direct, thus eliminating dollar exchange and present excessive profits to American companies. The recent nationalization of Brazil's oil industry, as was explained in the American press, obeyed military and naval considerations. But it was nowhere explained that the act was motivated by the growing fear of aggression from Argentina. Brazil, whose potential oil fields are not developed and not proven, lacks this one essential product at present. She does not wish to be dependent upon Argentina for a supply, and is attempting to build up especially close relations with Venezuela and Colombia, the two biggest oil countries of South America.

Argentina is in many ways in the more strategic position. It has been able to drive a wedge through the center of the continent, much as Germany in the Old World seeks to drive a wedge through the Balkans to the Mediterranean.

Another curious phenomenon of this general alignment is that, with regard to European influences, Germany is strongest in Brazil, Chile, Colombia and Venezuela. Italy and England are strongest in Argentina, Uruguay, Perú and Paraguay.

10

More recently, to complete her encirclement of Brazil and to isolate it, Argentina has made increasing overtures to Chile. It would be unpleasant in case of trouble to have the third strongest nation of South America jump on her back. The outstanding dispute is the boundary difficulty in the far southern tip of the continent. Ill feelings have long been stirred up by paid propaganda in both nations and by munitions venders.

But in 1933 the two countries eased up their tariff war, and recently the Argentine Minister of Foreign Affairs, Cantillo, journeyed to Chile. A lot of long-suppressed good-will bubbled forth. The military cadets paraded, and General Quiroga, head of the Argentine army, presented a bronze statue of the hero of the Pampas, San Martín, who over a century ago crossed the Andes in Hannibal-style, but without elephants, and liberated Chile from Spanish rule. There was a whole lot of blah-blah about peace and democracy.

An Argentine military attaché, charged with espionage, went hurriedly home, and in the blare of trumpets, the Chileans decided to forget the matter. It was also decided to arbitrate the Beagle Channel dispute. It is too soon to know whether Argentina has really cracked the Brazil-Chile alliance. The dispute over the Beagle Channel is now to be arbitrated.

Recently Argentina has also made overtures to Colombia. A Colombian financial mission recently visited Buenos Aires. A favorable trade treaty has been arranged by which, according to the Colombian Minister, Argentina "will get the smoothest coffee in the world" from the most "effective democracy with free press and guaranteed suffrage." That is coffee with a real aroma indeed.

This, too, fits in with Argentina's efforts to split away Brazil's allies, isolate her, encircle her. It conceals for the moment the wide crack yawning down the center of the continent and helps demagogues prate about peace and friendship.

Unless the tensions of South America become too unstable, for the moment, Argentina is quite likely to try to maintain the status quo, while pushing these sundry aims. For the time being she will likely try to wedge Chile and Colombia further from Brazil, while continuing her economic invasion of Bolivia and southern Brazil itself.

In the meantime, in this effort, up to a certain point she even coöperates with Brazil, for both are pushing the Black League alliance of semi-Fascist dictatorships to maintain all the governments firmly in power against possible revolts. This also gives Argentina a chance to rush her big armament and naval program.

11

The United States, with her vast investments, her predominant financial position, her need for raw materials to the south, is eager for this sort of Fascist-like peace, stability of the present harsh dictatorships, the maintenance of the status quo. And yet we, too, are playing the armament game. In thus imitating, of late, the Fascist countries, we too are helping to destroy the status quo. The United States has much to gain from such peace, even on such an unjust basis. If trouble comes in the southern continent, it will be a desperate affair. The Chaco War itself was one of the bloodiest and costliest affairs on record, and those two small countries engaged had none of the great resources of the larger countries. In such a major conflict, the various countries would inevitably seek alliances wherever they could find them. While the United States sought a formula for peace, the European countries would be meddling, driving ahead with arms, advice, aid. England has always meddled. Germany, France and Japan are today far more daring in their meddling than England.

One clear fact stands out. The South American countries are not arming against Europe, against Fascism; they are arming, often with the aid of Fascism, to maintain dictatorial governments, and against the menace of their own neighbors. It is the dreary spectacle we already know so well in Europe, of balance of power, armament races, and international intrigue.[1]

Thus the most imperialistic of the countries, Argentina, is hastening to be beforehand. The outstanding feature of President Ortiz' government is armament. He stressed this the very day of his inauguration. He has been stressing it every day since. He has been part of the inner circle planning Argentina's forcible expansion. He is preparing for it.

Already having the strongest, most up-to-date navy in

[1] Would it not be too monotonous, it would be of value to point out similar intrigues in Central America: the imperialistic ambitions of Dictator Ubico of Guatemala, his building up of armed forces with German and Italian aid, his attempts to buy up elections and candidates in neighboring countries, as in the case of Dr. Rodolfo Espinosa of Nicaragua, his dream of conquering and welding Central America by force. There also is the story of the cross-intrigue of Martínez of Salvador, who controls Honduras, and who has similar Napoleonic ambitions. The key at present is Nicaragua. It is interesting to note that the thread of Nazi influence runs most strongly through Salvador and Honduras, while Italian influence is stronger in Guatemala.

southern waters, nevertheless Argentina plans to enlarge it still more. New warships are to be added, cruisers, destroyers, submarines and naval airplanes.

It is planned a bit later to build most of these vessels within the country, one step further in Argentina's general program of economic self-sufficiency. Up until now, England, the United States and Italy have been favored with such purchases. Now it is expected that Italian ship-builders will be brought in to start naval yards at home. Within ten years, Argentina expects to be a leading naval power.

Once the Bolivian penetration is consolidated, once her navy is in shape, then she will be ready for the great adventure.

On May 11, 1938, Ortiz reiterated his great faith in democracy, and told Congress to work instead of wasting time on debates on political questions. This is the same sort of democracy as was advocated by old Porfirio Díaz of México, who came into power with similar fixed elections. It is the constant theme, work and no politics, of the barbarous dictator of Trujillo of the Dominican Republic. Ortiz' words are in fact copied almost directly from an early speech by Mussolini in Montecitorio. But Ortiz is preparing for the great day.

"Let no one imagine," said President Roosevelt, alluding to the threat of international terror and war, "that this Western Hemisphere will not be attacked."

But no European power is likely to be so mad with our own frontiers so exposed, to indulge in colonial conquest which would bring the immediate opposition of the United States. No, the game is far different, but no one in official quarters breathes a word of it. The game is propaganda-war, trade-war, armament sales, subtle undercover intrigue, in all of which we are playing a nasty part. The jealousies of South America give ample scope to such activities.

We will not be called upon to defend Latin America against Europe. Our problem will be undercover intervention in the name of non-intervention, in the very sacred name of the Monroe Doctrine itself, our problem will be to attempt peace between nations backed by European powers. If that fails, we shall be reduced to impotence, or else will have to choose sides, not with a united western world opposing a naughty Europe, but between American countries allied with different sets of European powers.

CHAPTER

XII

What Does Latin America Want?

No more pointed proof of the inability of highly industrialized nations to pursue a policy of isolation and self-sufficiency is presented than by the general international scramble to win South American raw materials, trade, and strategic control points.

Rubber, sugar, coffee, wheat, meat, hides, tin, wolfram, oil, nickel, manganese, copper, platinum, coconuts, sisal, gold, silver, medicinal herbs, hard woods, vegetable oils, cotton, corn, wool, linseed—these are a few of the products which are necessary to all nations, including the United States—which have an insufficiency of some of these or other products, both for peace-time industry and even more so for war purposes.

But it is perhaps worth while considering not merely the international scramble for dominance, but also to ask what the Latin-American countries want. What are their needs, their way of life, their hopes for the future? For in the answer to these questions will be found, in the long run, the determining factor in all the high pressure power-politics, the final dictator of the future. In the long run, the success or failure of Nazi or Fascist or Communist or American propaganda in Latin America will depend not upon the activities of outside nations, but upon the needs and inclinations of the Latin-American people themselves.

This is hard doctrine for us to swallow. It violates our Jehovah complex about Latin America. We have a feeling that we are entitled to the major share of Latin America's trade. We have a feeling that we are the arbiters of the two continents. Though we talk about the sovereignty of all the free nations of the Western Hemisphere, we do not really mean it; we feel that they should gladly and gratefully follow our guidance, especially in world affairs, that they should accept our ideas. We still feel that it is incumbent upon us to protect the whole Western Hemisphere against Europe. We feel that Latin America owes us allegiance, friendship and gratitude, and in the past few years we have been a bit puzzled as to why Brazil, for instance, should buy more goods from Germany than from us.

If we could only put ourselves in Latin America's place for a few minutes, we might look at international affairs far differently. If we were to imagine ourselves as Brazilians, living in Rio de Janeiro, growing cotton, or Argentineans, living on the Pampas, raising cattle, we would at once see the fallacy of most of our pretensions.

2

We soon find certain tendencies are common to all the countries of Latin America regardless of whether they are ruled by despotism like that of Vargas in Brazil, or near democracies, or radical democracies of a semi-socialistic nature, as in México.

One of the most important of these tendencies is that of economic nationalism. In varying degrees, the various Latin-American countries are promoting industrialization; increasingly they are practicing diversified agriculture, are attempting to lessen their dependence upon foreign trade, and to free themselves from the subservient role of being merely providers for the great industrialized nations.

The Mexican Six-Year Plan states: "México is compelled, on its part, to adopt a policy of economic nationalism as a measure of legitimate defense . . . not to place our country in isolation, but, . . . through revision of . . . foreign trade and . . . our regime of production, in order that national interests predominate."

The program demands an end of land monopoly; of monopoly of mineral resources by foreign concerns; the creation of native mining coöperatives; the building of smelters for common use, tolls to be fixed by the State; no oil to be extracted that is contrary to national interest; the stopping of all exploitation of national resources which are then elaborated abroad and reimported, unless they are processed in México; every impulse to be given to the importation of machinery for permanent production; the creation of new industries to substitute present imports.

"We must protect our national industries . . . Perú first!" editorialized *La Nacion* of Trujillo, Perú (February 5, 1934).

El Tiempo of Bogotá, warning against a careless favored-nation treaty with the United States, has declared:

"Until a few years back our international trade policy was restricted to seeking markets where our coffee could be consumed . . . our only exportable product. Today we have to give joint attention to that need and to the further need of protecting our incipient manufacturing industry.

"We are also confronted with the difficulty of harmonizing the conflicting interests of the United States and of Europe, both of which aspire to control the Latin-American markets by the customary procedure of entering into bilateral treaties. It is more than likely that the United States aspires to propose, perhaps impose, a policy of commercial compensations irreconcilable with the policy of free world-wide commerce."

La Opinión of Santo Domingo hopes that country can become the "Little Japan of the West Indies."

"Industrial development in our country has not had the precipitatedly rapid pace that it has had in other countries, but this does not mean that we have not had fair progress.

"Excepting the industry of machinery, scientific apparatus and chemical products, very few manufactures remain to be established in the country in order that we may be self-sufficient. The concentrated objective of the Government must be . . . to see that these new industries are established." One of the gaps still is the need for a cotton textile factory. "Why should we not have among us a factory of that sort, there being the advantage that our soil produces the raw material? . . .

"Every time a new factory is put up, it means a large amount of national funds kept from going abroad, a suspension of the emigration of national gold, a larger number of Dominican families that find work, a new market like a fountain of life for the raw material production of our farmers.

"Let us be fiery in protecting our national industry. . . . Let us be patriotic as fiercely as the Japanese are, and we shall become economically a Little Japan of the West Indies."

There are few things the southern countries are not now trying to produce from aspirin to railroad cars, from razor blades to airplanes, from typewriter ribbons to auto tires.

Take Brazil. Brazil has long been predominantly a one-crop country. Its great boom product for decades was rubber. More recently its great boom crop has been coffee. Brazil supplies nearly 70 percent of the world's coffee, could easily, were there no competition, supply the entire world's needs and have a surplus.

But gradually Brazil has been working out from under such an unbalanced national economy, which made her prosperity dependent upon the whim of the outside market price in a single commodity. In a few short years, Brazil has become one of the greatest cotton-producing countries in the world. Today more than 6,000,000 acres are under cultivation; 2,000,000 bales have been flung into the world market. In a few more years, Brazil can equal the production of the United States. Her yield per acre is much larger than ours; her costs of production are lower.

In a few more years, Brazil promises also to be a big tea-silk-and-rice exporting country. Her cattle and meat industry has expanded greatly. Her fruits are sold in Moscow and Glasgow. She produces more bananas probably than any other country. Her vegetable oils are finding more uses in the international market. Her iron—she has a fourth of the world's supply—and manganese deposits are being increasingly exploited. The prospects of an oil-boom are not far distant.

But not merely in raw products is change to be noted. In a few short years São Paulo has grown from a city of a few hundred thousand to a city of over a million inhabitants, one of the most highly industrialized cities in the world. Today Brazil, which less than a decade ago imported most manufactured articles, now supplies nearly all the needs of its forty-eight million inhabitants, in paints, cotton and woolen goods, biscuits, nuts, bolts, screws, buttons, cigarettes, matches, phonograph records. In 1920 Brazil had 13,300 industrial establishments. Today she has over 30,000.

Brazil today produces over 30,000,000 pairs of boots and shoes; and over 9,000,000 hats.

By 1928 Brazil had 346 textile mills with an annual production of 629,450,000 square yards valued at $112,000,000; in 1935, there were 510 mills, and Brazil now supplies most of her domestic needs and exports to five adjacent countries and to Cuba. She has 1,261 establishments producing machinery. There are 82 silk mills in São Paulo, with 2,846 looms. 3,500,000 pairs of silk stockings are turned out annually. São Paulo has eleven paper factories which supply nearly all national necessities except for news print. With the exuberant growth of cellulose plants, Brazil can easily become the greatest paper-manufacturing country in the world. Growing industries are those of jute, cement, rubber and woolen goods, iron and steel, chemicals.

Argentina, since 1929, has been pursuing a rigid program of economic self-sufficiency—the promotion of new industries, looking toward a diminution of its import needs. New industries are protected by tariffs, subsidies, exchange controls, import restrictions. Its textile spindles quadrupled between 1930 and 1936. It supplies all its own shoes and woolen goods, most of its cement and tires. It exports electric refrigerators.

In Perú, Italian capital and German technicians have put up a new airplane factory. It has carried on an intensive wheat-growing campaign. The Peruvian cotton industry (it grows its own cotton) has now ousted all but Japanese and fine quality goods from the local market. Woolen goods manufactures are expanding rapidly. Clothing, shoe, cement, paint, aluminum ware, flour, meat, furniture, glassware, are industries that almost supply native needs. Drug and chemical industries, toys, perfumes, hats, leather goods, are products being turned out in increasing quantities. The Grace Company has just put up a large paper factory.

Chilean industry, compared to the 1927-29 level (100), stood at 146 in 1936 and since has been expanding still more rapidly. Textile—wool, cotton, linen, rayon—and jute mills have expanded enormously in the past ten years. A new $2,500,000 cotton yarn mill, built in 1936, is said to be the most modern in the world. There are three big cotton-knitting plants and thirty smaller plants supplying all national needs. In 1935 (compared to 1928 as 100), Chilean textile production stood at 404, Great Britain's at 91.2, and the United States' at 59.8.

There are ninety shoe factories. 250,000 tons of cement are turned out annually. Explosives, chemicals, furniture, paper, lumber, sugar-refining, perfumery, enamel-ware production, supply most or all of the national needs. Glassware, now exported to various outside countries, has pushed United States glass products out of the Peruvian market. There are 579 flour mills. Chile has large iron and coal deposits. A new smelter has been set up at Valdivia. The iron and steel industry is expanding rapidly. The country now makes most of its own steel railway freight cars. Curtiss-Wright corporation has erected an aircraft factory at Loa Cerillos with a 50-plane capacity. Native industry is now demanding more and more protection against the "dumping" of American, German and Japanese goods.

"There can be sensed an almost feverish activity tending to make Chile as far as possible self-supporting," declared the *Latin-American Digest*, October 18, 1933, and for years *El Mercurio*, among the twelve newspapers of the world having largest circulation, has been promoting this goal.

José Miguel Bejarano, Mexican delegate to the Montevideo Pan-American Conference, returning through Bolivia, remarked—though he condemned severely the war with Paraguay:

"The greatest advantage that the Chaco War has brought to Bolivia has been to foster her economic development, and Bolivia is now practically self-supporting. An extensive campaign is being waged by the government to increase the production of the three most important items formerly constant in her import shipments: cotton, sugar, and rice. . . .

"In the outskirts of La Paz a new cotton mill has been erected: the last word in machinery and construction, it need not envy the most modern mill in New England. Two large woolen mills are also working to capacity, and all uniforms, overcoats and blankets issued by the army are now of Bolivian manufacture."

Jump far north to Cuba. Despite the American efforts to chain Cuba to a one-crop sugar economy, new industries slip into the corral. One picks up such items as that in May: the Technical Tariff Commission allowed duty-free importation of equipment and machinery for the installation of an electric lamp factory. The new plant will manufacture bulbs, sockets and all electric apparatus for completely assembling lamps.

In México the production of footwear, auto tires, canned fruits, perfumes, matches, cement, beer, soap, paper, biscuits, cigars, cigarettes, drugs, glassware, pottery, furniture, oil, gasoline, sisal, meet or can meet all native needs. The steel and iron industry, with native capital, centering at Monterrey, is constantly expanding and can supply practically all building needs. México manufactures all its own munitions and a goodly share of its explosives. It builds many of its own freight and passenger cars.

Textile production has grown prodigiously, and México

has undersold the United States with cotton goods in the Central American market. Woolen fabrics are today almost the equal of those anywhere and cost a sixth as much as imported cloth. The shoe industry is growing, and low-grade workmen's shoes are even exported into Texas.

Four airplane factories operate. Canadian capital has just contracted to go into partnership with the government to erect a fifth, which will begin exporting within two years.

Much of this nationalistic effort concerns itself with native control of industry, the creation of Mexican instead of foreign ownership.

3

The Latin-American countries have lost much of their fear of, also their admiration and respect for, foreign capital. The unmitigated faith of the world in the prosperity, power, and happiness of the great industrial nations has vanished. The southern countries look north to the United States and no longer see much to admire in our social system: 13,000,000 men unemployed, endless bloody strikes, crime waves, political demagogy and confusion, inability to balance the national budget, devaluation of the dollar, the abandonment of gold payments, the corruption and jailing of high business heads, farmers increasingly dispossessed of their lands, horrible emaciated faces of southern share-croppers, lynching of Negroes—all in all the southern peoples do not hold an attractive picture of the great land of the free. The Latin-American countries no longer see any rhyme or reason in imitating our economic or political system.

At the Montevideo Conference, Dr. Puig Casauranc declared:

"I have lived for years in the United States." He hinted at our evil race prejudices, but he saw also "the hopefulness, the desire for happiness of the American people, struggling and laboring and saving for an untroubled old age. And I can affirm . . . that now an enormous majority of all the middle and sub-middle classes and of skilled laborers, almost all that the men who could by dint of work, of effort and intelligence—wearing out their bodies and their brains —carve out for themselves or for their children a better future, almost all those men have been robbed of their efforts, of their sacred savings during the last twenty-five years—the savings of a whole generation—by the international super-banker corporations."

No, they are not anxious to emulate that sort of thing down south. They are experimenting, seeking new formulae in accord with their own needs and temperament.

Doctor Leonidas Anastasi of the La Plata University, one of the leading Latin-American authorities on constitutional law, and very much a Tory, is nevertheless not enamored of the American system.

"We must remain faithful to the idea expressed by Saenz Peña when he said that he wanted an America dedicated to humanity not to a portion of humanity alone chosen on grounds of conceit.

"Let us avoid as if it were a pestilence that type of citizen which the North American novelist Sinclair Lewis had depicted."

The prominent Argentine sociologist, Luis Franco, has declared: "The fault that has driven Yankee civilization to the border of utter failure is all too visible: its formidable lack of balance between the world of facts and the inner world. Its transient opulence and its inner poverty of spirit."

Today the Latin-American countries wish above all to gain control of their own resources, and are not stopping in most cases to ask whether the measures they take conform to capitalist folklore, or are ethical according to the standards of American business and law. Ownership in fee simple has little meaning for southern dictators. It had little meaning in Indian law. It has little in Spanish law.

A few years ago foreign capital and the foreigner were above the law. Today they are lucky if they even get fair protection under the law. Today foreign capital in Latin America is definitely on the defensive.

In country after country the officials, if cautiously, have declared that they do not want foreign capital on the old pre-war basis. They do not want the stealing away of the national resources, the shipping of wealth abroad without commensurate return. Capital, foreign or native, must now contribute permanently to building up the economy of the country where it lodges. It must subject itself to controls and regulation. It must provide higher wages. It must largely employ native labor. It must submit to national planning. It must reinvest its profits in the country.

Doctor Augusto S. Boyd, Minister of Panamá, speaking over a Washington short-wave broadcast, May 17, 1938, declared that Latin America no longer wanted foreign capital "invested solely with extortionist purposes, but on the basis of proportional benefits to the country lending its soil and its men and to the company that exploits them." Mild enough language, but behind it lurks the determination everywhere to put national needs above those of private capital from abroad.

We have heard of México's expropriation of land, sugar production, oil and railroads. But Bolivia has confiscated all Standard Oil holdings. Brazil has just nationalized foreign oil plants. In the future only Brazilian citizens may engage in the industry; and production and selling controls similar to those in México have been set up. The Standard Oil of New Jersey at once stopped further work on the construction of a $500,000 refinery now taken over.

A few years ago on the coast of Colombia, the United Fruit Company was the law. Officials, military commanders, judges, senators, bowed to its will. Investigations came along. The manager of the company was put under arrest. Serious charges were lodged against him. He was finally released and forced to leave the country. Now Colombia is nationalizing the banana industry.

Argentina has nationalized most of her oil resources, has placed the private holdings of the Standard Oil Company under such strict regulation as to make them little more than an adjunct of governmental enterprise. A British-owned railway has been taken over, amount of payment to be announced later. Rigid controls have been placed over the meat-packing industry to protect the native growers, and the government expects to take over a packing plant and run it itself.

Little Ecuador has even had the temerity to confiscate concessions when the contracts have not been strictly lived up to. Native lawyers have been deported for defending such foreign companies.

In Chile, the government has turned its guns on the American and Foreign Power Company by bringing ruinous suits for violations of the exchange-control law. With this as a leverage, the government obliged the company to resume construction of a new generating plant and to go into a new combine with all other concerns—the *Compañía Chilena de Electrícidad*. The government placed seven directors on the new board of eleven and divided up the profits three ways: one-third to the government, one-third to the new concern, and one-third for reduction of service costs.

In the nitrate industry, the government also now dominates. When synthetic nitrates put the skids under the Chilean industry, the Guggenheims, having secured a new process for the natural product, organized the famous Cosach combine, a bit of financing that was the scandal of the two continents. But except for brief semi-recovery, the nitrate production in Chile has been in a bad way. Gustavo Ross, the financial brains behind the Chilean nationalization program and governmental control of private industry, himself a wizard entrepreneur worth millions, took the nitrate industry in hand by forcing all concerns to subordinate themselves to the Chilean Nitrate and Iodine Corporation, the government keeping six of the eleven directors' seats, Ross himself acting as chairman. This company assigns quotas, sells all products and takes 25 percent of the profits.

In the oil industry, Ross and the government set up the COPEC, which has allotted itself a third of the market previously divided by the West India Oil and Shell Mex on a monopoly concession.

In the copper industry, the government forces the American companies, if they wish to ship out their profits, to buy American dollars at twenty-five percent above the market price. The proceeds from this and the new oil arrangements are used to retire Chilean bonds. One-half goes to purchasing the bonds at their ten-cents-on-the-dollar price on the open market. The other half goes to the payment of interest to the extent possible (less than one percent).

The government has also taken over the British Trans-Andean Line, and has added it to the government-owned network of railroads, one of the finest equipped and best run systems in the world, with excellent, fast, streamlined trains.

4

With respect to foreign debts, the Latin-American countries, despite defaults and scaling down, have in general a far better record than powerful Europe.

But some new practices give the bankers headaches.

In the old days the banker, we will say, placed a 6 percent loan at 96. Probably he also deducted the first year's interest, pulling the amount actually paid over down to 90. He also deducted his commissions, etc. These bonds were then sold to the American public, with the attraction of a year's interest in advance for perhaps 102 or 104.

The banker wrote up a glowing prospectus with plenty of high-power romance fluttering in the corners. The true economic facts about the country, the instability of its dictatorial government, were mostly concealed. In this way securities were passed on to small local banks, to the corner dentist, to the merchant and candlestick maker. The bonds, naturally, went into default.

The local bank failed, so in the last analysis the poor depositors paid for bonds whose gilt edges they had never even fingered. The price of the bonds sank to ten cents on the dollar. The big international banks began raking them in again.

Then they would have a heart-to-heart talk with the State Department. Diplomatic pressure would back up negotiations for a settlement. After long bickering, a deal would be made, say at 40 or 60 or 80 cents.

Thereupon a new bond issue would be floated. The American sucker would again absorb the new issue. The bank would once more reimburse itself for the payment of the old bonds, thus making a profit of from 100 to 800 percent. The country might get a few million dollars; but its debt load would become more absurd than ever. This merry rigamarole was repeated indefinitely, to the injury of American investors and foreign peoples.

The Latin-American countries are not so amenable to this process any more. They have learned to shave loan payments down to benefits received or in accordance with national capacity to pay. "We must put our national defense before payment of debts," recently stated a member of the Peruvian cabinet.

The various countries no longer see why they should pay the piper for bankers' speculation, especially as the original bondholders are thereby not benefited. They see no reason why they should pay off at par when the bankers buy in the paper at a few cents on the dollar.

Recently Costa Rica calculated that the average sales price of her bonds on the New York Stock Exchange during the past two years has been 31 cents. She offered to settle with the bankers for this price. They refused. As a result the price dropped to 17 cents. Costa Rica now buys in her own bonds quietly at that figure on the open market. In March she spent $2,000,000 for this purpose.

Chile, we have seen, follows a similar policy. So do other countries. It peeves the bankers—but it is merely their own game.

Such developments as these cut into the old-time trade and investment possibilities of all nations, and they point to the fact that Latin America in the near future will achieve far greater economic independence from all the countries, including the United States. This will mean still more independent foreign policies.

5

Tariffs, exchange controls, capital export taxes, force capital reinvestments, managed currencies, special anti-foreign taxes, governmental fostering of labor unions to harass foreign companies, favored freight rates, trade subsidies, tariffs for national goods, have buttressed up the war for economic independence. Some countries require that, in various industries, a certain percentage of the profits be invested in the country.

The major industry of Bolivia is mining, mostly in foreign hands. The government has prescribed that 50 percent of the value of all exports must be spent in purchase of Bolivian money, i.e., reinvested in the country or spent for Bolivian goods.

Similar laws have been enacted in México. Others are pending. Other governments require that such profits be taken out, not in the form of money, but by the purchase of local goods. National commissioners set import quotas in various industries and for given countries. Numerous regulations hedge the buying of foreign exchange about in such ways as rigidly to control commerce. Many of the countries impose high capital export taxes.

Taxes are often directed against foreign monopoly enterprises. Costa Rica this May upped her assessment on Electric Bond and Share Company properties from $1,417,857 to $3,259,976 and made it retroactive. *El Dia* of Costa Rica had repeatedly warned the country against letting its power resources get into foreign hands. In an editorial, March 12, 1934, it pointed out that Costa Rica has no coal or oil (explorations for the latter are again being made), and therefore should jealously guard and develop for the country's own interest the considerable hydro-electric power available. "We cannot dispose of what belongs to the future without incurring grave responsibilities, . . . ought not to dispose of it in any form under any condition," and hailed the law nationalizing electric power. This law has been largely evaded, but the question still moves the public, and President León Cortés Castro has recently suggested that eventually the right solution may be the nationalization of the industry under the National Electric Board which already has large powers of regulation.

Colombia has just established a National Junta of Cotton Import control made up of officials, growers and workers.

The National Bank of Uruguay is empowered to regulate all foreign trade, to assign quotas to each country, and to indicate the amounts of any given product that can be imported during a given period. The quota assigned shall be not less than 75 percent of the value of the goods bought from different countries.

Three types of foreign exchange exist: the official rate for purely governmental trading, the controlled rate for commerce, and the free rate for certain non-competitive goods. At this writing—May—as yet no quotas this year had been assigned to American goods, which are piled up in the warehouses. American purchases have declined heavily; German purchases have increased, so that it is almost impossible to buy dollars, though Aski marks can be obtained in almost unlimited amounts.

Argentina, in April, 1938, took steps to control abuses of regulated exchange by prescribing penalties for all who took out permits and failed to use up to 90 percent of the amount granted.

A few years ago, influenced by England, Argentina went on a quota basis, awarding import permits to the businessmen of each country only up to the amount of Argentine goods purchased by that country. Subsequently this was modified to an exchange control, which in practice provided a premium to the importer on all exchange up to an amount that equalized trade. Sales by a given foreign country in excess of that amount had to be financed by purchases of exchange in the open market at about 20 percent higher than the official rate.

In spite of this handicap, American goods have been jumping the hurdle. The first four months of this year, the United States sold 64,000,000 pesos more than it bought. In May, alarmed by this, the Argentine government refused to grant much dollar exchange and announced it would probably revive the old quota system. This will especially benefit England and Germany and put the United States down to fourth place in the market.

Bolivia fixes three types of exchange. 100 bolivianos per pound sterling are prescribed for imports of articles of prime necessity, such as sugar, rice, flour, milk, meat, etc. Other articles of prime necessity to be indicated from time to time by the Minister of Hacienda may be imported by payment of an exchange rate of 120. Free exchange rates—higher than this—are allowed on permits to import other goods not listed.

Ecuador, with iron-clad control of foreign exchange (though the Germans have recently been given a special concession), places a 50 percent surtax on all goods from countries whose sales exceed purchases by 30 percent.

Chile forces arbitrary exchange rates in accordance with national trading needs and permits exchange according to a well-worked-out system of import quotas, directing purchases to essential needs and to indicated countries.

Every country in South America except Perú strictly controls foreign exchange and attempts to make imports and exports from any given country balance by granting or withholding exchange permits. Every Central American country except Salvador and Guatemala—which have devised other controls—follow the same policy.

The old laissez faire world, upon which Hull so valiantly bases his faith in his favored-nation treaties, no longer exists in Latin America any more than it exists in most of the world. The free market is gone, never to return in our day.

6

Not only need we not expect, as Mr. Hull stated, pointing to our 1937 increase of trade with Latin America, that those countries will limit their commercial relations with Europe all of a sudden, but we should expect to see those relations increase rather than decrease.

Is it necessary to remark that we have no need for Argentine wheat, corn, wines, little need for few of her major products? She must sell them abroad, and whatever devices, propaganda, coercion or other weapons we use, we cannot hope to win permanently more than a certain minority percentage of Argentina's market. To gain more would merely mean costly and useless effort without corresponding rewards or lasting gain. The main reason for our unusual temporary expansion last year in that market has been due to armament sales more than to legitimate commerce. Brazil must sell her cotton and many other products to Germany and Japan.

Latin-American nations, like the other countries of the world, are going to buy from those who buy from them. They are going to buy where the buying is cheapest and more advantageous. This is good business. It is in accordance with our own cherished principles of business—except for being government-enforced—and to expect Latin America to sacrifice her economic advantages to us because of some mythical gratitude is an absurdity that would only occur to a statesman.

Foreign trade today is a species of war, political monopoly and barter. This inevitably has led to political influences that scarcely existed a few decades ago, nor can we expect Latin America to cut such bonds. If we do, we are merely heading into war; and in the long run, even with war, we would only temporarily halt natural commercial relations of Latin America with the rest of the world.

Latin America, in fact, knows the people of Europe far better than she does Americans. The large European colonies bring intimate contacts and understanding. In 1935-36, for instance, 250,000 Europeans emigrated to South America, as compared to only 12,000 Americans, many of whom did not become permanent residents.

Our own third largest market is Japan, and we sell Japan much more than we buy. Japan indeed is in large part responsible for much of our improvement in world trade. It is due to this that we have perhaps been slow to apply the neutrality act to the conflict in the Orient. We have no desire to destroy our market in Japan or our commercial intercourse with that country. Yet, strangely enough, we become hugely alarmed because Japan buys and sells goods in South America. We have a lurking feeling that that is unfair to us. But Latin America would never have the presumption to try to destroy, change or limit our profitable relations with the Orient.

By reason of our overshadowing political influence, our need for raw materials, the superior quality of certain American products, the need of Latin America for machinery and manufactured products, we are normally assured—regardless of foreign competition and propaganda in South America, regardless of our own dull and patronizing propaganda there—of a big share in the market to the south.

Nor will the Latin-American dictators—however much they may dislike our brand of democracy and our political system and our propaganda—likely offend us more than they have to. They are going to ply us for a long time to come with sweet words. They need the American market as well as the European market. They know that in case of a European war, the trade currents with peaceful United States would set in strongly again, as they did after the last war. The one point is that Latin America is not desirous of putting all her trade in one basket, be it the United States, Germany or England.

That being the case, the barrier to German or Italian or British propaganda in Latin America will not be the American counter propaganda, our counter trade drive, nor our sale of American munitions in the name of peace, all of which to Latin America is also "foreign," but in the natural patriotic resistance of the Latin-American peoples and governments to outside meddling.

Certain dictators are going to flirt with the Fascist countries regardless of us. Latin America is going to make European alliances if they are convenient. In fact that is far more likely to be done by the type of dictators we support there than it would be by democratic countries. Our naval missions and our arms promotions are creating or helping to maintain the type of dictatorial government that will gladly plunge its country into any mad adventure or alliance in a reckless gamble to retain unjust power.

The point that we curiously forget with regard to Latin America is that there we also are foreigners, aliens, that our radio messages, press, movies, educational missions and what not are as alien as the similar efforts of European powers. Mr. Roosevelt may continue to talk in the name of all the governments of the Western Hemisphere, but the fact remains that most of those governments still fear us more than they do Europe. Such patronizing merely promotes the Fascist cause in the southern countries. The governments of the latter are not going to antagonize us, but they wish to diversify the investments in their country. They do not want to see themselves hog-tied by American capital as is Cuba. They wish, first of all, to promote the expansion of native capital, and to the extent that that is impossible, they wish diversified capital: American, British, German, Italian. Why kid ourselves?

If nothing else, relationships with Fascist powers give them a bigger bargaining power with the so-called democratic nations.

7

The real barrier to the eventual purpose of German, Italian, British and American propaganda in Latin America is the normal desire of the southern lands for true sovereignty and independence. For that reason the Latin Americans are equally suspicious of our official propaganda, in some cases more so. More and more Latin America's relations with outside nations are likely to be bounded by the claims of the various nations for respect for their national sovereignty. Already German propaganda seems to have overshot its mark. Brazil is strictly limiting the scope of alien propaganda. It has forbidden the maintenance of foreign-language schools subsidized by alien governments, it has imposed the teaching of Portuguese in all private schools for children up to the age of fourteen.

America rejoices at this new turn in Brazilian politics. We forget that this will also affect numerous American schools, and numerous American missionary establishments. Long ago in México and other countries such regulations were imposed. In México, the American school had to quit using texts which the government there claimed misrepresented the Mexican-American War and Mexican history. All private schools must now abide by the legal program of instruction.

Sharp criticism of Nazi methods has occurred in the Argentine and Chilean papers. Humorously enough Argentina has forbidden the singing of all foreign national anthems.

Beyond a certain point Naziism and Fascism are not likely to prosper in Latin America.

First of all, many governments are so superficially similar to Nazi and Fascist regimes that the new doctrines present little novelty. Basically, though, the dictatorial governments of Latin America are not Fascist, even though most of them are totalitarian and function with only one party through military control and force. To call them Fascist is merely to confuse all terminology, Communist-style. It is to obscure the political processes of semi-colonial and raw-product countries, largely still agrarian in economy, yet entering upon various phases of industrialization and independent nationhood.

Nationalism in such countries becomes a revolutionary doctrine in a sense that it never does in highly industrialized or European countries. It becomes a weapon of partial liberation. It is a method by which foreign controls are eliminated and profits of foreign-owned companies are kept within the country for further development. It largely evades the class conflicts within the country. Whatever sort of economy or government exists, it tends to bring certain benefits to all in the shape of public works, improvements and national goods—though local governing inefficiency and dishonesty frequently offset much of the gain that might be expected. For a time, in relatively backward countries, the problem of efficiency makes it a tossup whether the country is better off trying to run its own industries or paying the price of foreign ownership and operation. But cast on their own initiative, such peoples learn rapidly. Nationalism seeks to promote independence. It should not be confused with Fascist nationalism.

Italian Fascism was compounded of four direct-action forces: the arditi, or discharged shock-troops, unable to find their way back into employment; the Sempre Pronto Blue Shirt Nationalists; the Syndicalists, or direct-action labor groups; and the militant squadri of middle-class youths, also unable to find lodgement in the customary professions because of the bad post-war economic conditions.

In most of the Latin-American countries such groups, to the extent that they exist, play a widely different role and have widely different aspirations. The regimes, with few exceptions, are already militaristic. In other words, the racial and cultural conflicts in Latin America have created disorders which have made the tradition of the strong nondemocratic government one of long-standing persistence. It is the army of the State itself which revolts and puts in a new leader. This is not Fascism, it is the old Roman Praetorian-guard tradition.

The nationalistic trends, however, embrace all classes. Even the most reactionary governments, when it comes to a question of native labor against foreign labor, or even foreign capital versus native labor, are gradually beginning to decide in favor of their own nationals. Many such reactionary regimes have actually granted labor more rights than the ineffectually organized labor groups have been able to gain through their own weak organizations. In fact, in few of the countries is there as yet a large proletariat in the Marxian sense.

In Europe, labor feels that it can increase its share of the national income and wealth only by seizure of the State or by seizure of existing private property. In Latin America the same pressure does not exist. Land-monopoly, it is true, has created an artificial pressure, as in the case of the early American colonies. But sparse settlement still makes many economic solutions possible. In an expanding industrial system, such as exists in the Latin-American countries, whatever course economic and political events take, the worker now sees the possibility of a better standard of living. The alternatives are still wider than in Europe.

As native industry develops, its only serious enemy is foreign capitalism. More and more it backs nationalist programs.

Previously in Latin America there were great social gaps, with a very insignificant middle class. Now the middle class is everywhere expanding. Its aims are far different from those of European middle classes whose very existence is threatened by the collapse of capitalism in the Old World and the class-war between the owners of industry and the proletariat. The middle class to the south is, rather, against militarism and the old feudal aristocracy. It represents a laissez faire force, and the whole industrial development tends to crack the old molds of feudal and ecclesiastic monopoly of power.

And so, in Latin America, the militaristic regimes are more often those of the traditional feudal and military elements rather than the newer groups, rising to importance.

They cannot by any stretch of imagination, in most cases, be considered Fascist, despite their occasional alliances, as of Batista in Cuba, with powerful foreign capital.

Thus, by and large, the native Nazi and Fascist organizations in Latin America merely represent monkey-dressed fads or serve small cliques to maintain their political bartering power. They do not and cannot represent a national imperative. If some governments have briefly taken the slogans of Fascism, as Vargas in Brazil and Franco in Paraguay, it is merely an aping of an alien creed that does not and cannot have the same implications—like a general trying to imitate a Roxy usher.

In fact the various Latin-American governments, with few exceptions, have stolen most of the Fascist thunder for other purposes than Fascism. Even semi-Socialistic states, like México, pursue a nationalist program, and all slogans include the new middle class and the army as proletarian allies against foreign capital. This has Fascistic notes, but it is not Fascism; and the component forces, whatever the similarities, have far different aims and function in a different way.

If, in this book, I have frequently been guilty of speaking of Fascist governments to the south, this has been merely a convenient but no exact handle. It merely serves to prove the inadequacy of much of our political and sociological terminology, and to the blurring of all analyses, the destruction of all finesse of classification and of the most elementary understanding of political phenomena, a process of befuddling to which both the Communists and Fascists have greatly contributed, and yet which is not half so gross as our State Department's general lumping of all countries in the Western Hemisphere in the "democratic" column. It merely reveals how one arm of our government has been reduced, in the hurly-burly of the times, to base its appeals and even its policies on the grossest demagogy.

8

But the real bulwark in Latin America against alien ideologies, including our own, is in the people themselves. The people of Latin America, so oppressed by their own semi-Fascist governments, are not kindly toward the Fascist powers. Wherever they have been given a chance to express their true opinions, they have indicated clearly that they have no sympathy for Fascism, but desire more democracy and more liberty—a process actually obstructed by our own State Department by its false labels and ill-considered support to such tyrannies as those of Brazil, its support of re-armament and its power-politics.

The answer to present events eventually rests with the people of Latin America. The people of Latin America still have ahead of them a titanic struggle for freedom, political and economic. Only in México have the people forged ahead to assert to some extent their own freedom, to control foreign capital, to improve the standards of the workers and the peasants, to build up a more independent economy, and to create a new nation founded on popular rights.

Elsewhere the people still have before them the task of getting rid of military dictatorships, of promoting democracy, of abolishing the centuries-old system of monopoly land-holding, of creating proper labor codes, of abolishing age-old political and economic inequalities. That, and not the international politics, is the true sphere of coming Latin-American effort.

In this struggle, many sinister outside forces will be at work. Unfortunately, the people of Latin America are not likely in those struggles to turn to the United States, which now so supports the governments which oppress them. As a government or as a people, we have rarely shown great sympathy for the struggles of the Latin-American people to achieve free governments and liberate themselves from the military tyrannies that weigh them down.

The people of Latin America can hardly accept with pleasure the words of President Roosevelt that they already have democracy and freedom. They at least know better.

A great destiny awaits the people and the countries of Hispanic America. They have great contributions to make to the cultural wealth of mankind. They stand on the brink of momentous new discoveries in political, economic and social organization. Alien forces that warp their growth and obstruct their self-discovery will be pushed aside. The impending struggles for freedom in Latin America bear in embryo the mature development of now submerged races and cultures. The struggle of the people of the southern countries against militarism, against feudal enslavement, against mass serfdom, against foreign domination, against ecclesiastical exploitation—that is the only *real* struggle that exists in Latin America, that is the only struggle of importance.

INDEX

A.B.C., 144, 229, 231, 234
Academy of Natural Sciences, 200
Acre Province, 20
Agüero, Felix, 336
Aguirre Cerda, Pedro, 154
Airplanes, 14, 82, 91, 173, 250, 284, 287, 316, 317, 346, 356, 358, 361
Alagoas, 52
Albizú Campos, Pedro, 240
Alessandri, Pres., 55, 80, 98, 136, 153
All-American Cables, 187, 280, 314
Alvear, Marcelo T. de, 319
Amazon, 15, 21, 45, 114, 328, 332
American and Foreign Power Company, 117, 187, 196, 281, 364
American Arbitration Association, 190
American Federation of Labor, 210
American Manufacturers Export Association, 189, 190
American Mercury, 180
American Mission to Lepers, 205
American Philosophical Society, 209
American Popular Revolutionary Alliance, Cf. APRA
American Smelting and Refining Co., 277
Amkino, 137
Amtorg, 140
Anatasi, Dr. Leonidas, 362
Andes, 20, 44, 51, 63, 117, 316, 319, 340, 345, 348
Anglo-Brazilian Chronicle, 119
Anglo-Brazilian Graphic, 119
A Noite, 54
Anti-Imperialist League, 137, 148, 175, 211
Antilles, Cf. West Indies

Antofagasta, 339
APRA, 101, 145, 147, 150, 152, 182
Aracena, General Diego, 56, 100
Arbaiza, Genaro, 180, 213-15, 285, 286
Arboleya, Atalaya, 165-66
Arequipa, 49, 76, 101
Argentina,
  agriculture, 48, 297, 324, 325, 331
  airplanes, 54
  alfalfa, 325
  area, 325
  armaments, 54, 124-25, 167, 316, 324, 326, 349, 350
  army, 83, 166, 320, 321, 326
  automobiles, 92
  aviation, 54, 63, 64, 90, 94, 96, 199, 267, 275, 279, 280, 287, 316, 317, 324, 326
  banking, 22, 48, 53, 88, 89, 113, 114, 321
  Black League, 273, 317, 349
  Bolivia, 112, 129, 302, 323, 327, 328, 337-42, 343-46, 349, 351
  boundaries, 284, 345, 348
  boycott, 80
  Brazil, 54, 284, 312, 326-27, 330-35, 343-44, 346, 348, 349
  British, 120, 300
  cable service, 179, 280
  capital, 323, 336
  Catholics, 72
  cattle, 126, 300, 325, 336
  Chaco, 89, 323, 328, 339-43
  Chile, 284, 343, 345, 348, 349
  civil liberties, 248
  climate, 324
  coal, 330

Argentina, Continued
  Colombia, 348-49
  Communists, 144, 154
  Concordia Party, 98, 319
  Conservative Party, 98, 319, 320
  corn, 325, 371
  cotton, 325, 327
  currency, 369, 370
  debts, 319
  democracy, 249, 273
  dictatorship, 166, 172
  economic nationalism, 321, 325, 330, 351
  Ecuador, 327
  education, 75, 93
  England, 55, 80, 93, 103, 129, 130, 131-32, 300, 316, 318, 322-24, 326, 331, 340, 341, 348, 351, 364, 369, 370
  Fascism, 97, 98, 103, 166, 172, 249, 318
  Fascists, 80
  fisheries, 17, 297
  France, 64
  Franco, 161, 164
  Germans, Germany, 48, 52-54, 63, 72, 75, 80, 82, 83, 120, 122, 133, 300, 326, 370
  Guardia Argentina, 98
  hides, 300, 325
  immigration, 48
  imperialism, 112, 124-25, 129, 316-52
  independence, 110
  industries, 325, 326
  investments, 22, 52, 55, 300, 318, 322, 326-27, 336
  iron, 330
  Italy, 48, 52, 53, 54, 63, 72, 75, 80, 82, 83, 96, 99, 103, 104, 120, 131, 300, 316, 323, 326, 348, 351
  Japan, 17, 19, 21, 22, 24
  Jews, 69, 71, 134
  labor, 80, 92
  Legión Cívica, 98

Argentina, Continued
  loans, 111, 178
  meat, 21, 132, 282, 364
  munitions, 82, 341-42
  Navy, 112, 124-25, 350
  Nazis, 69, 71, 72, 80, 320, 334
  newspapers, 69, 109, 134, 319, 375
  oil, 52, 340-41, 343, 345, 364
  Pampas, 337
  Paraguay, 112, 129, 302, 323, 324, 328, 334-37, 340-42, 344
  Perú, 327, 346
  Poles, 48
  politics, 318, 319, 324
  population, 325
  propaganda, 69, 71
  public works, 319
  quebracho, 89, 336
  radio, 93
  railroads, 319
  rivers, 327
  roads, 319
  Russians, 48
  Soviet Union, 141-42
  Spain, 48, 161, 164
  steamship service, 90, 114, 115, 143, 283, 336
  students, 205
  sugar, 325
  tariffs, 345
  United States, 122, 129, 131, 177, 245, 259, 273, 287, 310, 311, 319-20, 322-24, 326, 351, 370-71
  Uruguay, 112, 127, 129, 323, 327, 333, 334-35, 344
  wheat, 126, 132, 297, 322, 324, 327, 371
  wine, 89, 325, 371
Argentine Navigation Company, 115
Argentinisces Tageblatt, 69
Arias, Harmodio, 240, 241
Armaments, 124-25, 213-14, 258, 283-88
  Argentina, 82, 167

Armaments, *Continued*
Brazil, 62, 82
Chile, 56, 82-83, 346
Colombia, 346
Ecuador, 82
Guatemala, 82
Italy, 99
Latin America, 250
Nicaragua, 82
Paraguay, 337
Perú, 367
United States, 283, 303, 310-11
Venezuela, 82, Cf. Munitions
Asia America, 40
Aski Marks, 52, 53, 54, 57, 58, 60,
262, 264, 369
Associated Press, 118, 178, 180, 181
Asunción, 38
Atlantic Gulf and West Indies
Steamship Company, 283
Automobiles, 24, 55, 270
tires, 24, 356
Aviation, 115-16
Argentina, 54, 56, 64, 65, 100,
275, 277, 279-80, 316-17
Bolivia, 63-64, 345
Brazil, 63, 64, 90, 95, 96, 100,
279-80, 345
Caribbean, 278
Chile, 56, 63, 83, 96, 277, 359
Colombia, 63, 65
Cuba, 277-78
Dominican Republic, 278
Ecuador, 65
England, 115-16
France, 64, 279-80
Germany, 54, 56, 63-65, 83, 276-
80, 344-45
Italy, 83, 90, 95, 96, 99, 100,
101, 279, 280
México, 361
Panamá, 276-77
Paraguay, 99, 279
Perú, 64, 95, 100, 101, 276
Puerto Rico, 278

Aviation, *Continued*
United States, 54, 56, 64, 65,
100, 275-80, 316-17
Uruguay, 63, 90, 96, 280
Aviation Corporation of America,
278
Ayala, Eusebio, 336

Balbo, 95, 99
Baldomir, 334
Banana, 21, 51, 150, 263, 357, 364
Bandera Roja
Chile, 152
Cuba, 149, 150
Banking, 22, 48, 366-67
American, 282
Argentina, 22, 53, 88, 89, 282,
321
Bolivia, 338
Brazil, 22, 53, 88, 89, 282
Central America, 282
Chile, 53, 88, 89, 282
Colombia, 88, 282
Cuba, 282
Ecuador, 88
English, 282
French, 282
German, 48, 53, 282
Haiti, 282
Japanese, 22
México, 53, 282
Panamá, 282
Paraguay, 53
Perú, 53, 88, 89, 102, 288
Puerto Rico, 282
Salvador, 58
Spanish, 282
Uruguay, 22, 53, 88, 282, 364
Venezuela, 282
Barnes, Harry Elmer, 220
Barrett, 185
Barrows, David P., 187, 212-13
Barter systems, Cf. Trade
Batista, Fulgencio, 60, 149, 165,
166, 188, 208, 224, 231, 234-
36, 301, 378

Bauer, Dr. Von, 277
Beagle Channel, 345, 348
Beaverbrook, Lord, 115
Becker, Archbishop Joâo, 103
Bejarano, José Miguel, 359
Bemis, Samuel Flagg, 213
Benavides, Oscar, 43, 101, 102, 145, 152, 167, 170, 274, 300, 346
Berlin, 63, 64, 65, 72, 74, 75, 83, 276
Beteta, Ramón, 200
Bethlehem Steel Company, 282, 286
Black League, 159, 166, 249, 273, 317
Boersen Zeitung, 61, 79
Bogotá, 42, 184, 241, 309, 355
Bolivia
　Argentina, 112, 129, 322-23, 327, 337-42, 346, 351
　armaments, 124-25
　army, 82, 99
　aviation, 63, 64
　banking, 338
　Brazil, 334, 338, 340, 343, 349
　cattle, 339
　Chaco War, 84, 125, 337, 339, 343
　Chile, 332, 338, 339, 343
　coffee, 339
　Communists, 154
　cotton, 339
　currency, 370
　education, 76
　England, 129, 339, 340, 341
　Fascism, 249
　Germany, 49, 63, 64, 82, 334
　investments, 126, 337-44
　Italy, 99
　Japanese, 19, 20
　mining, 338
　oil, 338, 340-43
　Paraguay, 334, 337, 340, 341
　Perú, 338
　railroads, 117, 338, 339
　rice, 370

Bolivia, Continued
　United States, 126, 259, 338, 340
　Uruguay, 334
　vanadium, 126
　wolfram, 126
Bolivar Simón, 110
Bolsheviks, Cf. Soviet Union, Communists, etc.
Bolshevique, El, 151
Bordenave, Dr., 336
Borodin, 135
Brazil, 18-19, 21, 33, 50, 52, 53, 54, 60, 61, 75, 76, 78, 79, 89, 91, 96, 126, 134, 142, 181, 189, 287, 295, 312, 332, 334, 337, 358
　agriculture, 19, 89, 357
　American naval mission, 285
　Argentina, 127, 284, 302, 310, 326, 330, 332, 334, 343, 347-49
　armaments, 62, 125, 285, 286, 310
　aviation, 63, 64, 90, 95, 96, 100, 279
　banking, 22, 59, 77, 88, 89, 113, 114, 282
　Bolivia, 334, 338, 340, 344, 349
　British, 120
　cable services, 60, 115, 179, 280
　Chile, 345, 347, 349
　coal, 54, 332
　coffee, 21, 50, 53, 54, 357
　Colombia, 321, 347, 349
　Communists, 144, 153, 155
　copper, 52, 332
　cotton, 21, 29, 43, 51, 53, 61, 87, 297, 299, 357, 371
　dictatorship, 78, 79, 157, 164, 166, 169-70, 172, 187, 224, 249, 273, 274, 354, 379
　Ecuador, 347
　England, 54, 84, 112-15, 118, 119, 122, 125, 127
　Fascism, 169-70, 249
　Fascists, 77, 78, 79, 378

Brazil, *Continued*
Franco, 161, 163, 164
Germany, 50, 51, 53, 54, 61, 62, 63, 67, 68, 71, 73, 74, 76-79, 82, 83, 98, 120, 312, 322, 334, 347, 348, 354
industry, 331, 357-58
Integralistas, 76-77, 98
investments, 51, 52, 89
iron, 52, 302, 358
Italy, 86, 87-89, 90, 95, 96, 98, 99, 104, 120, 125, 322
Japanese, 18-19, 20, 22, 29, 33, 43, 51, 120
Jews, 81, 287
labor, 19
loans, 178
manganese, 332
mining, 67, 118
munitions, 43, 76, 77, 82, 99
Nazis, 71, 72, 76, 77, 78, 312, 313, 334
Navy, 43, 77, 99, 125, 285
oil, 52, 332, 340, 347, 363
Paraguay, 334, 335, 337, 340
population, 332
Portugal, 160, 163
propaganda, 61, 62, 67, 73, 76, 374
radio, 60-61, 67, 73, 181
railroads, 54, 117, 344, 347
rubber, 20, 21, 43, 282, 285, 356-57
silk, 357, 358
Spain, 161, 163, 164
steamship service, 90, 114, 115, 286
students, 74, 105
sugar, 21, 89
tea, 357
textiles, 358
trade, 53, 54, 122, 265, 358
tin, 332
United States, 53, 61, 62, 78, 79, 100, 122, 125, 169, 172, 187, 267, 273, 287, 288, 297, 299,

Brazil, *Continued*
301, 310, 311, 313, 321, 322, 354
Uruguay, 127, 334, 335
Venezuela, 347
Brazilian Press, 119
Brazilian Review, 118 n.
Briceño, Julio E., 32
British Honduras, 129
Browder, Earl, 147, 148, 212
Brown, James Scott, 186
Buell, Raymond Leslie, 163, 172, 207
Buenos Aires, 20, 22, 24, 46, 63, 64, 69, 87, 89, 91, 92, 95, 99, 105, 115, 116, 117, 125, 130, 134, 135, 149, 154, 166, 213, 249, 277, 279, 280, 319, 321, 325, 327, 329, 333, 340, 341, 346
Colegio Americano, 204
Empire Trade Exhibition, 105, 107
National Palace, 316
newspapers, 319
Pan-American Conference, 145, 159, 167, 205, 247, 248, 251, 272, 308
province of, 103, 145
Buenos Aires Herald, 119
Bunau Varilla, 84
Burgos, 165
Busch, Germán, 151
Butler, Nicholas Murray, 186

Cable services, 60, 115, 178-179, 280-81, 288
Caffery, Jeffersons, 208, 222, 231, 233, 235, 301
Callao, 22, 111, 114
Calles, Plutarco Elias, 75, 136, 137, 147, 227
Canada, 106, 113, 114, 116, 173, 227, 272, 281, 324, 361
Canal Zone, 13, 14, 19, 20, 42, 240, 241, 277, 297

Cantil, José María, 103, 323, 348
Capitalism, 157, 134, 220-21, 363
Carbó, Segio, 229
Cárdenas, Lázaro, 140, 168, 201
Carnegie Endowment for International Peace, 186, 205
Carnegie Institute, 200, 296
Caribbean, 16, 18, 49, 88, 90, 116, 121, 177, 207, 214, 248, 274, 275, 278, 281, 283, 323, 344, 356
Carson, James S., 180, 187-189, 191, 196, 197, 198
Catholic Church, 37, 62, 72, 92, 96, 97, 134, 161, 179, 205, 206, 215, 227
Cattle, 126, 142, 300, 325, 339, 357
Cedillo, Saturnino, 81
Cement, 24, 58, 357, 358, 360
Central America, 17, 18, 20, 32, 35, 40, 50, 58, 73, 84, 88, 90, 99, 121, 150, 161, 179, 183, 206, 237, 238, 239, 282, 288, 302, 350, 361, 371
Chaco, 42, 45, 82, 112, 125, 151, 302, 323, 328, 337, 339, 340, 341, 342, 343, 344, 350, 366
Chamber of Commerce, 22, 38, 175, 190, 198, 289
Chicama Valley, 20, 56, 83
Chile, 17, 24, 48, 51, 52, 55, 62, 73, 78, 89, 91, 97, 99, 100, 110, 118, 120, 142, 153, 154, 157, 162, 248, 295, 300, 348, 349, 358, 359, 364, 365, 375
  agriculture, 48-49
  Araucanos, 48
  Argentina, 249, 284, 343, 345, 347, 348
  armaments, 124-25, 250
  army, 82, 153, 346
  aviation, 56, 82, 83, 96, 100, 103, 250, 346, 359
  banking, 53, 88, 89, 113, 282
  Bolivia, 332, 338-39, 346
  cable service, 179, 280-81

Chile, Continued
  copper, 55, 300
  currency, 91, 189, 358, 364, 365, 370
  debts, 178, 365, 367
  England, 54, 55, 82, 91, 97, 112, 121, 124-25, 365
  Fascism, 98, 249
  Franco, 160, 161
  Germany, 45, 48, 51, 53-56, 62, 73, 75, 79-80, 82-83, 91, 97, 120, 121, 162, 348, 359
  iron, 282, 300, 359
  Italy, 55, 87-91, 96, 99, 100, 103
  Japan, 17, 19, 22, 24, 38, 120, 359
  Navy, 99, 124-25
  Nazis, 72, 79-80, 98, 154
  nitrates, 52, 99, 300, 332, 365
  Perú, 88, 248, 332, 346
  propaganda, 62, 73
  railroads, 339, 365
  trade, 54, 55, 121, 359, 370
  United States, 124, 153, 359, 364
Chilean Review, 119
Chimbote, 19, 20
China, 28, 34, 35, 40, 43, 44, 54, 62, 135, 136, 185
Civil liberties, 146, 152, 153, 154, 169, 201, 248
Clarendon-Mosquera treaty, 123
Cleveland, Grover, 129, 177
Coal, 54, 330, 332, 359, 368
Coffee, 50, 59, 102, 124, 215, 220, 224, 262, 299, 339, 349, 353, 355, 357
Colombia, 17, 24, 35, 44, 49, 50, 51, 52, 54, 57, 58, 63, 65, 88-89, 110, 113-15, 118, 123, 124, 129, 150, 151, 156, 184, 197-99, 264, 265, 282, 284, 346, 347, 348, 355, 364, 369
  Germany, 49, 51, 52, 54, 57, 58, 63, 67, 84, 264, 348
  Japan, 18, 19, 24, 30

Colombia, *Continued*
  United States, 58, 129, 150, 151,
    241, 309-310, 321, 355, 364
Comercio, El, 92
Comintern, 133, 134, 135-43, 163
Committee on Coöperation with
  Latin America, 202
Committee for Cultural Relations
  with Latin America, 205-7
Committee on Industrial Organiza-
  tion (C.I.O.), 211
Committee on Inter-American Re-
  lations, 189
Communism, Communists, 80, 133,
  135-58, 168, 175, 194, 211-12,
  216, 294, 301, 353, 378
Communist International, Cf. Com-
  intern
Communist International, 145, 149
Confederación Latino Americana,
  142
Coolidge, Calvin, 177, 226, 232
Copper, 52, 55, 300, 332, 353
Corn, 126, 325, 353, 371
Corumbá, 52, 63, 64
Costa Rica, 17, 19, 33, 34, 35, 38,
  49, 117, 150, 156, 165, 248,
  259, 265, 270, 368
Cotton, 19, 20, 21, 27, 28, 29, 31,
  51, 53, 58, 89, 123, 297, 299,
  325, 336, 337, 339, 353, 354,
  356, 369, 371
Crítica, La, 80, 319
CROM, 137-41, 210, 211
Crowder, 282
CTM, 34, 69, 141, 144, 147, 148,
  211
Cuba, 16, 18, 24, 30, 33, 47, 60,
  91, 104, 112, 114, 115, 117,
  144, 146, 148, 150, 153, 157,
  162, 164-67, 183, 188, 193,
  194, 199-200, 209, 224, 227-
  36, 263, 274, 280, 281, 282,
  298, 301, 304, 358, 360
  American capital, 202, 281, 374,
    378

Cuba, *Continued*
  iron, 282
  population, 236
  United States, 177, 199-200, 207-
    09, 218, 227-36, 243, 244,
    250, 255, 256, 263, 264, 270,
    298, 301, 304, 310
Curaçao, 115, 281
Currency, 25, 83, 91, 189, 192,
  252, 254, 256, 257, 262, 264,
  265, 358, 364, 368, 369-70
Current History, 213, 286
Cuyamel Fruit Company, 284, 302
Czechoslovakia, 124, 274

Daily Worker, 212
Darío, Rubén, 24
Davidson, Viscount, 112
Debts, 84, 100, 177, 217, 238, 253,
  254, 255, 264, 268, 319, 365,
  366, 367
De Céspedes, 228, 229, 230
Democracy, 41, 64, 78, 79, 98, 131,
  134, 155, 156, 157, 159, 165,
  166, 167, 169, 172, 174, 217,
  240, 247, 272, 276, 287, 291,
  294, 300, 303, 306, 315, 348,
  354, 373, 378, 379, 380
De Pinedo, 99
Detweiler, Chas. S., 202
Diario de Costa Rica, 34
Díaz, Porfirio, 47, 177, 351
Dickman, Enrique, 80, 334
Dictatorship, 41, 78, 79, 97, 134,
  156-59, 161, 162, 164-70, 172,
  188, 210, 224, 238, 274, 276,
  291, 298, 300-04, 351, 354,
  373, 379
Diffie, Baylie, 220
Dollar diplomacy, 79, 239, 282, 343
Dominican Republic, 32, 49, 50,
  82, 141, 150, 161, 166, 214,
  259, 271, 278, 282, 356
  dictatorship, 166, 224, 274, 301,
    302, 351
  Germany, 49-50, 60, 82

Dominican Republic, Continued
  Japan, 32, 356
  manufacturing, 356
Duggin, Stephen P., 188

Ecuador, 17-18, 24, 43, 50, 57, 82,
    88, 99, 113, 147, 151, 284,
    327, 347, 364, 370
  Germany, 43, 47, 49, 57, 65, 82,
    83, 370
  Japan, 17-18, 24, 33
  Perú, 99, 347
  United States, 57, 259
Electric Boat Company, 100, 124
Electric Bond and Share Company,
    187, 277, 281
Electric resources, 117, 191, 192,
    291, 364, 368
El Paso, 177, 242
England, 14, 18, 54, 55, 59, 63, 73,
    84, 100, 104-32, 136, 159,
    162, 177, 179, 240, 275, 293,
    323, 331, 339, 348, 349, 350,
    359, 373, 374
  Argentina, 103, 105, 107, 126,
    129, 300, 318, 326, 331, 337,
    341, 348, 351, 364, 369, 370
  banking, 113-14, 282
  Brazil, 54, 84, 91, 112, 126, 127,
    331
  Chile, 54, 55, 82, 91, 112, 365
  Colombia, 54, 58, 129
  Germany, 62, 66, 84, 104, 122-
    24, 128, 169-71, 322
  imperialism, 112, 134, 243
  investments, 40, 109-14, 121,
    318, 326, 337, 341, 374
  Italy, 93, 126, 128, 130, 131,
    169-71, 323, 333, 334
  México, 59, 84, 111, 112, 128
  munitions, 82, 124-25, 274, 351
  Navy, 84, 112, 126
  Perú, 54, 339, 348
  propaganda, 62, 66, 118-19, 181,
    293, 373
  Spain, 127, 131, 162, 169-71

England, Continued
  trade, 12, 25, 30, 54, 58, 59,
    105 ff., 119, 121, 129, 130-33,
    258, 271, 300, 322
  United States, 54, 121-24, 126,
    128, 129, 130-33, 169-71, 177,
    311, 337
  Venezuela, 54, 129, 177
Erie Canal, 329, 330
Espelucín, 152
Espiritu Santo, 52
Estigarribia, 336
Estrada, Genaro, 140
Ethiopia, 62, 91, 93, 96, 104, 127,
    169, 218
Exchange controls, Cf. Currency

Fabra, 181
Fascism, 134, 144, 149, 150, 151-
    53, 159-60, 165-74, 275-315,
    318, 350, 374, 375, 378
Fascist Action for Italians in South
    America, 86
Fascists, 56, 80, 123, 127, 131,
    139, 169-74, 225, 261, 273,
    313, 349, 353, 374, 378, 379,
    Cf. Germany, Italy, etc.
Faucett Aviation Co., 279
Federal Council of Churches, 205
Federzone, Luigi, 86, 94, 163
Fellowship of Reconciliation, 206
Films, Cf. Movies
First National Bank of Boston, 282
Fishing industry, 13, 16-18, 298
Flores da Cunha, 77
Forbes, Lord, 115
Foreign Policy Association, 70, 163,
    206, 207, 209
Foreign Trade Association, 189
Foreign Trade Review, 189
France, 25, 33, 37, 51, 62, 115,
    118, 128, 162, 240, 279, 280,
    283, 299, 302, 326, 329, 333,
    337, 350
Francia José Gaspar Rodríguez, 334

Franco, Francisco, 62, 93, 96, 97, 154, 159-74
Franco, Luis, 363
Franco, Rafael, 336, 378
Frank, Waldo, 188
Frente a Frente, 148
Fresno, Governor Manuel, 103, 154
Fruit, 24, 48, 142, 235, 297, 302, 357, 360
Futuro, 148, 304

Galapagos Islands, 17
Galván, Ursulo, 137
Gamio, Manuel, 75
Gayde, Virginio, 86, 87
General Electric Company, 73, 196, 289
Germans, Germany, 14, 18, 32, 45-88, 96, 100, 120, 124, 127, 128, 150, 159, 162, 163, 165, 166-79, 283, 290, 293, 294, 295, 299, 308, 310, 312, 314, 315, 322, 326, 334, 336, 337, 345, 369, 370, 373
  Argentina, 48, 50-54, 68, 69, 71, 72, 75, 80, 82, 83, 122, 300, 326
  aviation, 83, 95, 100, 115, 279, 280
  Brazil, 47, 48, 50-54, 61-64, 67-79, 82, 83, 98
  Chile, 48, 50-56, 62, 63, 72, 73, 75, 79, 82, 83, 91
  imperialism, 134, 163, 168
  investments, 150, 163
  Jews, 61, 68-70
  munitions, 43, 52, 82, 124, 125, 173, 274
  news, 60, 61, 118, 179
  Perú, 45, 47, 49-56, 62, 64, 75, 83, 95, 100
  propaganda, 180, 182, 293, 297, 310, 312, 314, 373, 374
  Spain, 160, 162, 163, 166-74

Germans, Germany, *Continued*
  trade, 31, 45-85, 91, 121-24, 130, 150, 159, 163, 168, 257-63, 265, 300, 302, 373
Gestapo, 66, 68, 69
Gildermeisters, 51, 52, 83
Goebbels, 60, 73, 310
Gôes Monteiro, 77, 345
Golden Rule Foundation, 205
Gold Shirts, 80
Gómez, Juan Vicente, 151
González Marín, General, 160
González von Marées, 80
Goyaz, 52
Grace Line, 23, 113, 197, 278, 282, 283, 359
Grau San Martín, Ramón, 148, 149, 208, 228, 229, 230, 231, 232, 233, 234, 237, 238
Great Britain, Cf. England
Grove, Marmaduke, 80, 152
Guatemala, 32, 59, 73, 81, 82, 87, 88, 96, 97, 102, 113, 146, 164, 170, 172, 224, 265, 274, 284, 301, 302, 311, 314, 350, 371
Guayaquil, 33, 47, 65
Guaymas, 17
Guedalla, Philip, 120
Guerrero, Xavier, 138
Guggenheim, Harry, 236, 277, 298
Guggenheim interests, 282, 365
Guggenheim scholarships, 205, 296
Guggiari, José, 87
Guianas, 90, 129, 177
Guiteras, Antonio, 149
Gulf Stream Magazine, 190

Haiti, 50, 97, 114, 144, 150, 183, 213, 214, 259, 265, 274, 281, 282, 302
  United States, 97, 177, 183, 202, 218, 226, 227, 265, 310
Haring, Clarence H., 212
Harris, H. L., 196
Hartford Foundation, 206

Havana, 117, 228, 277, 282
  Evangelical Congress, 203
  German Minister, 162
  Jigg's café, 229
  Marianao Casino, 162
  O'Reilly Street, 229
  Pan-American Conference, 177,
    205, 226
  University of, 208
Havas, 60, 118, 178, 181
Howard, Roy, 180
Haya de la Torre, 144, 145, 152,
  303
Henequén, 51, 58, 136, 353, 360
Herald Tribune, N. Y., 215, 287
Hernández, Francisco Alfonso, 233
Herring, Dr. Hubert Clinton, 205-
  207, 342
Hides, 53, 58, 141, 220, 270, 300,
  325, 353
Hitler, 46, 49-52, 56, 62, 65, 68,
  69, 75, 85, 103, 156, 165, 167,
  168, 170, 182, 267, 272, 287
Hochstein, Joshua, 188
Honduras, 37, 49, 350
Hoover, Herbert, 177, 188, 226,
  227, 232, 236, 238, 245, 296
Hughes, Charles Evans, 212, 226
Huidobro, Vicente, 103
Hull, Cordell, 45, 53, 59, 166, 171,
  173, 196, 200, 205, 218, 236,
  249, 251, 252, 255-57, 260,
  262-65, 268-71, 286, 290, 294,
  297-98, 309, 311, 320, 321,
  371

Ibañez, Carlos, 80, 153, 154
Ibañez, Father Pedro, 161
Ibero-American Institute of Great
  Britain, 119
Ica, 20, 89
Ickes, Secretary, 239, 297
Iguasu, 45, 327
Immigration, Cf. Various countries
Imperialism, Cf. England, Germany,
  United States, etc.

Indians, 37, 47, 48, 51, 76, 150,
  151, 157, 158, 363
Información económica y estadística,
  58
Inman, Samuel Guy, 40, 70, 146,
  186, 202, 203, 204, 205
Institute of Current World Affairs,
  201
Institute of International Education,
  205
Instituto de las Españas, 205
Instituo Interuniversitario Italiano,
  93
Integralistas, 76, 77, 169, 312, 334,
  336, 345
Inter-America, 212
Inter-American Commercial Arbitra-
  tion Council, 189
International News, 118, 180, 183
International Students' Congress,
  205
International Telephone and Tele-
  graph Company, 179, 190,
  280, 281, 314
Investments, Cf. England, United
  States, Germany, etc.
Iquitos, 114
Irigoyen, Hipólito, 318
Iron, 282, 300, 302, 330, 331, 332,
  357, 358, 359, 360
Italy, 14, 41, 69, 86-104, 127, 131,
  134, 146, 159, 160, 162, 166,
  170, 284, 285, 308, 323, 337,
  350, 383
  Argentina, 80, 87-92, 94-98, 103,
    104, 131, 300, 318, 323, 326,
    351
  aviation, 83, 90, 94, 95, 99-101,
    115, 279, 286, 287
  banking, 88-90, 92, 102
  Brazil, 86-91, 96, 99, 100, 114,
    125
  Chile, 55, 83, 87, 89, 91, 96, 97,
    99, 100, 103
  England, 104, 126, 128, 130-31,
    322-24

Italy, *Continued*
  Ethiopia, 91, 96, 104, 168
  Franco, 160, 162, 163, 169-71
  investments, 87, 88, 102, 181, 326
  munitions, 43, 58, 99-101, 102, 124, 125, 173, 274, 288, 351
  Nicaragua, 58, 97, 102, 265, 288
  Perú, 88-96, 99-104, 152, 170, 287
  propaganda, 86, 92, 93, 118, 182, 290, 310, 374
  trade, 33, 91, 122, 130-31, 160, 257, 258, 260
  Uruguay, 87-90, 92, 96
Ito, Kuro, 31
Iuamtorg Corporation, 98, 142-43

Jalisco, 138
James, Earl K., 271
Japan, 13-44, 51, 56-58, 59, 62, 69, 80, 106, 120, 122-25, 130, 150, 165, 170, 185, 212, 218, 293, 300, 311, 337, 350, 356, 371
  Brazil, 18-22, 29, 33, 43, 51, 120, 371
  Chile, 17, 19, 22, 23, 28
  fishing industry, 13-18
  labor, 19, 20, 23, 26, 28, 33, 35
  México, 18-20, 32-39, 120, 212
  Panamá, 13-14, 17, 19, 22, 24, 32, 120
  Perú, 17-24, 29, 33, 34, 42-44, 120, 123, 152
  propaganda, 26, 35, 36, 93
  textiles, 23, 31, 33, 34, 123, 255
  trade, 12, 22-26, 29-30, 32-44, 53, 54, 56-59, 69, 91, 93, 97, 122-25, 130, 146, 150, 165, 257-60, 300, 302
Japanese-Argentina Society, 37
Japanese Central and South American Export Association, 25
Japanese-Salvador Coffee Propaganda Society, 31

Jenks, Leland, 208
Jews, 61, 68-72, 134, 249, 287
Jiménez, President, 150
Jones-Costigan Act, 234-36, 263
Jones, Grosvenor, 199
Jones, Henry L., 189
Jones, Thomas Jesse, 205
Juiz de Fora, 52
Jungles, 20, 21, 45, 328
Justo, President, 80, 98, 249, 318

Kane, L., 17
Kasuga, Tsuyoshi, 31
Keith, Sir John, 119
Keith, Minor C., 186
Kellogg, 226
Kemmerer, Professor Edwin, 198, 199
Kennedy, 282
Kent, Duke of, 119, 122
Key West, 278
Kitagawa, 37
Klinger, Umberto, 90
Knights of Columbus, 206
Knox, Philander P., 282
Knudt, General, 82
Konishi, Yasuhei, 36
Kraevsky, 142-43, 209
Krupps, 52, 76, 82
Kubota, Tsunetaro, 31

Labor, 19, 20, 23, 26, 28, 34-35, 80, 92, 148, 194, 210-13, 221, 368, 379
  organizations, 156, Cf. CROM, CTM, etc.
Laborde, Hernán, 140, 211-12
Lafitte, Elias, 153
Lamas, Saavedra, 167
Land problems, 92, 156, 158, 161, 353, 363, 377, 379
La Paz, 64, 338, 339, 340, 344, 360
La Plata, University of, 362
La Quiaca, 338
Las Palmas, 100

Latin-American Bondholders' Association, 238
Latin-American *Digest*, 42, 230, 245, 359
Latin-American Society of Great Britain, 119
Latin American World, 116
La Unión, 62
League Against War and Fascism, 150
League of Mental Hygiene, 205
League of Nations, 30, 97, 127, 129, 342
Leahy, Admiral, 306
LEAR, 148
Leguía, Juan, 20
Lenin, Nicolai, 135, 136
Leticia, 42, 43, 145, 284, 346
Levin, Jack, 193
Lewis, John L., 211
Lewis, Sinclair, 362
Lima, 20, 24, 46, 50, 64, 88, 89, 92, 94, 95, 100, 101, 204, 276, 283, 309, 311
  University of, 205
Lindbergh, Charles, 177
Lisbon, 300
Lobo, Fernando, 289
Lombardo Toledano, 34, 141, 147, 211, 304
London, 114, 126, 139, 178
Longo, 103
López, Carlos Antonio, 334
López, Francisco, 335
López Meva, Manuel, 166
Lufthansa, 63, 64
Lugones, Leopoldo, 334
Lumber industry, 89, 142, 178, 339, 353, 359
Lynch, Reverend Frederick, 186

Machado, Gerardo, 148, 177, 199, 209, 210, 228, 230, 236, 277, 280, 281, 298
Machete, El, 137, 148
Mackay, Dr. John, 205

MacKenzie College, 204
Madeira River, 344
Madrid, 108, 109, 159, 300
Magallanes, 56
Magdalena River, 15
  highlands, 45
Magellan, Straits of, 43, 346
Majes Valley, 51
Makar, Dr., 139-40
Managua, 102
Manchester Guardian, 78
Manchuria, 30, 97, 218
Mancisidor, José, 148
Manganese, 21, 300, 332, 353, 357
Manufacturing, Cf. respective countries
Marañón River, 45
Mariátegui, José Carlos, 144
Marof, Tristán, 151
Marti, 232
Martin, C. C., 187, 188, 191
Martínez, Pres., 30, 148, 232, 237, 238, 301, 350
Martínez Fraga, Pedro, 188
Marx, Karl, 133
Mason, Frank D., 293
Matto Grosso, 52, 327
Maverick, Maury, 291, 312
Mazatlán, 32
McAdoo, Wm. G., 290
McBee, Silas, 186
McCoy, General, 295
McDonald, James G., 70
McGregor, John D., 197
McLean, Dr. J. H., 205
McLoughlin, 362
McNab, "Sandy," 313
McNich, Frank R., 289
Meat, 21, 84, 142, 235, 282, 300, 353, 356, 357, 364, 370
Mediterranean, 126, 163, 168, 347
Meiggs, Henry, 117
Mella, Julio Antonio, 138, 145, 148
Mendieta, Carlos, 207-8, 231-34
Mendoza, 89, 319
Mercurio, El, 359

Merrill, John L., 187-89, 197, 198
Mestizos, 37
Metapa, 24
Mexicali, 80
Mexican Labor Confederation, Cf. CTM
Mexican Labor News, 148
Mexican Labor Party, 136
Mexican Life, 81
Mexican Nationalist Union, 81
Mexican Regional Confederation of Labor, Cf. CROM
México, 17, 18, 20, 32, 39, 47, 50, 51, 53, 69, 71, 80, 83, 114, 116, 118, 128, 137, 138, 145, 158, 179, 182, 193, 205, 207, 248, 256, 268, 282, 286, 295, 299, 313, 351, 354, 360, 361, 363, 368, 375, 378
  Catholics, 205, 227
  Communists, 135-42, 144, 147-48
  England, 59, 84, 110-12, 114, 118, 120, 121, 126, 128
  Fascism, 102, 140, 165, 167
  Germany, 47, 50-53, 59, 69, 71, 81, 83, 85, 165
  Italy, 88, 92, 102, 162
  Japan, 17-20, 32, 37, 39, 47, 120
  labor, 34-35, 37, 69, 138, 141
  land problems, 50, 59, 137, 227, 243, 355, 363
  nationalism, 158, 355, 378
  Nazis, 71, 72, 80, 81, 102, 165
  oil, 33, 52, 59, 84, 99, 118, 126, 128, 211, 242, 243, 299, 313, 360, 363
  silver, 243, 363
  Spain, 47, 51, 156, 162, 165, 173
  trade, 121, 137, 256, 259, 266, 267, 355, 360, 361
  United States, 85, 121, 126, 128, 173, 177, 201, 226, 259, 266, 267, 299, 301, 304, 313, 337, 361, 375
Mexico City, 20, 117, 138, 140, 141, 204

Mexico City, *Continued*
  Brown House, 81
  Uruguay Street, 81
México-Japanese Society, 37
Meza, Congressman, 79
Miahanovich, Nicolás, 115
Miami, 275, 276, 277, 316
Michoacán, 19, 32
Middle-class, 145, 376
Militarism, 134, 377, 378, 379, 380, Cf. Armaments, munitions, dictatorship, etc.
Minas Geraes, 52
Mining, 118, 138, 282, 338, 355, 368
Miranda, Francisco, 109
Miro Quesado, Carlos, 92
Missionaries, 175, 202-4, Cf. Protestantism, etc.
Mississippi, 324, 328, 329
Mitsubishi, 43
Mollendo, 339
Monroe, James, 127
Monroe Doctrine, 85, 124, 129, 181, 218, 226, 276, 304, 307, 352
Monterrey, 360
Montevideo, 62, 90, 115, 116, 142, 204, 269, 280, 286, 306, 333
  Pan-American Conference, 196, 249, 359, 361
  Soviet Legation, 142
Montgomery, Captain J. F., 277
Moon, Dr. Parker, 220
Morales, Angel, 92, 102
Morgan, House of, 226
Morgan, J. P., 186
Morgenthau, 243, 287
Morocco, 240, 302
Morones, Luis N., 137
Morrow, Dwight W., 138, 140, 201, 281, 296
Moscow, 135, 143, 148, 153, 357
Movies, 67, 73-74, 137, 162, 163, 202, 295, 374
Munitions, 23, 31, 35, 43, 56, 76-7, 81, 82, 83, 99, 100, 102, 124-

25, 162, 164, 168, 170-73, 213-14, 274, 283-88, 308, 311, 313, 314, 316, 324, 337, 342, 351, 360, 373

Munro, Dana, 212, 213

Mussolini, Benito, 62, 86, 87, 91, 93, 94, 95, 97, 101-04, 127, 130, 131, 156, 167-68, 170, 182, 203, 218, 304, 351

Mussolini, Bruno, 90

Nacion, La (Trujillo), 33, 355, (Buenos Aires), 109

Natal, 90, 116

National Broadcasting Company, 288-89, 290, 293

National Catholic Welfare Conference, 206

National City Bank, 189, 278

National Conference for Educational Broadcasts, 288

National Foreign Trade Council, 189, 190

National Radio Association, 292

National Socialists, Cf. Nazis

Nationalism, economic, 157, 158, 225, 252, 294, 325, 351, 353-71
  Argentina, 321, 358, 364, 369-71
  México, 355, 360-61, 363, 364, 368

Navarro Montalvo, Francisco, 165

Nazi Jugend, 81

Nazis, 49, 50, 62, 65, 67-82, 85, 92, 98, 104, 144, 156, 160, 165-71, 301, 312, 314, 334, 353, 375, 378
  Jews, 70 ff.

Negroes, 147, 332

Nequén province, 52

Neutrality, 85, 91, 130, 162, 168-74, 322

New Deal, 198, 231, 239, 241, 242, 268

New Masses, 212

News Chronicle (London), 78

Newspapers, 62, 71, 76, 93, 192, 319, 375

News services, 36, 38, 60-62, 86, 118, 178, 180, 181, 288

New Orleans, 329, 332

New York, 50, 64, 75, 87, 114, 140, 153, 160, 162, 188, 270, 291
  India House, 197, 293

New York Shipbuilding Company, 285, 286

NYRBA, 279

Nicaragua, 24, 31, 49, 58, 82, 84, 97, 102, 113, 129, 151, 164, 213, 265, 288, 302
  trade, 258, 259, 261, 265
  United States, 31, 58, 97, 151, 177, 202, 212, 218, 226, 227, 229, 258, 288

Nickel, 52, 353

Nitrates, 52, 99, 282, 300, 332, 365

North American Cultural Institute, 204

North American Newspaper Alliance, 180

Norton, Charles, 213

Nova Scotia, Bank of, 114

N.R.A., 226

Nueva Democracia, La, 204

Nye, Senator, 171
  investigation by, 284, 286, 298

Oaxaca, 47

Ocumare, 110

Obregón, Alvaro, 223

Oil, 21, 32, 35, 52, 59, 84, 92, 99, 118, 126, 128, 142, 169, 184, 211, 242, 243, 264, 268, 332, 338, 339-41, 343, 345, 347, 363, 364, Cf. respective countries

Olguín, E., 101

Olney, 129, 177

Opinión, La (Chile), 152, (Santo Domingo), 356

Orient-Orientals, 15, 18, 43, 71, 372
Ortiz, Jorge, 94
Ortiz, Roberto, 80, 166, 249, 287, 316, 321, 323, 350, 351
Ortiz Rubio, 140
Ostria-Gutiérrez Treaty, 343

Palacios, Alfredo L., 224
Palmer, A. K. C., 197
Pampa(s), La, 89, 324, 331, 337, 354
   Territory of, 80
Panamá, 13-17, 20-22, 24, 32, 35, 47, 49, 59, 62, 63, 67, 93, 94, 114, 120, 129, 173, 177, 205, 240-42, 244, 248, 259, 276, 277, 282, 288
Panama American, 241
Panama Canal, 17-18, 43, 84, 100
Panama City, 14, 16
Panamá evangelical congress, 202
Panamericana, 188
Pan-American Airways, 64, 65, 116, 190, 192, 196, 275-80, 296
Pan-American Center, 197
Pan-American Confederation of Labor, 210, 211, 249
Pan-American Conference, 146, 159, 167, 287, 311
   Buenos Aires, 146, 247, 301
   México, 145
   Montevideo, 304, 306, 359, 361
   Lima, 311
Pan-American Grace Airways, 197, 277, 279
Pan-American Information Service, 191-92
Pan-Americanism, 24, 62, 130, 146, 159, 160, 167, 176, 195, 197, 297, 307
Pan-American News Service, 180
Pan-American Society, 185, 187, 189, 197, 205, 314
Pan-American Student, 188
Pan-American Students' League, 187, 314

Pan-American Trust Co., 196
Pan-American Union, 176, 185, 187, 205, 212, 288, 289, 296, 342
Pan-Japanism, 38
Pan-Pacific Exposition (Japan), 38
Pará, 21
Paraguay, 19, 21, 42, 43, 49, 52, 53, 87, 89, 112, 113, 115, 117, 124, 129, 154, 248, 259, 323, 326, 327-28, 334, 336, 337, 340-42, 343-45, 347, 348, 360, 378
Paraguay River, 99, 327, 340, 341, 344
Parahyba, 52
Paraná River, 327
Pardo de Zela, F., 100
Paris, 64, 178, 300
Paro, Luis de, 289
Patagonia, 45, 115, 214
Patria, 63
Pavia, Félix, 336
Peace, 159, 167, 213, 214, 286, 304, 315, 348, 349
Pedro II, 335
Pelligrini, General, 90
Pende, Dr. Nicolà, 86, 87
Pernambuco, 179
People's Mandate for Peace, 213
Pershing, 85, 177
Perú, 17, 18, 20, 22, 24, 29, 34, 42-45, 47, 49, 51, 52, 53, 54, 56, 62, 75, 83, 88-89, 92, 94, 95, 96, 99, 100-02, 110, 111-14, 117, 118, 120, 126, 144-45, 147, 150, 152, 157, 161, 163, 172, 194, 249, 259, 266, 276, 279, 281, 282, 284, 287, 297, 300, 301, 310, 324, 332, 338, 346, 355, 358, 367, 370
   Germany, 18, 45, 47, 49, 51-56, 62, 83, 95, 100, 120, 347, 348, 358
   Italy, 44, 88, 89, 91, 94-96, 99, 100, 101, 102, 104, 120, 152, 170, 287

Perú, Continued
  Japan, 17, 18, 19-22, 24, 25, 29,
    33, 34, 42, 43, 44, 56, 57,
    120, 152
  Spain, 161, 163, 164
  United States, 44, 45, 100, 259,
    266, 273, 285, 287, 311, 327,
    358
Peruvian Corporation, 112, 117,
    339
Petskovsky, 136-37, 139
Philippines, 29, 236
Piahuy, 63
Picón-Salas, Mariano, 48, 49
Pierce, Palmer C., 187, 188
Pierson, Lee, 289
Pierson, Lewis Eugene, 277
Pilcomaya River, 327
Piura, 20
Plata, La, River, 15, 90, 270, 326,
    335
  region, 332
Platt Amendment, 177, 202, 227,
    236, 249, 299
Ponce, 240
Ponce, Francisco, 102
Popolo d'Italia, Il, 86
Portes Gil, Emilio, 138, 139
Porto Alegre, 76, 104, 115
Porto Esperança, 344
Portugal, 110, 160, 163, 280
Power Trust, 192-94, 209, 368, 369
Praderas Múñoz, 162
Prensa, La, 40, 269
Prestes, Carlos, 155
Primo de Rivera, 190, 203, 280
Progressive Education Association,
    200
Propaganda, 25, 26, 36, 66, 68, 69,
    72, 77, 164, 179, 181, 193,
    203, 206, 216, 284, 293, 351,
    353
  anti-Semitic, 68, 70-72
  Brazil, 34, 38, 61, 62, 67, 68
  British, 118-19, 293, 374
  business, 183, 197, 198, 288,
    314, 341

Propaganda, Continued
  Franco, 159-74
  Germany, 60-62, 66, 69, 70-73,
    74, 75, 78, 79, 81, 104, 182,
    293, 310, 353, 374
  Italy, 86, 92, 93, 96, 182, 293,
    310, 374
  Japan, 25, 35, 36, 38, 293
  United States, 36, 60, 66, 118,
    168, 175-216, 284, 288-89,
    310, 314, 353, 371, 374
Pro Patria, 148
Protestantism, 70, 146, 179, 186,
    202-04, 205
Puerto Casada, 336
Puerto Goiba, 344
Puerto Pinasco, 52
Puerto Rico, 114, 144, 177, 202,
    239, 240, 250, 278, 280, 281,
    297
Puerto Sastre, 336
Puerto Suárez, 344
Puig Casauranc, 253-54, 268-69,
    306, 361
Puntarenas, 19, 33

Quebracho, 45, 89, 270, 336
Quezaltenango, 47, 50
Quiché, 47, 317
Quiroga, General, 348

Race conflict, 72, 157, 361, Cf.
    Jews
Radio, 17, 60-62, 65, 73, 83, 93,
    119, 181, 197, 198, 270, 288-
    93, 314, 363
  Germany, 60-62, 65, 67, 68, 73,
    83, 288, 290, 310
  Italy, 93, 288, 290, 310
  Japan, 37, 288
  propaganda, 143, 270, 288-93
  United States, 72-73, 288-93,
    314, 374
Radiobras, 115
Radio Corporation of America, 189,
    281
Radio sets, 24, 71, 73

Radio teletype, 60
Railroads, 55, 59, 116-17, 138, 163, 332, 336
  Argentina, 55, 336, 338, 339, 364, 365
  Bolivia, 338, 339, 344
  Chile, 55, 56, 365
  Germany, 54-56
Rand, 279
Raw products, 51, 82, 84, 126, 141, 170, 221, 253, 325, 357, 372
Reber, Col. Samuel, 189
Red Flag, 149, 150
Rengo, 181
Reuters, 60, 118, 178, 181
Review of the River Plata, 119
Riacho Dolce, 52
Rice, 20, 21, 235, 357, 360, 370
Rio Bonito, 52
Rio de Janeiro, 25, 46, 62, 63, 64, 77, 90, 95, 116, 120, 204, 280, 291, 301, 333, 354
  Guanabara Palace, 77
  Japanese Embassy, 38
Rio Grande do Sul, 67, 75-77, 327
Rivadivia, 341
Rivera, Diego, 138, 145
Robertson, Sir Malcolm, 120
Rockefeller, Percy, 278
Rockefeller Foundation, 201, 209
Rodríguez, President, 111
Röhm, Captain, 82
Rome, 93, 94, 100, 102, 103, 104, 314, 323
  University of, 86
Roosevelt, F. D., 24, 40, 55, 91, 130, 155, 159, 166, 167, 176, 198, 208, 218, 219, 222, 226, 228, 229, 230, 232, 236, 237, 238, 241, 242, 243, 244, 245, 246, 247-74, 289, 290, 296, 299, 301, 302, 311-12, 317, 322, 346, 351, 374, 380
Roosevelt, Theodore, 177
Root, Elihu, 177
Rootes Securities, Ltd., 16
Rosas, 333

Rosenberg, Alfred, 66
Rosenthal, Baron von, 83
Ross, A. E., 207
Ross Santa María, Gustavo, 153, 365
Rothschild, Lionel N. de, 119
Rothschilds, 124
Roumania, 84, 126, 192
Royal Bank of Canada, 114
Royal Dutch Shell, 118
Rowe, Dr. L. S., 289
Rubber, 21, 43, 282, 353, 356, 357, 358
Rumbo, 148
Russia, Cf. Soviet Union

Saenz, Vicente, 165
Saenz de Sicilia, 97
Saenz Peña, 362
Salamanca, 161, 339
Salazar, Belisario, 102
Salgado, Plinio, 76
Salochi, Gino, 102
Salvador, 30, 31, 51, 58, 59, 85, 96, 99, 113, 117, 146, 150, 151, 164, 301, 371
  Germany, 31, 51, 58-59, 85, 350
  Japan, 30, 31, 40, 59, 99
  trade, 30-31, 59, 266
  United States, 31, 59, 202, 266
Sánchez Cerro, 43
Sánchez Sorondo, 321
Sandino, Cesar Augusto, 151
Sanhaber, Herr, 66
San José, 33
San Martín, 348
Santa Catharina, 52, 75, 327
Santa Clara, 117
Santa Cruz, 63, 339, 341, 345
  Republic of, 360
Santiago de Chile, 25, 56, 61, 117, 204, 280, 345
Santo Domingo, Cf. Dominican Republic
  University of, 205
Santos, 54, 90

Santos, Eduardo, 197
São Paulo, 19, 55, 87, 204, 327, 332, 344, 357, 358
    State of, 52
    University of, 38
SCADTA, 63, 277
Schoup, Dr. Carl, 199
Shulenberg, Count, 67-68
Schwab, Charles, 187
Seigle, Octavio, 167
Seligman, Professor R. A., 199
Selva, Salomón de la, 230
Sempre Pronto, 95, 376
Seone, Manuel, 147
Serfdom, 27, 150, 156, 161, 380
Sevilla, 190
Sheffield, Ambassador, 227
Shell Mex Oil, 365
Shipping, Cf. Steamship services
Silk, 21, 23, 24, 27, 357, 358
Simpson, Eyler N., 201
SIPA, 187, 191-94
Siquieros, David, 138, 142
Sisal, Cf. Henequén
Soares, Macedo, 345
Sociedad de Amigos de Alberto Torres, 33
Sonora, 19, 81
Sosa, Julio, 102
South American Journal, 119
South American Trading Agency, 142
South Pacific Mail, 119
Soviet, El (Colombia), 151
Soviet Red Aid, 137
Soviet Russia, 14, 48, 62, 93, 135-51, 168, 169, 293
Spain, 37, 48, 51, 62, 97, 103, 126, 128, 143, 159-74, 280, 304, 329
    Church, 97
    England, 108-9, 110, 131, 169, 171
    Franco, 159-74
    Germany, 160, 162, 163, 165, 168, 169-74

Spain, Continued
    Italy, 97, 131, 160, 161, 162, 163, 168, 169-74
    Loyalists, 62, 159-74
    Soviet Union, 168, 172
    United States, 169-74, 315, 337
Stalin, 134, 170
Standard Fruit Company, 282
Standard Oil Company, 171, 282, 340-41, 343, 363, 364
Standard, The, 119
Steamships, 22-3, 62-63, 84, 87, 90, 114-16, 142-43, 336
    United States, 63, 114, 270-71, 282-83
Steel, 24, 52, 100, 358, 360
Stefani, 181
Steichner, Hans, 67
Stinnes, Hugo, 52
Stone, Chas. A., 278
Strauss, 186
Strikes, 66, 138, 148, 149, 150, 152, 153
St. Thomas, 281
Stuttgart, Institute of, 67
Sucre, 338, 339
Sugar, 20, 21, 51, 58, 89, 137, 141, 215, 234, 236, 239, 267, 360, 363, 370
    Cuba, 91, 255, 263, 282, 360
Sun, The, 119
Syndicato Condor, 63-64

Tablada, José Juan, 39
Tacna-Arica, 124, 284, 302
Taft, William Howard, 177
Tanin, 21, 337
Taquari River, 327
Tariffs, 30, 33, 91, 193, 251-71, 291, 345, 358, 368
Tarija, 339
Tchitcherin, 136
Tea, 300, 357
Tegucigalpa, 88
Tehuantepec, Isthmus of, 19
Telégrafo, El, 33
Teotihuacán, Valle de, 75

Tenuco, 48
Terra, Gabriel, 59, 143, 155-56, 249, 334
Texas Oil Company, 197
Textiles, 23, 33, 34, 51, 58, 89, 123, 124, 339, 357, 358, 360, 361
 Brazil, 51, 357, 358
 Japanese, 23-31, 34, 123, 255
Thompson, Wallace, 189
Thomson, Charles, 206
Thyssen interests, 336
Tiempo, El (Bogotá), 42, 241, 309, 355
Times of Argentina, 119
Times of Brazil, 119
Times (New York), 58, 187, 341
Tin, 126, 220, 332, 353
Titicaca, Lake, 112, 339
Tobacco, 91, 234, 325, 363
Tokio, 24, 32, 37, 40
Totalitarianism, 41, 77, 294, 320, 324. Cf. Fascists, Fascism, Nazis, Germany, Italy, Brazil, etc.
Trade, 53, 60, 252, 300, 306, 351
 barter, 30, 31, 53, 60, 130, 257, 263, 309, 310, 348, 372
 boycott, 80
 embargo, 130
 quota, 123, 369, 370, 456
 subsidies, 25, 53, 60, 261, 263, 358, 368
Transocean, 61, 62, 181
Trens, 182
Tribuna, La, 34
Trinidad, 64, 115, 116
Trippe, Juan Terry, 275, 276, 278
Tropical Life, 119
Trotsky, 143, 145, 146
Trotskyites, 145, 149
Trujillo (Perú), 33, 355
Trujillo, Rafael Leonidas, 49, 82, 102, 166, 214, 224, 274, 301, 302, 351
Truskonov, 137
Tsars, 134, 139

Tucker, Elizabeth Ann, 290
Tucum, 52
Tumaco, 65

Ubico, Jorge, 102, 170, 224, 274, 301, 350
Uchyama, K., 16
Ufa, 74
Ugarte, Manuel, 334
United Fruit Company, 51, 186, 192, 196, 197, 238, 266, 282, 284, 296, 302, 364
United Press, 118, 202
United States, 13, 16, 18, 21, 25, 28, 29, 31, 32, 33, 40, 43, 44, 53, 55, 56, 57, 59, 60, 61, 62, 63, 66, 73, 78, 79, 81, 91, 93, 95, 109, 110, 111, 115, 116, 118, 121, 122, 123, 124, 125, 126, 128, 129, 130, 131, 133, 136, 146, 147, 148, 149, 160, 167, 168, 169, 170, 171, 177, 178, 183, 199, 202, 213, 217, 225, 232, 233, 238, 240, 242, 244, 247, 251, 253, 254, 255, 259, 263, 264, 265, 266, 274, 275, 282, 283, 284, 285, 286, 287, 288, 289, 291, 292, 293, 297, 298, 300, 301, 306, 307, 308, 309, 310, 313, 314, 315, 316, 317, 319, 323, 324, 351, 357, 359, 361, 372, 373, 380
 Argentina, 91, 259, 266, 282, 314-317, 322, 326, 351, 370
 Bolivia, 126, 259, 338, 340
 Brazil, 53, 61, 79, 91, 100, 282, 285, 313, 322
 Chile, 55, 56, 282, 364, 365
 Colombia, 44, 241, 264, 265, 282, 309, 310, 355, 364
 Cuba, 33, 59, 61, 149, 177, 202, 218, 227-36, 241, 243, 244, 263, 282, 298, 299
 good-neighbor policy, 24, 40, 160, 167, 170, 175, 216, 222, 232, 241, 287, 288, 291, 293, 297, 303

United States, Continued
　Haiti, 97, 118, 177, 183, 202,
　　213, 226, 259, 265, 282
　intervention, 31, 40, 41, 97, 118,
　　130, 149, 151, 176, 177, 183,
　　202, 203, 212, 213, 218, 219,
　　220, 226, 228, 238, 243, 245,
　　299, 304, 305
　investments, 55, 110, 112, 113,
　　121, 227, 236, 239, 253, 275,
　　282, 326, 327, 340, 341, 364
　México, 44, 111, 118, 128, 242,
　　259, 266, 282, 313, 337, 378
　Nicaragua, 31, 97, 151, 171, 177,
　　202, 212, 213, 218, 226, 259,
　　265
　Perú, 43, 95, 113, 259, 266, 282,
　　285
　propaganda, 36, 60, 61, 62, 66,
　　72, 73, 93, 168, 270, 284, 288,
　　299, 351, 373, 374
　radio, 72, 73, 288-93
　Spain, 160, 168-71
　State Department, 18, 19, 167,
　　169, 171, 172, 173, 176, 201,
　　224, 227, 228, 237, 239, 243,
　　270, 274, 284, 285, 289, 290,
　　291, 292, 298-99, 310, 313,
　　314, 322, 378, 379
　trade, trade treaties, 25, 28, 29,
　　31, 33, 55, 57, 59, 60, 79, 91,
　　121, 122, 193, 220, 221, 225,
　　226, 235, 251-71, 294, 306,
　　309, 310
Urabas Gulf, 51
Uriburu, General, 98, 142, 318, 319
Uruguay, 19, 22, 49, 92, 96, 117,
　　126, 151, 161, 164, 179, 229,
　　248, 249, 280, 300, 327, 333,
　　335, 344, 369
　Argentina, 112, 127, 129, 323,
　　334, 344
　aviation, 63, 90, 96
　banking, 22, 53, 88, 113, 114,
　　282, 369
　Brazil, 333, 334, 335, 336, 341
　Communists, 144, 153, 155, 156

Uruguay, Continued
　England, 54, 112, 113, 123, 129,
　　333
　Germany, 49, 53, 54, 123, 334,
　　347, 369
　Soviet Union, 141, 143, 155-56
　steamship services, 90, 115, 142,
　　143, 283
　trade, 54, 123, 141-43, 369
　wheat, 126, 300
Uruguayan Navigation Company,
　　115
Uruguay River, 327

Valdivia, 48, 359
Valenzuela, 339, 340
Valparaiso, 135
Vanadium, 126
Vanderlip, 186
Van Dyke, W. B., 189, 196
Vargas, Getulio, 70, 76, 77, 79, 85,
　　154, 155, 169, 170, 187, 249,
　　274, 286, 301, 304, 312, 354,
　　378
Vargas, Jorge, 94
Varona, Enrique José, 232
Vasconcelos, José, 182
VDA, 67-68
Vegetable ivory, 23
Vegetable oils, 42, 43, 235, 300,
　　353, 357
Venezuela, 49, 50, 61, 82, 97, 99,
　　110, 113, 114, 117, 118, 126,
　　129, 151, 177, 282, 283
　England, 58, 84, 129, 177
　Germany, 49, 54, 65, 88, 84, 347
　Italy, 88, 97, 99
　Japanese, 18, 37, 40
　oil, 84, 99, 118, 347
　trade, 54, 266
　United States, 129, 177, 259, 266
Vera Cruz, 83, 117, 128, 140, 162
Vickers, 82, 124
Villanueva, Manuel, 162
Villa Bella, 344
Villegas, Silvio, 199

Voncassel, H. H., 78
Voz, La, 50

Wabayashi, Takahiro, 32
Wages, 23, 155, 156, 220, 312
Wallace, Henry, 202, 297, 330
Washington, 15, 75, 241, 242, 270, 277, 291, 310
Wast, Hugo, 71
Welles, Sumner, 169, 171, 222, 223, 228, 229, 230, 231, 252, 255, 289, 290, 292, 294, 301, 304, 307, 310, 313, 322
West Coast Leader, 119
West India Oil Company, 365
West Indies, British, 106, 113, 115, 129, Cf. Caribbean
Wheat, 84, 126, 136, 297, 300, 322, 324, 326, 353, 371
Whitney, Cornelius Vanderbilt, 278
Wilson, Woodrow, 97, 177
Windsor, Duke of, 105-09
Winship, Governor, 239

Wolff Service, 60, 179
Wolfram, 126, 220, 332, 353
Wood, General, 228
Wool, 27, 30, 31, 270, 325, 353, 359, 360
Workers University of México, 148
World-Telegram, 291
World Peace Foundation, 205, 212
World Wide Broadcasting Foundation, 73, 288, 289

Yacimientos Petrolifercos Fiscales Bolivianos, 343
Young, Evan E., 196
Yocupicio, 81
Yucatán, 51
Y.M.C.A., 202
Y.W.C.A., 202

Zarahof, 124
Zeesen, 72, 93
Zeppelin, 63
Zubizarreta, Gerónimo, 337